COLLECTED WRITINGS OF W. D. GANN

VOLUME 3

THE MATHEMATICAL FORMULA FOR MARKET PREDICTIONS

THE MASTER MATHEMATICAL PRICE TIME & TREND CALCULATOR

BY

WILLIAM D. GANN

COSMOLOGICAL ECONOMICS

WWW.COSMOECONOMICS.COM

www.CosmoEconomics.com

This Series is Published by the:
Institute of Cosmological Economics

Cosmological Economics
is an imprint of:
Sacred Science Institute
www.SacredScience.com
institute@sacredscience.com
US: 800-756-6141 θ Intl: 951-659-8181

COSMOLOGICAL ECONOMICS

THE MASTERS OF TECHNICAL ANALYSIS SERIES

The Masters of Technical Analysis Series brings together a collection of the most important classical and modern works on technical analysis and financial market forecasting. These classic works from the Golden Age of Technical Analysis were carefully selected by the late Dr. Jerome Baumring of the Investment Centre Bookstore in the 1980's, as representing the most valuable and important works in technical analysis ever written. They were included as the foundational source texts for his program in advanced financial market analysis and forecasting, and serve as the ideal foundation for any analyst seeking a thorough education in market theory and technical trading.

The Golden Age of technical analysis was a period from the early 1900's through the 1960's where the foundational theories of modern financial analysis were initially developed. The ideas and technologies developed during this fruitful period have formed the basis for most modern technical market theory, which is considered to be mostly a repetition or reworking of these past ideas and techniques developed by the Old Masters of the Golden Age. In these historical works can be found the timeless trading wisdom which has laid the foundation for all modern investment theory and literature. These techniques are as useful in today's markets as they were in the past, providing rare and valuable insights, tools and strategies that give the modern trader an edge over traders and investors that are unaware of these time honored tools.

Each quality reprint of these classical texts has been reproduced as an exact facsimile of the original text, maintaining the original layout, typeset, charts, and style of the author and time period, helping to preserve and communicate a sense of the feeling of the original work that a reproduction in modern format does not capture. Many of these rare works and courses were originally printed in only very small private editions or as correspondence courses, so that the originals were easily lost or destroyed over time. Our reproductions of these important source works have been printed on acid free paper and bound in a quality hardcover format that will compliment any trading library and help to preserve this important resource for generations to come.

The series is also currently being digitized and archived for permanent digital preservation by the Institute of Cosmological Economics, creating a searchable reference library of market wisdom accessible globally and available in new digital formats to keep the knowledge fresh and accessible through new devices and technology as we advance further into the information revolution. To see our full catalog of hardcover reprints, new publications, and digital editions please visit our website at www.CosmoEconomics.com.

The Mathematical Formula For Market Predictions

Included with this Course is

an Electronic Set of the

Mathematical Calculator

Master Chart Overlays

For Purchasers of this Course

Please Contact us to receive

a Download of these Overlays at:

Institute of Cosmological Economics

WWW.COSMOECONOMICS.COM

INSTITUTE@COSMOECONOMICS.COM

951-659-8181 or 800 756-6141

Master Mathematical Formula
And Calculators Course
W. D. Gann

W. D. Gann Mathematical Formula For Market Predictions

The Master Mathematical Price, Time, And Trend Calculators

Chapter 1	*Mathematical Formula For Market Predictions* A marketing brochure describing the Master Mathematical Calculator's importance
Chapter 2	*The Master Mathematical Price Time And Trend Calculator* This is one of the two rarest and most valuable of Gann's courses, unpublished since his advertisement in the above brochure containing complete instructions for the following: - Master Time And Price Calculator, Square of 12 (144) - Master Time And Price Calculator, Square of 9 (90)
Chapter 3	*How To Use The Master Calculator May Soy Beans* Instructions on how to use the Calculator for Soy Beans
Chapter 4	*Master Calculators For Weekly Time Periods To Determine The Trend Of Stocks And Commodities* Instructions for the use of the following included calculator - Time and Price Calculator- Square of 52, Weekly time periods
Chapter 5	*May Soy Beans Square Of 67 Time Periods For Days, Weeks, Months* Instructions for the use of the fourth calculator included in this course - Calculator for Daily, Weekly, Monthly Time Periods, May Soy Beans
Chapter 6	*The Basis Of My Forecasting Method For Grains– Geometrical Angles* A. For Stocks B. For Commodities. For the further elaboration of the calculators we have included in this course on geometrical angles, a fundamental element of the calculators
Chapter 7	*Resistance Levels* We have also included this course on Resistance Levels for a deeper explanation of the Calculators, and of the important points to consider.
Chapter 8	*Time And Price Resistance Levels* This course includes both Time And Price Resistance Levels
Chapter 9	*Enhanced Master Charts* Master of "12" Chart – Square of 9 – Six Squares of 9 – 2 Hexagon Charts – Master Chart of 360° – Master 360° Circle Chart Squared – Spiral Chart – NYSE Permanent Chart – US Steel Name Chart – US Permanent Chart – Price And Time Spiral Charts – 15° Hourly Spiral Chart – Square of 4 – May Soy Bean Master Chart – Master Egg Chart – Coffee Rio Conic Chart – May Wheat Geometric Chart – Even Squares – Gann Scientific Forecast – May Soy Beans

Chapter 1

Mathematical Formula For Market Predictions

MATHEMATICAL FORMULA FOR MARKET PREDICTIONS

Time Cycles Tell the Trend of Commodities, Stocks and Business

To make success investing in stocks or speculating in commodities you must have a well defined plan and must know the rules that have stood the test of time for 50 years or more. After you learn the rules you must eliminate guess work, hope and fear and follow rules and you will make profits.

When you buy a course of instructions look up the record of the man who has discovered and developed it and if he has made a success with it and made money you can afford to buy the course and follow the rules.

W. D. GANN'S RECORD FOR 52 YEARS

1902 August 15th made first trade in commodities and started studying mathematical principles to determine the future trend.

1905 September 12th the daily Texarkanian of Texarkana, Texas, printed an article giving Mr. Gann's view on Cotton prices.

1907 he predicted the panic in stocks and the decline in commodities and made large profits.

1908 May 12th left Oklahoma City for New York City. August 8th made one of his greatest mathematical discoveries for predicting the trend of stocks and commodities. Started trading with a capital of $300 and made $25,000. Started another account with $130 and made $12,000 in thirty days time.

1909 December the Ticker magazine (now the magazine of Wall Street) printed an article "remarkable predictions and trading record". The article was written by the late R. D. Wyckoff, owner and editor of the Ticker Magazine at that time.

The following is a copy of part of the article:

"In order to substantiate Mr. Gann's claims as to what he has been able to do under this method, we called upon Mr. William E. Gilley, an Inspector of Imports, 16 Beaver Street, New York. Mr. Gilley is well known in the downtown district. He himself has studied stock market movements for twenty-five years, during which time he has examined every piece of market literature that has been issued and procurable in Wall Street. It was he who encouraged Mr. Gann to study out the scientific and mathematical possibilities of the subject. When asked what had been the most impressive of Mr. Gann's work and predictions, he replied as follows:

" 'It is very difficult for me to remember all the predictions and operations of Mr. Gann which may be classed as phenomenal, but the following are a few: In 1908 when Union Pacific was 168⅛, he told me that it would not touch 169 before it had a good break. We sold it short all the way down to 152⅝, covering on the weak spots and putting it out again on the rallies, securing twenty-three points profit out of an eighteen-point move.

" 'Mr. Gann's calculations are based on natural law. I have followed his work closely for years. I know that he has a firm grasp of the basic principles which govern stock market movements, and I do not believe any other man on earth can duplicate the idea or his method at the present time.

" 'Early this year he figured that the top of the advance would fall on a certain day in August and calculated the prices at which the Dow-Jones averages would then stand. The market culminated on the exact day and within four-tenths of one per cent of the figures predicted.'

" 'You and Mr. Gann must have cleaned up considerable money on all these operations,' was suggested.

" 'Yes, we have made a great deal of money. He has taken half a million dollars out of the market in the past few years. I once saw him take $130, and in less than one month ran it up to over $12,000. He can compound money faster than any man I ever met.

"'One of the most astonishing calculations made by Mr. Gann was during last summer (1909) when he predicted that September wheat would sell at $1.20. This meant that it must touch that figure before the end of the month of September. At twelve o'clock, Chicago time, on September 30th (the last day) the option was selling below $1.08, and it looked as though his prediction would not be fulfilled. Mr. Gann said, 'If it does not touch $1.20 by the close of the market it will prove that there is something wrong with my whole method of calculation. I do not care what the price is now, it must go there.' It is common history that September wheat surprised the whole country by selling at $1.20 and no higher in the very last hour of the trading, closing at that figure.'

"So much for what Mr. Gann has said and done as evidenced by himself and others. Now as to what demonstrations have taken place before our representative:

"During the month of October, 1909, in twenty-five market days, Mr. Gann made, in the presence of our representative, two hundred and eighty-six transactions in various stocks, on both the long and short side of the market. Two hundred and sixty-four of these transactions resulted in profits; twenty-two in losses.

"The capital with which he operated was doubled ten times, so that at the end of the month he had one thousand per cent on his original margin.

"In our presence Mr. Gann sold Steel common short at 94⅞, saying that it would not go to 95. It did not.

"On a drive which occurred during the week ending October 29th, Mr. Gann bought Steel common at 86¼, saying that it would not go to 86. The lowest it sold was 86⅛.

"We have seen him give in one day sixteen successive orders in the same stock, eight of which turned out to be at either the top or the bottom eighth of that particular swing. The above we can positively verify.

"Such performances as these, coupled with the foregoing, are probably unparalleled in the history of the Street.

"James R. Keene has said, 'The man who is right six times out of ten will make his fortune.' Here is a trader, who, without any attempt to make a showing (for he did not know the results were to be published), establishes a record of over ninety-two per cent profitable trades.

"Mr. Gann has refused to disclose his method at any price, but to those scientifically inclined he has unquestionably added to the stock of Wall Street knowledge and pointed out infinite possibilities.

"We have requested Mr. Gann to figure out for the readers of The Ticker a few of the most striking indications which appear in his calculations. In presenting those we wish it understood that no man, in or out of Wall Street, is infallible.

"Mr. Gann's figures at present indicate that the trend of the stock market should, barring the usual rallies, be toward lower prices until March or April, 1910.

"He calculates that May wheat, which is now selling at $1.02, should not sell below 99c and should sell at $1.45 next spring.

"On cotton, which is now at about the 15c level, he estimates that, after a good reaction from these prices, the commodity should reach 18c in the spring of 1910. He looks for a corner in the March or May option.

"Whether these figures prove correct or not will in no sense detract from the record which Mr. Gann has already established.

"Mr. Gann was born in Lufkin, Texas, and is thirty-one years of age. He is a gifted mathematician, has an extraordinary memory for figures, and is an expert Tape Reader. Take away his science and he would beat the market on his intuitive tape reading alone.

"Endowed as he is with such qualities, we have no hesitation in predicting that within a comparatively few years Wm. D. Gann will receive full recognition as one of Wall Street's leading operators. R. D. W."

December, 1909—The Commercial West Magazine and other newspapers carried articles about W. D. Gann's successful speculation.

1914—Predicted the World War and the panic in Stocks.

1918, March—Issued a prediction indicating the end of the war and the Kaiser's abdication, 1918. This prediction was accurately fulfilled. The Beaumont Journal, Houston Post, New York Herald and many other leading newspapers commented on this prediction.

1919—The Annual Forecast issued in the fall of 1918 indicated a big boom in oil stocks as well as a general bull market in stocks which was accurately fulfilled.

1920, November—Issued an Annual Forecast on Stocks for 1921 predicting a panic and extreme low for stocks for August. Also predicted improvement in business starting in the summer of 1921. Many newspapers commented on these forecasts.

1922—Predicted better business conditions. The Los Angeles Sunday Times and many other newspapers carried his article.

1922, December 6—The Daily Northside News of New York carried an article headed "Gann Foretold Course of Stocks." The Morning Telegraph also gave W. D. Gann credit for forecasting bull market in stocks for 1922.

The Angelina County News of Lufkin, Texas, Mr. Gann's home town, gave wide publicity to his accurate predictions.

The Boston American, Evening Telegram of New York in March, 1923, commented on W. D. Gann's mathematical ability.

1923—Wrote "Truth of the Stock Tape." This book pronounced by experts as the best book ever written on the Stock Market. It was favorably reviewed by the Wall Street Journal, Financial Times of London and other newspapers in Canada and the United States.

Predicted a crop failure and a big advance in Cotton for 1923. Cotton prices advanced 17c per pound between August and November 30, 1923. Mr. Gann made enormous profits trading in Cotton during this period. Below we quote from a letter:

W. D. GANN STARTED AN ACCOUNT WITH $973.00 AND MADE OVER $30,000.00 IN SIXTY DAYS' TIME

(Read the Letter Below Confirming This)

New York, N. Y., March, 1933

Dear Mr. Gann:

I am very glad to write you a letter stating my personal observation of the application of your system to trading in Cotton.

On November 30, 1923, starting with a capital of $973.00, you showed a clear profit of over $30,000 at the close of business on January 28, 1924. This profit was made through the purchase and sale of contracts for the delivery and sale of cotton on the New York Cotton Exchange through one of the leading New York brokerage offices. I personally know of all the trades made in this commodity for the account, having received advises of your operations, from the broker on the day following the day each trade was made.

On January 29, 1924, a check for $24,764.04 was drawn against the account and delivered to a person with whom I am personally acquainted.

I am glad to add that I had one of your cotton forecasts for the year 1923, and the diagram prepared by you foretold, without exception, the days on which all the major and minor moves of the market would start and finish.

With best wishes, I remain

Very truly yours,

C. M.

1924—Forecast big advance in Wheat.

In the fall of 1925 issued an Annual Forecast predicting a big decline in Cotton for 1926.

December, 1926—Cotton was selling for 12½c per pound. He wrote an article entitled "King Cotton to Regain His Throne." Newspapers throughout the South printed this forecast. The forecast for Cotton in 1927 indicated a big advance, calling final high for September, 1927. Cotton advanced to 24½c a pound in September, 1927. One client in Alabama wrote, "You had the Cotton forecast 100% accurate."

September, 1927—The New York Morning Telegraph concluded an article with the following: "Mr. Gann may not bet a success as a novelist but he is unique. I am convinced that there is no man alive who could compete with him on his own ground." (Meaning Wall Street).

Most Remarkable Forecast

1928—In November W. D. Gann issued an Annual Forecast predicting the end of the great bull market in stocks for September 3, 1929, and the greatest panic in history to follow. We quote from this forecast, "September—One of the sharpest declines of the year is indicated. There will be loss of confidence by investors, and the public will try to get out after it is too late. Storms will damage crops and the general business outlook will become cloudy. War news will upset the market and unfavorable developments in foreign countries. A 'Black Friday' is indicated and a panicky decline in stocks with only small rallies. The short side will prove the most profitable. You should sell short and pyramid on the way down." Many newspapers commented on the accuracy of this forecast.

The newspapers in Bombay, India, commented on Mr. Gann's accuracy in forecasting the decline in Cotton prices.

Wall Street Stock Selector

In the spring of 1930, Mr. Gann wrote, "Wall Street Stock Selector," which was published in June, 1930. In this book he had a chapter headed, "Investors' Panic," which described conditions just as they occurred during 1931, 1932 and 1933. We quote from the book, pages 203-04:

'The coming investors' panic will be the greatest in history, because there are at least 15 to 25 million investors in the United States who hold stocks in the leading corporations, and when once they get scared, which they will after years of decline, then the selling will be so terrific that no buying power can withstand it. Stocks are so well distributed in the hands of the public that since the 1929 panic many people think that the market is panic-proof, but this seeming strength is really the weakest feature of the market."

The predictions in this book were remarkably fulfilled by panicky declines in stocks during 1930 to 1932.

In April, 1930, when this book was written the Dow Jones 30 Industrial Averages were selling at 297½. They declined to 40½ on July 8, 1932.

"Thousands of people have bought this book and profited by reading and studying it. The book has been favorably commented on by such papers as the Financial Times of London, England, Wall Street Journal, New York Daily Investment News, Coast Investors, and many other newspapers and magazines throughout the world.

Member of Commodity Exchanges

1931—In March W. D. Gann was elected to membership on the New York Rubber Exchange, The New Orleans Cotton Exchange and later became a member of the Commodity Exchange of New York.

In 1941 was elected a member of the Chicago Board of Trade.

He was in good standing when he sold his membership.

1932 Stock Forecast

"On February 10, 1932, Mr. Gann said that Stocks were bottom for a big rally. His 1932 Stock Forecast, issued October 21, 1931, called March 8 for last top for another big decline. During the latter part of June, 1932, and early July he strongly advised buying stocks, stating that final bottom had been reached, as shown by his market letter issued July 8, the day that most stocks reached final bottom. We quote from page 6 of the 1932 Forecast: "The latter part of June, July, August and September are the most active and bullish months of the year, when sharp advances will be recorded. First extreme high is indicated around September 20 to 21, when stocks should make extreme high for the year. Then follow a decline, reaching bottom around October 4 to 5."

"Between July 8 and September 8 many stocks advanced 20 to 60 points. The market reached high of a secondary rally on September 23 from which a big decline followed, making low in the latter part of November and early December, as indicated in the Forecast."

"On March 1, 1933, by the use of his Master Time Factor Mr. Gann forecast bottom for stocks and commodities and advised buying for a big advance, as shown by the market letters issued March 1 and 3 given below. This is another proof of the great value of Mr. Gann's discovery of a Master Time Factor."

1932, December—The New York Daily Investment News printed an article written by W. D. Gann entitled, "New Era of Prosperity will be Born in 1933 Student of Cycles Declares in Forecast." This prediction was fulfilled by the Roosevelt Boom.

1933, March—W. D. Gann bought an airplane to tour the country to make crop surveys and study business conditions. His 1933 Stock and Cotton Forecast were fulfilled with remarkable accuracy. The 1933 Stock Forecast called for top July 17 and a sharp decline to July 21st. The Dow Jones Industrial Averages reached high July 17th and a wide open break followed. The Averages declined 25 points in 4 days.

W. D. Gann's Trading Record

Mr. Gann made large profits speculating for his own account in Stocks, Cotton and other commodities during 1933. Below we publish a record taken from brokers' statements, showing the trades made by Mr. Gann for 3 years. This is proof that he can and does make money by following his own rules and methods.

1933—From August 1 to December 31, total number of trades 135 of which 112 showed profits and 23 losses. Percentage of accuracy on total number of trades, 83%. Percentage of profit to losses, 89.9%.

Total number of Trades for the year 1933, 479 of which 422 were profits and 57 losses. Percentages of accuracy, 88.1%. Percentage of profits on capital used 4,000%, or 40 to 1.

1934—January 1 to December 31, total number of Trades, 362. COTTON, 147 trades of which 135 shows profits and 12 losses. GRAINS, 170 trades of which 161 shows profits and 9 losses. RUBBER, 23 trades of which 21 showed profits and 2 losses. SILVER, 7 trades. All showed profits; no losses. SILK, 4 trades, 3 showed profits, 1 loss. STOCKS, 11 trades; 10 profits and 1 loss. Total for the year, 362 trades of which 337 showed profits and 25 showed losses. Percentage of accuracy on total number of trades, 93.09%. Percentage of profits to losses, 93.10%. Percentage of profits on Capital used, 800%, or 8 for 1.

1935—Total trades in Cotton, Grain and Rubber, 98, of which 83 showed profits and 15 showed losses. Percentage of accuracy in total trades, 85%. Percentage of profit to losses, 82½. Percentage of profit on capital used, 336%.

Stocks, total trades 34, of which 29 showed profits and 5 showed losses.

Percentage of accuracy on total number of trades, 85.5%. Percentage of profits to losses, 83%. Percentage of profits on capital used, 100%.

During 1935 W. D. Gann visited all of the Latin American countries to study crop conditions and business conditions.

1935, March 31—The Buenos Aires Herald carried an article about W. D. Gann's record of accurate forecast. W. D. Gann was in Buenos Aires at the time this article was written.

Writes New Books

1936—"New Stock Trend Detector" was written by W. D. Gann. This book was a further advance over "Truth of the Stock Tape" and "Wall Street Stock Selector" and contained an actual trading record for 10 years in Chrysler Motors according to the rules set down in these books.

1936, July—Bought special built all-metal airplane, "The Silver Star," for making crop surveys.

1937—Wrote and published a book, "How to Make Profits Trading in Puts and Calls." Scientific Stock Forecasting again proved equal to the test of predicting a bear year, sharp declines coming in March and September. A maximum decline of 80 points was called for and the actual decline from the March high to the November low was 82 and a fraction points.

These books were favorably reviewed by the Wall Street Journal, The New York Daily Investment News and various other newspapers.

In the 1936 Grain Forecast predicted crop failure and higher prices.

1936, November—Issued the Annual Forecast for 1937 and predicted a panic in stocks. The decline was very severe and lasted into March, 1938, with the Dow-Jones Averages declining 97 points.

1937, November—The Milwaukee Journal gave Mr. Gann credit for predicting the 1929 and 1937 crashes in the Stock Market and the accuracy of his timing. Mr. Gann made large profits selling stocks during 1937 and the certified public accountant has seen the statement of these profits.

1939, July—Bought a new Fairchild airplane to use for business purposes in making crop surveys. He predicted the beginning of World War II and made large profits buying grains.

1941, September 14th—Mr. Gann forecast the top for Soy Beans and sold short, making large profits on the decline. Prices declined to October 17, 1941, being down 48c in 30 days' time.

New Commodity Book

In the fall of 1941 W. D. Gann wrote "How to Make Profits Trading in Commodities." This book has been pronounced the best book ever written on commodities and has been reviewed by many newspapers.

1946—Predicted a big advance in stocks and cotton and the big decline which followed.

Figured the exact date, October 15, 1946, for the big decline in cotton. Prices declined nearly 16c per pound in three weeks and he sold short all the way down.

Trading Record

October 1, 1946, to December 30th—One account started with a capital of $4,500 showed a gross profit of $18,981.30. Total losses $1,165. Net profit $17,816.30 or approximately 400% on the capital used.

Another account started with a capital of $6,000. Gross profits $19,-972.75. Total losses $634.75. Net profits $19,338.00. A percentage of over 320% on the capital used. Other accounts which he handled showed profits as great as these.

W. D. Gann has always made a success trading in very active fast-moving markets and has made a great record for predicting the extreme high and extreme low on commodities and stocks. These accurate predictions are based on his discovery of THE MASTER TIME CYCLE which repeats at certain intervals.

1949—Wrote "45 YEARS IN WALL STREET," giving new rules for stock trading. The International Mark Twain Society awarded Mr. Gann an Honorary Membership in the Society based on the merits of his book, "45 YEARS IN WALL STREET." This book was favorably received by investors and traders throughout the country and is still selling. It has been favorably reviewed by newspapers and magazines.

1951, June 6th—On his 73rd birthday completed writing a new edition of "How to Make Profits Trading in Commodities," giving new rules bringing this book up to date and giving the benefit of his years of experience.

76th Year Trading Record and New Discoveries

Mr. Gann is active and keeps up to date. During his 76th year he made a new discovery and completed two MASTER CALCULATORS for saving time and getting accurate indications on the trend of stocks and commodities. In the spring of 1954 he completed a MASTER THREE-DIMENSION CHART which proves the relative position of TIME, PRICE and VOLUME which produces VELOCITY or SPEED and shows when the trend is changing to a very fast active advancing market or a slow upward movement.

The relative position of PRICE TO TIME TELLS the TIME CYCLES when prices decline very fast or move very slow. History repeats in the stock or commodity markets but you must learn the rules and the GREAT TIME CYCLES in order to take advantage of rapid advances and declines and make profits.

Many people have the idea that W. D. Gann is old and in his dotage and that he cannot still make money trading in the market.

From September 30, 1953, to October 26, 1953, he made 26 trades in Grains, 25 showed profits and one trade showed a small loss of $40. During this same period he made six trades in Eggs, five showed profits and one trade showed a small loss.

We have stated before that W. D. Gann has nearly always been right when there was big advances and big declines in Commodities and Stocks and in markets of this kind you can make LARGE PROFITS ON SMALL RISKS by following the rules which he has discovered and which he follows himself.

1954, April 27 to May 7—W. D. Gann made 17 trades in Coffee, Soy Beans, Rye and Eggs. Sixteen of these trades showed profits and one trade in eggs showed a small loss.

April 27, 1954, he sold July Soy Beans short at 412 and on May 5 bought in these beans at 485½, making a profit of 26½c per bushel in eight calendar days. He placed a stop loss order on the trade at 416, limiting the risk to 4c per bushel, and made 26½c per bushel or a gain of 6½ times the risk. He sold more Soy Beans at 400½, 395½, 390½, 392½ and bought them in or covered shorts at 384, 387 and 388¼. After he covered the shorts July Soy Beans rallied to 395¾ on May 6 and he again sold short at 392½ on May 7. The above record cf trades shows that W. D. Gann is still active and he is nearly 76 years of age and follows his own rules and makes profits. With some of the money he made trading in Coffee and Soy Beans he bought a fast express cruising boat and named the boat "The Coffee Bean."

You can make money following the same rules that Mr. Gann followed and the rules are not hard to learn.

1954 Coffee Trades

Coffee prices advanced the most rapid in the spring of 1954 and reached the highest prices in history.

1954, April 2nd—Coffee prices reached the highest in history at the opening. The last advance started October 13, 1953, when December coffee was low at 56.70. April 2, 1954, December Coffee high 95.20. Up 38½c per pound in less than six months and up 30c per pound since January 19, 1954.

W. D. Gann's MASTER TIME CYCLE and MASTER THREE-DIMENSION CHART indicated that December Coffee would be high on April 2nd at 95.20. When it reached this price he gave an order to sell short. The market broke very rapidly and he sold December Coffee at 94.31, and on April 14, 1954, bought December Coffee at 84.05 which was the extreme low for the decline at that time. He made 1,036 points profit in 12 calendar days. Based on the risk or stop-loss order he made 1,000% on the risk and the gain in percentage on the capital used was 140%.

April 15th sold December Coffee at 87.75. April 21st bought December Coffee at 85.50. A profit of 225 points in seven days. These were not all of the profitable trades that he made in Coffee. He traded in July and September Coffee also.

This is proof that his mathematical rules work accurately in extreme wild markets and when his rules indicated high for Coffee April 2nd, W. D. Gann had the faith in his knowledge and the nerve to sell Coffee and make quick profits. This record answers the question that he can and does make profits at the age of 76 by following his rules. You can learn these rules and make profits in Rye, Soy Beans, Wheat, Cotton, Coffee, Cocoa and other commodities. You must learn to follow the rules strictly, eliminate hope and fear and protect your capital and profits with stop-loss orders and success is assured.

We will not sell the course of instructions or teach the mathematical formula for market predictions just to get money, which we do not need or have to have; we will only sell the courses to people who meet our requirements, and if we feel after a thorough investigation that a man or woman cannot make a success investing or trading we will refuse to teach them the courses.

WHAT PEOPLE WHO HAVE USED W. D. GANN'S SERVICE AND COURSES SAY OVER A LONG PERIOD OF YEARS

New York, October, 1931

You predicted the end of this terrible condition as being October 3rd, 1931. It happened one hour later . . .

Someone ought to tell the world about you and your knowledge over a nationwide hookup and offer them proof in form of your "Tunnel Through the Air." I am sure we would have better preparations for another October 3rd, 1931, in the future.—G.F.

New York, October, 1931

Dear Friend Gann:

Again I must congratulate you on your marvelous predictions. I have followed your work closely for the past 23 years. I well remember that in the early part of 1909 you forecast the exact date in August when stocks would reach extreme high and came within about ⅛ of the exact high level for the Wall Street Journal railroad average. Twenty years later I saw your prediction fulfilled in September, 1929, when you said that stocks would make top and that the worst panic in history would follow, all of which has proved too true.

But the most amazingly accurate long-range prediction you have ever made was in your book, "The Tunnel Thru the Air," which you wrote in the early part of 1927. I have watched prediction after prediction fulfilled and have been especially interested in your forecast on the stock market for October 3rd, 1931. I had watched stocks go down and down as if no bottom was in sight and when last Saturday, October 3rd, stocks reached the lowest level in years, I said to myself, my friend Gann has called the turn and it's time for me to take my market basket to Wall Street and fill it with bargains. Monday, October 5th, arrived and stocks smashed to the lowest of the year. Today, at the close, I see that they are up 10 to 15 points from Monday's lowest. You missed the bottom by two days, counting Sunday. Well, that's pretty close when we consider you made the calculations 4½ years ago.

You have certainly demonstrated that when a man understands the practical rules and laws in the Bible, the future becomes an open book. May you live long and prosper, is my sincere wish for you.

Very truly your,

W. E. G.

(Telegram)

Santa Barbara, Cal.
February, 1931

Vanadium yielded about $40,000.00 in two weeks. J. H.

Following this telegram this same man wrote as follows:

I take genuine pleasure in sending you herewith New York draft for balance due on contract. As I said to Mr. E. this morning, "I have felt, ever since sitting at your feet, that I had obtained a full $4,000 worth of Comfortable Assurance alone, to say nothing of having had a net profit on my very first deal, alone, of just ten times that amount."

Our little Santa Barbara class will all make good; it takes some a bit longer than others, but as far as I am concerned, I just KNOW that I never need have financial worry, for you have given me a key-ring full of pass-keys which will unlock profits with a certainty. I would not take all that I have paid you for just one of those little pocket charts, which will do a lot of profitable trading, all by myself. J. H. B.

What one satisfied user writes to a prospect:

Cleveland, Ohio
December, 1933

I am in receipt of your letter of the 28th in reference to Mr. W. D. Gann and his mechanical trend indicator.

I have known Mr. Gann for a number of years and have followed and studied his services during this time. Some time ago, I took all the services that he offers, which was an outlay of considerable cash; however, I have found that the investment has proven most satisfactory and the cost is going to be a small item. Several of the courses were taken under his personal supervision, but I did have a lot of his work through correspondence. If you are not in position to take the services personally, I believe you can get your money's worth by correspondence. His services by correspondence are so detailed that it would be impossible for you to lose the thought he is trying to convey.

Mr. Gann is a man of considerable means and one of the most brilliant men I have ever contacted. He has made his entire fortune out of the market through the methods he will teach you and his market experience has been over a period of thirty years.

I hope I have given you the information requested; however, if you should like for me to answer further questions, it will be a pleasure to hear from you.

Yours very truly,

W. K. G.

Portland, Oregon
April, 1931

I have taken all the principal services, spending as high as four or five thousand dollars per year for these, and I think Mr. Gann has something that is so far in advance of anything else I have seen or worked with that there is no comparison.

W. P. H., Jr.

New Bern, N. C.
August, 1937

In reply to yours of the 19th.

I have known Mr. W. D. Gann for many years. I have been in his office on Wall Street, have seen him trade with his method and take the money out of the market. With it he has made a fortune in speculation. And he does not need the money he gets for his method or market service any more than Mr. Ford does for sale of cars.

His method has been used by me since 1927, successfully. In my opinion, it is the only one with which one can make money in the market and keep it. If you will follow his method and the rules he lays down, you will also make a success and I can assure you without it you will make a failure.

This statement is made after having read every book I could find on the subject, including the lives of all the big operators of the past and subscribed to every financial paper published and most of the market services.

Yours very truly,

C. K.

CERTIFIED PUBLIC ACCOUNTANT'S REPORT

January, 1933

The 400-share lot transactions were begun on June 4, 1931, and were completed on

December 28, 1932. This showed a net profit of $90,570, after deduction of $5,121 for commissions and taxes.

The $3,000 capital was used exclusively on the 100-share lot transactions and was withdrawn on February 27, 1931. All trading thereafter was done on accumulated profits.

I hereby certify that the schedules submitted correctly indicate the profits that could have been made by this Method.

Might I be allowed to place in this report my private opinion, that the Method, as you demonstrated it, is absolutely foolproof. It requires simply the original capital as provided for by the Method, which is plainly stated in the rules, and thereafter to follow the simple instructions explicitly without any human-made deviations from the rules. If the user of this Method will only remember this one simple suggestion of mine, there is no question nor any doubt but that it will make money for the user.

It is amazing to consider what has been accomplished with so small a capital in such a short period of time by simply following mathematical rules, so easy to memorize that a grammar school boy or girl could follow them.

I am making this digression in my report to you because I bought the Method in 1930 and am using it with good results myself. I have bought and examined the new and improved Method and consider it about 100% better than your Method was in 1930. You are at liberty to use this and I will be very glad to recommend the system.

Respectfully submitted,

S. J. M.

Certified Public Accountant

August 5, 1933

Covering the period from April 1st to July 31st, 1933, you made a total of 344 trades in stocks, cotton, rubber and grain. 310 of these trades showed profits and 34 showed losses. Your percentage of accuracy was 89% on the total number of trades. The capital wih which you operated was increased 26½ times. On each $1,000.00 capital with which you started, you made a profit of $26,500.00 net. This was after paying all taxes, interest and commissions and deductions of all losses.

Yours very truly,

S. J. M.

Certified Public Accountant

New York, N. Y.
May, 1933

I have examined the brokers' statements and trades made by W. D. Gann during the month of April, 1933. They show profits as follows:

Cotton Account	$ 8,136.29
Rubber Account	1,387.01
Grain Account	758.30
	$10,281.60

During that time there was only one loss of $39.25, and the above profits are net after payment of brokers' commissions. There were other trades in cotton, rubber and stocks at the end of the month, that had not been closed out, which showed profits.

When the trading on the above account was started, the greatest risk taken was $800, or in other words, if the stop loss orders had been caught, the loss would have been $800.

C. L. G.

New York, N. Y.
January, 1946

I knew of no one with a deeper understanding of the basic causes of trends in the stock and commodity markets than W. D. Gann and through the years have developed a high regard for his ability to successfully forecast long range movements. He is a practical economist of the first rank. Some of his forecasts for a year ahead, have been so precisely accurate as to attract the attention of leading newspapers that have featured them in large space stories.

Mr. Gann now spends a large part of his time in Florida supervising his extensive realty interests, and the business is ably conducted by John L. Gann, assisted by Miss Gilson, both of whom have had many years of training under the direction of Mr. W. D. Gann, and both of whom are thoroughly qualified in knowledge and character to advise and guide investors in stocks, bonds and commodities.

Yours very truly,

W. M. P.

Miami, Fla.
January, 1946

Gentlemen:

I take pleasure in stating that I have known W. D. Gann, John L. Gann and C. L. Gilson of W. D. Gann & Son, Inc., for more than ten years and that they all are persons of integrity, high moral character and proven ability. John L. Gann was a captain in the late war and returned with citations of merit. None of these parties are related to me by blood or marriage.

I have been receiving the W. D. Gann financial service for about eighteen years and it has been very valuable to me. I consider it the best service available. It was one of the very few that warned in no uncertain terms against and ahead of the market crash in 1929.

As to my background, I am a substantial

stockholder and director in:

Pepsi-Cola Bottling Co., of Atlanta, Atlanta, Ga.

Southern Discount Co., 220 Healy Bldg., Atlanta, Ga.

Consolidated Distributors, Inc., Atlanta, Ga.; Macon, Ga.; Jacksonville, Fla., and Tampa, Fla.

Very truly yours,

C. K.

Los Angeles, Cal.
January, 1946

Dear Sirs:

I have transacted business with the firm W. D. Gann, Inc., for approximately 24 years and it is indeed a pleasure to be able to deal with a firm for almost a quarter of a century with complete satisfaction.

I consider each of its members, W. D. Gann, Mr. John L. Gann and Miss C. L. Gilson to be honest, reliable, and trustworthy.

My experience has been satisfactory to the extent that I am still a client of theirs and hope to continue so in the years to come.

Yours very truly,

M. F.

San Francisco, Cal.
February, 1949

Today, I completed my 1948 Federal Income Tax Return, which shows my total dividends amounting to over $4,050.—the result of careful investments and wise speculations during the past decade, which I attribute to Mr. Gann's forecasts, letters and supplements.

W. T. P.

Miami, Fla.
November, 1951

Dear Sirs:

In 1926 I read a book, Truth Of The Stock Tape, written by W. D. Gann, three years before. I was deeply impressed by it. The next year I met Mr. Gann and since then, I have read with pleasure and profit, all the books written by Mr. Gann on the stock and commodity markets. What I learned from these books has paid me off in cash.

I have known Mr. Gann, intimately, 24 years. I never knew of a man who was such a fiend for research work and this would includes Mr. Thomas Edison. Mr. Gann believes, and so did Mr. Edison, to do what was thought impossible, just takes more time and work, than any one else has tried. Men like these go on and prove it.

Very truly yours,

C. K.

New York, N. Y.
November, 1951

I have studied Mr. Gann's books, courses and rules on stocks and commodities for more than a year.

It is a pleasure to recommend Mr. Gann's work to you and to urge study by those interested in the stock and commodity markets.

The courses of instruction are of great value to those with only a casual interest in the markets as well as to the specialist who needs to know.

MATHEMATICAL PREDICTION FORMULA

The four factors: TIME, PRICE, VOLUME and SPEED have been supplemented by a fifth factor, MASS PRESSURE.

TIME

Time is the essential element. Time cycles which he has developed cover the great time cycle and its important harmonics. Time cycles for stocks, commodities or business can be calculated and projected 100 years or more in advance, subject to minor corrections and variations.

He has proven a TRUE TREND LINE as well as a relatively TRUE TREND LINE when prices are advancing, and a relatively TRUE TREND LINE when prices are declining. He has developed rules and indexes which show whether high or low prices will culminate on the true trend line or the relatively true trend line.

A time variable and price variable has been worked out to exact mathematical points.

PRICE

Mr. Gann has developed rules which show the relation between time and price and what happens when prices complete a cycle before time expires.

There is a rule for determining when prices are in balance with time and when prices are out of balance with time. Prices are sometimes behind time and sometimes ahead of time.

TRANSITION PERIODS IN TIME AND PRICE

Rules have been developed showing how long prices and time remain in the transition period. All of the rules prove that TIME is the essential factor and that prices conform to time when a TIME CYCLE is complete.

VOLUME

Volume is the driving power which moves prices up or down, regardless of whether buying or selling is based on supply and demand or not. The increase in volume increases the velocity of prices in an advancing or declining market.

SPEED

Speed or velocity is a movement in price during a unit of time.

MASS PRESSURE

The fifth factor, mass pressure, shows when

the public becomes over-optimistic and buys on hope, and after a certain cycle of time, the public becomes pessimistic and sells because they fear prices are going lower. The mass pressure curve can be calculated 100 years or more in the future, as it is subject to only slight variations and minor corrections at fixed time intervals.

Mr. Gann has formulated and arranged MASTER CHARTS AND TABLES which save time and give greater accuracy with less work. With his mathematical formula and rules, the trend of stocks, commodities, business and crops can be predicted with remarkable accuracy. These discoveries and developments are of great value to investors, traders and business men in all walks of life. I hope his great work will be carried on for the benefit of mankind.

W. G. T.

Thompson, N. D.
November, 1951

In the summer of 1948, I bought Mr Gann's book, "How To Make Profits Trading in Commodities" and "The New Stock Trend Detector" and the "Truth of the Stock Tape." I was so impressed with the practical and valuable rules in these books that I decided to take his courses of instructions covering Stocks and Commodities. I began studying in December, 1948. The rules are all based on Mathematics and are practical and provable. If anyone will stick to the rules and leave out guesswork, they can make large profits trading in stocks and commodities.

After three years' experience, the rules have stood the test of Time, based on actual Market Movements.

Having taken various advisory services on the markets and reading books published by others on the subject, I am fully convinced that this is the best and most complete course available at any price. I highly recommend Mr. Gann's work to others and feel that if they study his rules and follow them, they cannot fail to make profits.

I hope that the work can be carried on for the benefit of business men, investors and traders.

A. O. K.

TO: Mr. C. R. L.

Dear Mr. L.:

I want to say a few words about Mr. W. D. Gann's course in Commodities. I feel that you and I as well as many others are fortunate in having a man like Mr. Gann to teach us in what it would take us years to learn by ourselves . . . It takes a man like Mr. Gann highly trained in mathematics to find the secrets that he can give to us.

I took the course in Commodities because I feel that it is less controlled than stocks and bonds . . . it is also faster and more interesting . . . you can delve in something slow like oats, or get something that will give you a run like soy beans. Wheat moves steady and about the right speed. From taking Mr. Gann's course I was able to sell December wheat short at 218—30,000 bushels and now it is around 200—$5,400 in about six weeks.

There is only one thing I had trouble with with his course . . . I could not believe it would work and being a skeptic I sometimes did not follow his teaching only to find that I should have . . . that cost me sometimes. I would advise you to take the course in Commodities and for six months after you get home cub trade . . . that is, trade in the minimum amounts that you can with the most backing until you get the feel and confidence in the teachings of Mr. Gann. Those little graphs in his book they work . . . I lost about three deals until I went back and studied and remembered what he said and then checked and saw that I could have made a lot of money except I was not confident until I saw it work on black and white.

I want to also take the Stock and Bond course as soon as I feel that I have mastered what he has given me . . . (he will give you enough to keep you busy for some time). Then when I get both courses I want to have short visits and talks with Mr. Gann to have him sharpen me up.

If you do not take his course the best advice I can give you is to stay away from stocks and bonds and commodities . . . it is like going into the jungle without a gun . . . he will make you safe and smart.

G. W. I. B.

ABOUT LOSSES. We have shown the record of W. D. Gann's profitable trades throughout the years. He wishes to show both sides and does not wish to mislead any one. He states that if he had never had losses himself he would never have learned how to prevent losses and teach others to protect their capital and profits and protect themselves from serious losses.

W. D. Gann states that in the early years of his trading he had many losses and at times had losses of as much as $10,000.00, $30,000.00, and at one time he lost $60,000.00. At another time he lost $50,000.00 following so-called inside information. This taught him a valuable lesson never to believe anything that he heard about what the market was going to do but to follow mathematical deductions which he could prove and knew would work.

In 1913 W. D. Gann lost all of the money he had in a brokerage failure; again in 1919 he lost another fortune which he had accumulated in a brokerage failure. He has been in two bank failures but regardless of all of these losses and misfortunes he has always been able to rely upon mathematical science and come back and make money again.

This is why he states that knowledge of the market is more important than money and with the proper knowledge and rules you will be able to protect yourself and prevent losses which W. D. Gann suffered when he was getting his experience and before he had learned all of the rules.

A great man once said, "One good piece of advice paid for is worth more than two that you receive free."

Do not depend on tips or so-called inside information, learn mathematical rules and SEE and KNOW for yourself and you will make profits.

No man ever became great or good except through many and great mistakes."—(Gladstone)

It is impossible to expect that you will never have any losses because small losses are about the only expenses in carrying on this profession of speculating and investing. The main thing for you to learn is to protect your capital and take small losses and when you get right to follow up with *stop-loss orders* and let your profits run and one big profit which can be easily made will overbalance three or more small losses and leave you away ahead. Again we repeat, follow all of the rules and not part of them, and you will make a success.

WHY TIME CYCLES PREDICT TREND OF COMMODITIES, STOCKS AND BUSINESS

After fifty-two years of experience and research going back hundreds of years, I have proved to my entire satisfaction that history repeats and that when we know the past, we can determine the future of prices. I have put TIME CYCLES to the test in my personal trading, and I have issued Annual Forecasts on Stocks and Commodities for more than 50 years which have proved accurate.

TIME CYCLES repeat because human nature does not change. That is why wars occur at regular CYCLES. Old men do not want wars, neither do they want to go into war after they have been through one. Young men fight the wars because they read history and want to be heroes. Leaders of nations appeal to the young men who have no experience, and induce them to fight. The same desire in men that urges them to risk their lives in war causes them to take a chance in business and in speculation. They take too many chances and get too optimistic after a long period of success in business and after prolonged advances in Stocks and Commodities.

Old men in business, after a prolonged period of prosperity, become too hopeful and get over-extended. It is easy to borrow money after a long period of business prosperity. People who borrow money on hope have to LIQUIDATE when FEAR overtakes them and conditions are at the worst. That is why CYCLES in business and the Stock and Commodity Markets have always repeated and always will.

Nature's laws are unchangeable and no man or set of men can change them. The New Dealers have not proved that they can stop inflation. They claim they can prevent DEPRESSION and PANICS, but no one has succeeded in doing it in the past and the next few years will prove that our Government leaders cannot stop a DEPRESSION by WASTE and SPENDING. The New Dealers have sown to the wind and must reap the whirlwind. During the past 20 years they have spent and wasted all the wealth that our country has accumulated during the past 175 years. Our Federal, State and private debts are the largest in history, and these conditions make the next few years the most critical in our history. The man who knows TIME CYCLES can predict the future, protect his capital and make money, while those who guess will lose. This is the time of opportunity to start to study mathematical, scientific rules for making accurate deductions to determine the trend of Stocks, Business, and Commodities.

April 5, 1954

W. D. GANN

OPPORTUNITIES FOR PROFITS

The greatest opportunities for profits occur at the end of great time cycles when advances or declines are very rapid and you can make large profits in a short period of time and then stay out of the market and wait for another opportunity.

Preparation for. Retiring

Business men, lawyers, doctors, engineers, accountants often wish to retire but they want something to do to keep them active and do not want to spend money out of their accumulated capital. By taking a coure of instructions after you retire you will have a new interest in life and can make an income from the market and enjoy greater pleasures.

Course for People in Trade Lines

We train men or women who are buyers or purchasing agents for large concerns and put in a complete set of charts and records and prepare the men or women who do the buying to get quick trend indications in a short period of time by the use of Master Charts, Master Calculators and the Master Three-Dimension Chart.

We teach the things that you need to learn and use in connection with your business.

If you believe in mathematics, which is the only exact science, practical and provable, and no matter what language men speak they all agree on mathematical rules. You can take this course knowing that it is the best because it is based on mathematics and has stood the test of time.

Our business is to teach you the mathematical rules so that you can determine the trend and know when to buy and sell for yourself.

"The Great Art or Learning is to understand but little at a time." (By Locke).

"All knowledge is hurtful to him who has not the science of honesty and good nature." (By Montagne).

W. D. Gann's greatest discoveries on Time Cycles have come from the Bible.

W. D. Gann is a Christian, a member of the Masonic Order and a Shriner. Special consideration and terms will be arranged for members of the Masonic Order to wish to take a course.

W. D. Gann Mathematiical Formula for Market Predictions

THE MASTER MATHEMATICAL PRICE, TIME AND TREND CALCULATOR

W. D. GANN'S latest and greatest invention for predicting the trend on stocks and commodities.

WHAT IT DOES. This Calculator is made of plastic and can be laid over a chart and it is easier to see through it than through glass.

This Master Calculator shows what these time figures are and what they mean.

1. It shows. major and minor time periods.
2. Locates a TRUE TREND LINE and a RELATIVELY TRUE TREND LINE for an advancing and a declining market.
3. The main trend and the proportion in minor time periods in days, weeks, months and years.
4. The Price Resistant Levels are shown and a Price and Time Balance.
5. The different divisions for Time and Price.
6. The Master Time Cycles and their relation to price levels and the indication where one time cycle ends and a new cycle begins.
7. The Number Seven is mentioned moro times in the Bible than any other number. The Master Calculator proves the importance of 7 in time periods, also 3, 9 and 12 which are referred to in the Bible. This Calculator accurately measures Price Time and Space for future indications of Time Trends.

8. The Master Calculator locates the Corner Stone, the Key Stone and the Cap Stone for price and time Trend. It proves the Master Number and Master Time Cycle and shows why and how they work on price.
9. The Master Calculator proves 9 divisions of time from one center or time factor and shows at a glance whether the price of stocks or commodities are in a weak or strong position.

The Value of Master Calculator to You

It is absolutely mathematically accurate and prevents you from making mistakes on price or time trend. It eliminates human judgment and guesswork and saves at least 75% of the time required to calculate trend indications. This is of great value to people who are busy and whose time is valuable.

One job of research work covering a period of 150 years required one man three weeks to complete. The Master Calculator covered the whole calculation in three hours' time and did not make one error. The man who did the research work averaged one error for every three years.

W. D. GANN has devoted over 52 years to research work on stocks and commodities and has spent a fortune to complete this revolutionary discovery.

The value of this Master Calculator to you cannot be measured in dollars. You have the use of it for your entire lifetime.

You receive with the Master Calculator complete written rules and instructions on how to use it.

We now have two (2) Master Calculators . . . Numbers 9 and 12. With these you can calculate quickly and accurately all future TIME CYCLES, PRICE and TIME RESISTANCE LEVELS. The new discovery used in connection with this Calculator forecast the big advance in Soy Beans from August 20, 1953, to March, 1954; also predicted that Coffee would advance to the highest prices in history in 1954. These Calculators gave these indications, based on the Master Time Cycle, as related to price.

One man who bought the Master Calculator says: "It is the greatest invention since the wheel. It saves me time and makes profits."

A cotton trader says: "I first took your course in 1927, and it has been of great value to me; but your new Master Calculator is the greatest discovery you have ever made, and the most valuable. It indicated top for March cotton at 4020 on September 8, 1952, and called for low at 3210 on January 12, 1953. March cotton sold at 3212 on January 12. That is plenty close for me."

The price of the Master Mathematical Calculator depends upon what courses you take in connection with it. It can be used on any commodity or on stock averages or individual stocks.

The Master Calculator can only be used with the Master Courses. It is not sold separate from the courses and cannot be used with the Mechanical Method.

We are making a special price to students who have taken the Master Courses on Stocks and Commodities. Please write if you are interested in the Master Calculator as we are having a supply made up and will reserve one for you.

COURSES OF INSTRUCTION BY CORRESPONDENCE OR PRIVATE INSTRUCTIONS

We have to develop different courses to fit the needs of different people. Busy men like Doctors, Lawyers and Engineers need a course that requires very little time to keep up every day to get market trend indications. People who have more time and who want to make speculation and investing in business need a different course. Large Business Institutions, of course, require a complete course covering everything. People in trade lines who have to purchase raw commodities need to be able to forecast the trend for several months in advance. We have special courses for people in these lines of business.

Course No. 1—SPECULATION A PROFITABLE PROFESSION. This is a new and up-to-date course completed in May, 1954. The course was gotten up principally to help people with small means to get a market education and start with a small capital which they can do and make a success if they follow the rules. This course for stocks is illustrated with 15 charts and you will receive one new chart, the *Dollar Trend*, which is much more accurate than the Dow-Jones Averages. This course on stocks is priced at $200.00 and it is not sold just to make a profit but to help the beginners get a start.

Course No. 2—THE MASTER FORECASTING COURSE ON STOCKS. This is a complete course and with this course you receive weekly and monthly high and low charts on individual stocks as well as the new chart, the *Dollar Trend*. The price of this course is $2,500.00.

COMMODITY COURSES: *Course No. 1*—SPECULATION A PROFITABLE PROFESSION. This course covers Soy Beans, Corn, Rye and Wheat. Examples are given which prove the rules and the charts show how the rules work. You receive complete set of rules and instructions and everything is made plain so that a beginner can understand it and make progress. The price of this course by correspondence is $200.00. With personal instruction $300.00.

Course No. 2—NEW TIME TREND INDICATOR. This is a more complete course than Course No. 1, but with this course you receive Course No. 1. This course covers all of the same commodities as covered in Course No. 1. The price of this course is $600.00 by correspondence or $800.00 with personal instructions. Suppose you buy Course No. 1 and pay $200.00 and later decide that you want Course No. 2: The $200.00 which you have paid can be applied on Course No. 2, and you would just pay $400.00 more for a correspondence course.

Course No. 1—COVERING COTTON, COFFEE, COCOA OR ANY OTHER COMMODITY, is $200.00 for each commodity.

Course No. 3—MASTER FORECASTING COURSE ON GRAINS, COTTON, COFFEE, LARD AND EGGS. With this course you receive a complete set of weekly and monthly high and low charts, also some daily charts. You receive two *Master Calculators* and other *Master Charts* and up-to-date *Timing Devices*. The price of this complete course by correspondence is $1,500. With personal instructions, $2,000.00.

GREAT MASTER COURSE—Covers 10 to 12 commodities, together with all the *Master Charts*, written rules and instructions and monthly high and low charts going back from 10 to 100 years. The price of this complete course with personal instructions is $5,000.00. The *Master Time Factor, Great Time Cycles, Master Charts Nos. 9* and *12* all go with this course.

With all Master Courses we send you a mass-pressure chart calculated for one year in the future. This is free.

W. D. GANN FOUNDATION, INC.
P. O. Box 399, Shenandoah Station
Miami, Florida
W. D. Gann Address: 820 S. W. 26th Road, Miami, Florida

Certified Public Accountant report verifying W. D. Gann's record is printed below:

JOSEPH ZITTRER
CERTIFIED PUBLIC ACCOUNTANT
388 MINORCA AVENUE
CORAL GABLES, FLORIDA
TELEPHONE 8-5278

Mr. W. D. Gann
820 S. W. 26th Road
Miami, Fla.

May 19, 1954

Dear Mr. Gann:

I have read the typewritten proof of the booklet which you intend publishing in the near future. While reading same I had before me your file containing many of the original testimonial letters, newspaper clippings, brokers statements and other data referred to in your booklet.

While practical considerations forbid detailed research into a remarkable history which spans more than half a century, I have delved sufficiently into the evidence submitted to convince me of the authenticity of the historical information contained in your booklet.

Very truly yours,
JOS. ZITTRER
Certified Public Accountant

JZ:f

CHAPTER 2

THE MASTER MATHEMATICAL PRICE TIME AND TREND CALCULATOR

W. D. GANN MATHEMATICAL FORMULA FOR MARKET PREDICTIONS

THE MASTER MATHEMATICAL PRICE TIME AND TREND CALCULATOR

This chart is made on transparent plastic so that you can place it over a daily, weekly, or monthly high or low chart and see at a glance the position on the time and price based on the geometrical angles. It is designed to give QUICK ACCURATE EASY CALCULATIONS: SAVE TIME AND PREVENT ERRORS.

This square of 12 is always important in working out time periods because there are 12 months in a year. The square of 144 is the GREAT SQUARE and works better than any other square both for TIME AND PRICE because it contains all of the squares from 1 to 144. This chart is divided up into sections of 9 both for time and price because 9 is the highest digit. Nine spaces on the daily chart equals 9 days, 9 weeks or 9 months in time periods and 9 equals 9¢ on grains, 9 points on stocks or 90 points on cotton on the daily high and low chart.

One column in the square of 144 contains 144. This would equal $144 on grain, 144 points on stocks or using a scale of 10 points to 1/8 inch it will equal 1440 points on cotton.

MASTER 144 SQUARE CONTAINS 324 square inches and each square inch contains 64 units which gives 20,736. This is 20,736 weeks or months and the proportionate parts of this are used for the measurement of time and price because this is the great cycle.

THE GREAT CYCLE OF THE SQUARE OF 144:

The time period of this square is 20,736 days, weeks or months. One-half is 10,368 days. One-fourth is 5,184 days. One-eights is 2,592 days. One-sixteenth is 1,296 days. One-thirty-second is 648 days and the one-sixty-fourth is 324 calendar or market days. 1/128 is 162 days and 1/256 is 81 days or the square of 9.

WEEKLY TIME PERIODS:

THE GREAT CYCLE in weeks is 2962 and 2 days and 1/2 of this period is 1481 weeks and 1 day. One-fourth is 740 weeks. One-eight is 370 weeks and 2 days. One-sixteenth is 185 weeks, 1 day. One-thirty-second is 92 weeks, 4 days and 1/64 is 41 weeks, 2 days.

MONTHLY TIME PERIODS:

THE GREAT CYCLE in months is 681 months and 23 days. One-half of this is 28 years, 5 months and 23 days. One-fourth is 14 years, 5 months and 8 days. One-eighth is 7 years, 2 1/2 months. One-sixteenth is 43 months and days. The weekly and monthly time periods from any major high and low and be checked to determine the future trend.

THE MASTER NUMBERS:

The Master Numbers are 3, 5, 7, 9 and 12. The No. 9 and its multiple is the most important because 9 digits added together equal 45. The next number of greatest importance is 7, the number mentioned more times in the Bible than any other number. There are 7 days in the week and 7 calendar days as well as 5 market days, and their multiples should be carried on your Daily, Weekly and Monthly Charts. The square of 7 is 49, which is a very important time period. The 2nd square of 7 is 98 and the third square of 7 is 147 and the fourth square of 7 is

196 and 196 is also the square of 14. The next number in importance is No. 5 which is the balancing number between 1 and 9. The square of 5 is 25 and the second square of 5 is 50 which is just 1 over the square of 7 making 49 to 50 very important for a change in trend. Three squares of 5 is 75 and 4 squares of 5 is 100 and 100 is the square of 10, which is also important for changes.

The No. 3 is mentioned in the Bible next to the No. 7 and 3 is important because 3 x 3 equals 9, the square of 3, and it is the first odd number that forms a square greater than itself. Three must be used in every way possible. 3 x 7 equals 21, 3 x 5 equals 15, 3 x 9 equals 27 and 3 x 12 equals 36, very important because it is the square of 6. The No. 12 is also spoken of in the Bible many times and is of great importance. Jesus selected 12 deciples. There are 12 months in the year, and 12 signs of the Zodiac. The important 12's in the square of 144 are 12, 24, 36, 48, 60, 72, 84, 96, 108, 120, 132 and 144. These are all important for both time and price in days, weeks and months.

Referring to the No. 9, 7 x 9 is 63 and is of great importance because the square of 8 is 64, therefore, around 63 to 64 is very important to watch the change in trend. 7 x 12 is 84 and this is of very great importance and the number next to this is 90, which is 10 x 9 and 90 is 1/4 of the circle, which is very important for time and price changes. Next in importance is 9 x 12 which is 108 or 3/4 of 144.

The importance of the circle of 360 degrees must not be overlooked in connection with the square of 144 because the proportionate parts of the circle agree with the parts of 144. 2 1/2 times 144 equals 360 and 1 1/4 times 144 equals 180, 1/2 of the circle, and 90 is 5/8 of 144. 9 is 1/16 of 144, 18 is 1/8, 27 is 3/8, 36 is 1/4, 45 is 5/16 and always very important for time and price changes and for resistance levels. 48 is 1/3 of 144 and 54 is 3/8 and 63 is 7/16, 72 is 1/2 of 144, 81 the square of 9, is 9/16 of 144 and 90 is 5/8, 99 is 11/16, 108 is 3/4, 117 is 13/16, and 126 is 7/8 and 135 is 15/16 of 144. These are the most important in the square of 12 and should be watched closely when time periods in days, weeks or months reach these points on the Master Calculator. Remember that you should always watch the Daily Chart for the first indication of the change in trend and at the same time look at the position on the Weekly Chart or 7 day time periods which is next in importance. The Monthly Chart is of the greatest importance for changes in the main trend.

THE IMPORTANCE OF 3 AND 5:

The movement in PRICE and TIME whether on a Daily, Weekly or Monthly chart has three important points, the PRICE, the TIME AND VOLUME of sales, the PITCH or TREND which is the geometrical angle which shows whether time is influencing and driving prices up or down on a slow angle or an acute fast moving angle. There are also four factors that influence prices, PRICE, TIME AND VOLUME AND VELOCITY. Time is the most important factor because when time is up volume increases and the velocity or speed of the market increases and the PITCH or TREND on the angles moves up faster or down faster.

There are three other important points to consider on a Daily, Weekly or Monthly High and Low Chart. These are the LOW PRICE, the HIGHEST PRICE and the RANGE or 1/2 between the high and the low.

FIVE FACTORS FOR TIME AND PRICE:

These are high, low, halfway point, opening and closing prices. The trend is indicated by the closing price, especially when the market is very active. If the price closes above the halfway point or near the high, the trend is up. If it closes below the halfway point or near the low, the selling is greater than the buying and the trend is down, at least temporarily. In connection with the Master Time and Trend Calculator apply all of the rules with the Master Time Factor and geometrical angles.

STRONGEST POINTS FOR TIME AND PRICE RESISTANCE:

In using the Master Square of 144, the strongest points are 1/4, 1/3, 2/3, 3/8, 1/2, 5/8, 3/4, 7/8 and the complete square of 144.

The points where the most angles cross are the strongest for resistance in PRICE and TIME.

TRIANGLE POINTS:

The triangle points or where the green angles cross are the most important. These are 72, 144, 36, 48, 96, 108 and, of course, 72, and at the end of the square of 144 at the top and the bottom.

SQUARES IN THE SQUARE OF 144:

These squares where the angles cross are of great importance for time and price resistance. These are 36, 45, 54, 63, 72, 90, 108, and at the top end of the square of 144 at the top and the bottom. When the price is at a point equal to 36 and the time periods in days, weeks or months is at 36, TIME and PRICE is SQUARE and it is important to watch for change in trend. With the square of 144 you can get any square from 1 to 144. Suppose you want to get the square of 72; you move across to 72 for time and if the price is at 72 moving up on the chart, PRICE and TIME has balanced, or squared out, and are at the 45 degree angle and at the half-way point on the Master Price, Time and Trend Calculator.

WHERE TO WATCH FOR CHANGES IN TREND:

Most changes in trend occur when the TIME PERIODS are at one-half of the square of 144 and at the end of a square or at the 1/3, 2/3, 1/4, and 3/4 points in the square of 144; you must always watch the square in time of the HIGHEST PRICE and the MINOR HIGHS and LOWS, also the square in TIME of the LOWEST PRICE and the SECOND OR THIRD higher bottom, and also the time required to square the Range and where this square works out in the Master Square of 144.

EXAMPLE: The lowest price that wheat ever sold was 28¢ per bushel in March, 1852. Therefore, every 28 months would square the lowest price. The highest price that wheat ever sold for was on May 11, 1917, when the May option sold at $3.25. Therefore, it would require 325 months to square the highest price. The lowest price that the May option ever sold was 44¢. Therefore, it would require 44 months in time to square the low price. The range between 44¢ and $3.25 is $2.81 which would require 281 months, 281 weeks or 281 days to square the range. You would look on the Master Chart and see that 2 squares of 144 equal 288, therefore, you would watch for a change in trend between 281 and 288 or near the end of the second square of 144. 7 x 44, the extreme low, equals 308, therefore, 6 1/2 times 44 would equal 286, which is within two points of the end of the square of 144 or the end of the second square making 286 an important time period to watch for a change in trend. In squaring the high of $3.25, the highest price for May wheat would be 2 squares of 144 and 37 over, therefore, when the time reached 36 days, weeks or months in the Master Square of 144 you can see that resistance would be met because moving up the time period of 136 you see that the 45 degree angle moving down from 72, which is the INNER SQUARE and the line drawn across from 36 on the price scale crosses at 36. In this way you can see that the Master Chart would indicate a resistance in time and price corresponding with the square of the highest price, the lowest price, and the Range. All other time periods from a high price, low price, or the range of any commodity or of the stock averages or individual stocks should be worked out in this same way.

You will succeed in using the Master Mathematical Price, Time and Trend Calculator by going over the charts and laying the calculator over them and working out past history. In this way you will learn just how it works and prove to yourself the great value of the Master Calculator.

HOURLY TIME PERIODS:

When Markets are very active and making a wide range in price, it is important to keep an hourly High and Low Chart, just the same as you keep the Daily High and Low Chart and the Hourly Chart will give the first change in trend.

There are 24 hours in a day, therefore, 6 days are required to pass through 144 and a total of 864 days to pass through the square of 144.

At the present time, all exchanges are open 5 days a week with the exception of holidays and most of them are open 5 hours each day. Therefore, it will require 28 days and 4 hours to pass through 144 at the rate of 5 hours per day and 5 days per week. Trading time for grains is 225 minutes or 3.75 hours per day or 38 days and 1 1/2 hours to pass through 144 at the rate of 3.75 hours per day and 5 days per week.

GREAT YEARLY TIME CYCLE:

To pass through the square of 144, which equals 20,736, it requires 56 years, 9 months and 23 days, which is a very important time cycle. Next in importance is 1/2 of this time period which is 28 years, 5 months and 8 days and 1/4 which is 14 years, 2 months and 19 days. The 14 year cycle is always very important because it is 2 seven year periods. 14 years equals 168 months and 169 months is the square of 13 making it very important for a change in trend and this is also an important time resistance point.

1/8 of the Great Cycle is 7 years, 1 month and 10 days and is quite important. 1/16 is 42 months and 20 days, 1/32 is 21 months and 10 days. This is an important time period because it is close to 22 1/2 months which is 1/16 of the circle of 360 degrees.

NINE SPACES AND NINE TIME PERIODS:

The chart being divided up into 9 sections gives all the squares of 9 for price resistance of time resistance which, as referred to above is 9¢ on the Daily Chart for grains and the same for Weekly and Monthly Charts; that is, 1¢ to each 1/8 inch. For different commodities, different scales are used. (See Special Instructions for the different commodities.)

The Chart being divided up into 9 sections gives 1/16th squares of 9 for price resistance or time resistance which, as referred to above, is 90 points on the Daily Chart, 135 on the Weekly Chart, and 270 on the Monthly and 2880 on the 20 point scale and 9 spaces equal

180 points.

The angles in red are all drawn on the squares of 9. The Inner Square of 45° is drawn from 72 because 72 is 1/2 of 144. These angles come out at 72, 144 and 72.

The straight lines are in green and are 1/3 of the square of 144 in price or time.

GREEN ANGLES;

The green angles are the angles of 2 x 1 which move up two spaces or 2 points in one period of the time. The other angle below the 45° angle is the angle of 1 x 2 which requires 2 time periods to move up 1 space or 1¢ per bushel on grains for each time period of 1 day, 1 week or 1 month. These angles move down from the top at the rate of 2 points or 2 spaces per time period or at the rate of 1/2 space, 1/2 point, or 1/2¢ per time period. The distance that the green angles and the red angles are apart determines how far prices can advance or decline.

When the market enters the INNER SQUARE it is important for a change in trend and time angles and Position in the square tell at the time it entered whether the price is going up or down. Also, when price breaks below a 45° on the INNER SQUARE it shows weakness in proportion to the time from high or low price.

WHEN TO START A NEW SQUARE:

When the time period of the Daily, Weekly or Monthly Charts has moved 144 you begin a new square. But to get the position you simply move the Master Square over,to 144 and place it over the chart to get the position in the next square.

STRONGEST AND WEAKEST POINTS:

Where the greatest number of angles cross or bisect each other in the square of 144 are the points of greatest resistance, such as where the 25 and 2 x 1 angles cross each other.

Study and practice on past action of the market and you will soon learn how to determine the trend very quickly by using the Master Chart.

HOW TO USE THE MASTER SQUARE OF 144:

Follow all rules on angles as given in the Master Forecasting course.

Place this chart at the bottom or 0 on the Daily, Weekly or Monthly Chart or place the bottom of the chart on the low price or SQUARE of the HIGH PRICE, the LOW PRICE, and the square of the RANGE and show where time and price balances.

When you figure the halfway point of the extreme high or the halfway point of the range, place either the top or the bottom of the chart on the halfway point and it will give the correct POSITION and TREND. However, if you will place the CENTER, or 72, on the halfway point in PRICE you will then get the correct position in time and can see how the price is working out with time in the MASTER SQUARE OF 144 and the INNER SQUARE which starts from 72, the gravity center or 1/2 point of the square.

CALENDAR DAYS AND MARKET DAYS:

For any kind of a chart, we move over one space for each unit of time. Therefore, it would require 144 market days or 144 calendar days to complete the square of 144. When prices pass out of one square into another, a change in trend usually takes place and the periods and geometrical angles on this MASTER CHART tell you which way the trend is going to change.

LEAP YEARS:

In calculating time periods to get exact number of days and weeks the LEAP YEAR must be figures and one extra day added. From 1864 the Leap Years were as follows: 1868; 1872; 1876; 1880; 1884; 1888; 1892; 1896; 1904; 1908; 1912; 1916; 1920; 1924; 1928; 1932; 1936; 1940; 1944; 1948; 1952.

POSITION WITH MASTER SQUARE:

To get the position with the MASTER SQUARE OF 144, lay it over the Daily, Weekly or Monthly and start from extreme low, extreme high, 0 or 1/2 point of the range or 1/2 of the high selling price. You can also place the top of the chart at the high selling price. In this way you can get the correct time and positions or angles at a glance.

Place MASTER CALCULATOR on January to get twelve year periods, each month same way.

You should have all time periods from important highs and lows calculated in days, weeks and month in order that you can look them up quickly on the MASTER CHART.

With all time periods brought up to date in this way, you can get the position on the MASTER CHART and the indicated trend without looking at a daily, weekly or monthly chart. You should have the time periods in months from every important top and bottom.

With the MASTER SQUARE OF 144, your work will be cut down but you must learn to practice and bring up all time periods and study the MASTER SQUARE and learn how to use it to get tops and bottoms accurately. Work and practice will bring PRECISION and PROFITS. I have done my part. It is now up to you to work hard and if you do, your success is assured.

HOW TO PLACE THE MASTER CHART SQUARE OF 144 ON CHARTS

To get correct positions on any of your charts, daily, weekly or monthly, you must place the MASTER CHART OVER THEM correctly. The top of the MASTER CHART has Price and Time Chart by W. D. Gann on it. Always place this on the bottom of your chart unless it is where you move up to a higher price when you place it at 72 or bottom marked "Bottom" 0.

Place the MASTER CHART at 0 on any of your other charts or at a low point on the same date of any high or low point. Place the MASTER CHART at 72 which is 1/2 of 144 or on any one-half point of the price range or 1/2 of the high selling price.

Always place the MASTER CALCULATOR on all previous highs and lows to get changes in trends and price resistance. Never overlook the extreme high and low price. Also, most important 1/2 of high to low and 1/2 of the highest price any commodity or stock ever sold.

TIME PERIODS AND PRICE RESISTANCE

The circle of 360º is most important for time cycles and price resistance. First, we divide the circle by 2 and get 180 which is one-half and is most important for time or price in days, weeks or months. Next we divide the circle by 3 and get the triangle points of 120, 240, and 360. Third, we divide the circle by 4 which gives 90, 180, 270, and 360, which are the squares and most important.

Divide the circle by 8 which gives 8 periods of 45 degree angles which are 45, 90, 135, 180, 225, 270, 315, and 360. Next in importance is to divide the circle by 16 which gives the angles of 22 1/2 degrees. We divide the circle by 32 and get the angles and time periods of 11 1/4 degrees and their multiples. Divide the circle by 64 which gives 5 5/8 degrees and their multiples.

The table below shows each division of 5 5/8 and we run down to 16 in the column which equals 90 or 1/4 of the circle and 16 is 1/4 of 64. This arrangement reading across gives each of the multiples and the figures between the heavy lines are among the ones which are the most important.

Table of 64th of the Circle

1.	5 5/8	17.	95 5/8	33.	185 5/8	49.	275 5/8
2.	11 1/4	18.	101 1/4	34.	101 1/4	50.	281 1/4
3.	16 5/8	19.	106 7/8	35.	196 7/8	51.	286 7/8
4.	22 1/2	20.	112 1/2	36.	202 1/2	52.	292 1/2
5.	28 1/8	21.	118 1/8	37.	208 1/8	53.	298 1/8
6.	33 3/4	22.	123 3/4	38.	213 3/4	54.	303 3/4
7.	39 3/8	23.	129 3/8	39.	219 3/8	55.	309 3/8
8.	45	24.	135	40.	225	56.	315
9.	50 5/8	25.	140 5/8	41.	230 5/8	57.	320 5/8
10.	56 1/4	26.	146 1/4	42.	236 1/4	58.	326 1/4
11.	61 7/8	27.	151 7/8	43.	241 7/8	59.	331 7/8
12.	67 1/2	28.	157 1/2	44.	247 1/2	60.	337 1/2
13.	73 1/8	29.	163 1/8	45.	253 1/8	61.	343 1/8
14.	78 3/4	30.	168 3/4	46.	258 3/4	62.	348 3/4
15.	84 5/8	31.	174 3/8	47.	264 3/8	63.	354 3/8
16.	90	32.	180	48.	270	64.	360

The squares from 1 to 10 are important to watch for time and price resistance as they are important degrees in the circle. These are: 1 - 4 - 9 - 16 - 25 - 36 - 49 - 64 - 81 - 100 - 121 - 144 - 169 - 196 - 225 - 256 - 289 - 324 and 361, which is the square of 19.

Divide the circle by 6 and we get two resistance and time periods which are not contained in the other table. These are 60 and 300.

It is also very important to divide the circle by 12 because there are 12 months in the year and this works out accurately for time periods. The following are the degrees not shown in the above table: 30 - 150 - 210 - 330.

Divide the circle by 24 which gives 15 degree periods in longitude and approximately 15 days in time. Because there are 24 hours in a day and the earth makes 1 revolution on its axis in 24 hours these periods are quite important. The following are not contained in the other table: 15 - 75 - 105 - 165 - 195 - 285 - 345.

Under the table of the 64th Circle reading across from left to right the 2nd column is always 90 degrees from the first. Example: The first is 5 5/8 and 17 in the next column is 95 5/8 or a gain of 90. Opposite 33 is 185 5/8 which is 90 from 95 5/8, opposite 49 is 275 5/8 or 90 from 185 5/8.

The column 1 under 8 between the heavy lines is 45 and the next one is 135, 225, and 315 each 90 degrees apart.

At the bottom of column 1 opposite 16 is 90 and reading across is 180, 270, and 360. These figures are all 45 degrees from the figures in column 8 which are the most important for time and price resistance.

To realize the value and importance of these degrees in the circle you take the price of highs and lows and the time periods, expecially in weeks and months and check them over and you will see how well they work out to these important degrees.

Remember you must always figure how many points or cents the prices are up from the extreme low or minor lows and how many cents it is down from the extreme highs or minor highs. Also, how many cents it is above or below the main halfway point or the minor halfway points or gravity centers. You will find that the important halfway points form very close to these natural degrees in the circle.

Example: May Soybeans extreme high 436 3/4, extreme low 67, gives the halfway point at 251 7/8. Look in the table and you find the 45th 64th at 253 1/8. This halfway point is very close. Next 1/2 of 436 3/4 is 218 3/8 and the 39th 64th is 219 3/8, very close to this natural resistance degree. The extreme low of Cash Beans was 44 and the halfway point between 44 and 436 3/4 is 240 3/8. 240 is 2/3 of a circle or a triangle point and 241 7/8 is the 43rd 64th of the circle. 44 the extreme low, was only 1 from 45, the important resistance level. 67, the lowest price May futures ever sold, is within 1/2 point of 67 1/2 which is 12/64 or 3/4 between 0 and 90 and 67 1/2 is halfway between 45 and 90 which was the cause of May beans making lows for 5 years between 67-69 which indicated the big advance that followed as there were triple bottoms between 67-69 in three different years.

Next consider the time periods December 28, 1932, was low on May Beans and December 28, 1947, was 15 years or 180 months which is 1/2 of a circle also 1/2 of the 360 degrees making this a very important time cycle. May beans reached extreme high on January 15, 1948, just 18 days beyond the even 15 year cycle. Check all other time periods and time cycles in the same way and you will find how well they work out in the circle of 360 degrees.

W. D. Gann

September 29, 1953

W. D. Gann

CHAPTER 3

HOW TO USE THE MASTER CALCULATOR MAY SOY BEANS

HOW TO USE THE MASTER CALCULATOR
MAY SOY BEANS

First it is important to know how to use the scale for prices. The scale is the same for grains, for all grains and stocks. The scale on the left side of the calculator runs from 0 to 144. If the price is above 144 you subtract 144 and then place the scale in the correct position.

EXAMPLE: When May Beans is selling above 288 this is 2 squares of 144 up from 0 and you place the Master Calculator with 0 on 288 at the time of any important high or low levels and you get the correct position and the indicated trend on the Daily, Weekly or Monthly Charts.

The scale on each side running from 0 up to 4320 is for cottom, eggs and other commodities. For cotton on the Daily Chart using a 10 point scale 1440 is the top of the chart of 144 spaces up. For the Weekly Chart using a scale of 15 points ot 1/8 inch the price at the top of the chart is 2160 and the second square is 4320 using a scale of 30 points for 1/8 inch on the Monthly Chart the top of the Master Calculator at 144 equals the price of 4320.

Using a 20 point scale the top of the chart equals 2880 and at 72 on the second scale up 72 equals 4320.

First it is always important to find out the price position in a square.
EXAMPLE: May Soy Beans extreme high 436-3/4. This is 3 x 144 which is 432 and 4-3/4 in the fourth square.

The extreme low on cash soy beans is 44¢. Subtract this form 456-3/4 gives a range of 293-3/4 which is 2 squares of 144 and 104-3/4 over. The extreme low for May Beans is 67¢. Subtract this from 436-3/4 gives 369-3/4 and 81-3/4 in the third square. Note that 81 is 9 x 9 and an important resistance level.

January 15, 1948 May Beans high 436-3/4, February 14, 1949 low 90½. A decline of 235¼. Subtract 144 gives 91¼ and 90 in the second square is a strong resistance level.
From the low of February 14, 1949 to February 6, 1951 hgih 344½ gives an advance of 143½ which was just inside this first square of 144 and was, therefore, a strong resistance and selling level. This price would come out at the top of the square at 144.

You should always keep up the important half-way points so that you can place the Master Calculator at 72 on the half-way point at the time period of any extreme high or low. ½ of 436 is 218-3/8 and ½ between 44 and 436-3/4 is 240-3/8. ½ between 436-3/4 and 201½ gives 319-1/8. Calculate all of the other half-way points in the same way.

WEEKLY TIME PERIODS. The time from one important top to a bottom and from bottom to bottom and top to top is very important in usint the calculator.

These time periods will show when you place the calculator on the chart at any top or bottom.

1948, May high to February 14, 1949, 38 weeks
1948, January 15, to October 16, 1950 low 232½, time 143 weeks
The low cane just at the end of the 1st square of 144.
1948, May to October 16, 1950, 125 weeks
1948, January to February 6, 1951, high 344½, 159 weeks
1948, May to February 6, 1951, 141 weeks
1948, January to July 9, 1951, low 269, 181 weeks
1948, May to July 9, 1951, 163 weeks
1948, January to December 10, 1951, 203 weeks
1948, May to December 10, 1951, 185 weeks
1948, January to August 13, 1951, 238 weeks
1951, February 6 to August 13, 1951, 79 weeks
1952, August 13, to February 13, 1953, 26 weeks
1949, February 14, to October 16, 1950, 88 weeks
1949, February 14, to February 6, 1950, 104 weeks
1949, February 14, to July 9, 1951, 126 weeks
1949, February 14, to December 10, 1951, 148 weeks
1949, February 14 to August 13, 1952, 183 weeks
1949, February 14 to February 13, 1953, 209 weeks

When the time period is more than 144 in time periods you subtract 144 and start the second square. 144 from 209 would give a balance of 65 in the 2nd square. You would, of course, look up the price on the time period of 65 to see the position on the Master Calculator.

By laying the top of the Master Calculator on 436-3/4 you will see that the green angle which is 2 x 1 moving down ½¢ per week crosses for the week ending March 7, 1953 at 267 weeks. ½ of this gives 303¼ and a price below this angle still shows down trend.

On February 6, 1951 high 344½ to March 7, 1953, time 108 weeks. One half of this is 54 and the angle crosses at 290½.

We can always add proportionate parts to the bottom or subtract from the top. To 201½ low we add 90 gives 291½. To 201½ we add 96 which is 2/3 of 144 and this gives 297½ as a resistance level. If we subtract 144 from 436-3/4 it gives 292-3/4.

If we subtract 48. Which is 1/3 of 144, from 344½ we get 296½ as a resistance level.

PRESENT POSITION OF MAY SOY BEANS: For the Weekly High and Low Chart place the bottom of the calculator at 0 on 201½ and you will see that November 17, 1951 is 144 weeks and ends the first square of 144. You then move your calculator over and place the bottom or 0 on 201½ at the end of the first square of 144 November 17, 1951. You will then see that the week ending March 7, 1951 is 212 weeks from Feb. 14, 1949 and the time is 68 weeks in the second square of 144. The price at 298 is at 96 on the price scale. This is the green line and is 2/3 of 144, a resistance and selling level. The red 45 degree angle from the top from 18 crosses 296 and the 45 degree red angle from 18 moving up crosses 296. Note that 18 is 1/8 of 144. Therefore, when the price of May beans is below 296 is the weaker position. 4 weeks later the time will be 72 weeks which is 1/2 of 144. This will be important for change in trend.

Next place the bottom or 0 on the Master Calculator at 232½, the low of October 16, 1950, and time is 124 weeks, which is the first square of 144 and a price of 300 is at 68 on the scale or 68 up in the square of 144. In two weeks it will be 126 or 7/8 of 144 which is important for a change in trend. When the price is below 295 it is below the green angle of 2 x 1 from 232½ and is a weaker position.

February 1, 1933 low 280, was on the 45 degree angle from 72. THIS IS THE INNER SQUARE AND IS VERY STRONG AND IMPORTANT. The price at 48 up is 1/3 of 144 and strong resistance and buying level. From 280 to 298 is 18 points up, 1/8 of 144, and normal rally.

Next place the calculator on 269, the low of July 9, 1951 and you will see that March 7, 1953 is on the 85th week and the price at 297 is at the 3 x 1 angle from 269 and 295 is on the red line 27 and also the 2 x 1 green line from 72 crossed at 297 making this a resistance level. And below 297 is a weaker position.

Next place the top of the calculator over 344½, the top on Feb. 6, 1951 and for the week inding March 7 is 108 weeks or 2/3 of 144. This indicates a time for change in trend. The price of 299 is on the red price line of 99, a resistance and selling level.

Next place the top of the claculator on 314½, the high of Aug. 13, 1952 and the time is 29 weeks. The green angle 2 x 1 from 144 or the top of 314½ crosses at 300 in the week ending March 7 making this a resistance and selling level. A price of 296½ is on line 126 down 18¢ from the high which is 1/8 of 144.

For August 13, 1952 place 72, the price scale, on 273½ which is 1/2 of 201½ to 344½. You will see that 298 is on line 96 which is 2/3 of 144 and the 45 degree angle from 126 crosses at 299 making this a selling level.

Place the Master Calculator, that is the top of the calculator, on 310, the high price of December 15, 1951. March 7, 1953 comes out on the 64th week which is the square of 8. The price line is on 132 which is 11 x 12 and is important for a change in trend.

TO GET POSITION FROM 0. For the week ending November 15, 1951 which was 144 weeks from February 14, 1949 when the low was 201½. As this was the end of the square of 144 you place the bottom of the calculator on a price of 288, which is 2 squares up in price, and you will see the position from 0 for the week ending March 7, 1953. The price of 297 is on 9 in the third square of 144 and 9 is 1/16 of 144. The 2 x 1 green angle from 144 to 0 crossed at 297 and in 5 weeks will be at 72 which is 1/2 of 144 and important for a change in trend.

MONTHLY INDICATIONS: You use the Master Calculator in the same way on the Monthly Chart to get the position for time and price.

December 28, 1952 low of 44. For the period ending March 28, 1955 is 243 months. You subtract 144 and this gives 99 in the second square. Set the Master Calculator at 0 on a price of 288 and on the 99th month and the price of 299 is at 9 in the 3rd square of 144. The second red angle comes out on 99 and this is 9 up in price which is 1/16 of 144. The 45 degree angle from 90 and the 45 degree angle from 108 on the Master Calculator crosses 299 making this a resistance or selling level.

Place the Master Calculator on 0 on 201½ and note that the 2 x 1 green angle crosses at 299 and the 45 degree angle from 344 crosses at 295. When the price is below 295 it is in a weaker position. A price of 296 is on line 96 which is 2/3 of 144.

1948, January 15, to March 15, 1953 is 62 months. Set the Master Calculator at 436 3/4. This will be on the time period 62 months and 297 which is 144 down at 436 3/4. Note the heavy red line 63 which is 7 x 9 is below 297 and in the second square of 144 down from 436 3/4 and when the price declines to 295 it will be in a weaker position.

On July 27, 1939 low 67¢ place the Master Calculator, that is 0, on 67 and Feb. 27th is 163 months and March 27, 1953 is 164 months. If we add 144 to 67 this gives 211 as the top of the first square in prices. Set the calculator on 211 and 164 is 20 months in the second square of 144. Note that the 45 degree angle from 108 crosses at 299 making this a selling level.

1920, February 15, high 405, time to Feb. 15, 1953 is 296 months or 2 squares of 144 and a 108 in the third square. Set the Master Calculator on 202½ which is 1/2 of 405 and place 108 for Feb. 1953 and this gives a price of 298 which is 96 on the scale and 2/3 of 144 the resistance level.

Set the calculator at 344½ for Feb. 6, 1951 and 299 is on 99 price scale and the 45 degree angle from 72 crosses at 297. This is the INNER SQUARE AND RESISTANCE LEVEL and when the price closes below 296 it is a weaker position and indicates further decline.

It is well to remember that at this time of the year a reversal in prices can take place or an advance can continue, therefore, a stop loss order of 3¢

above 299 should be used making the stop loss order 302, Should the price of May Soy Beans decline and close below 287 which will be back into the second square from 0 they will be in a weaker position. After March 15, if the price of May Beans is below 286 they will be below the 45 degree angle from Dec, 23, 1932 when the price was 44¢.

If you will practice with the Master Calculator and place it on all important tops and bottoms and half way points on the Daily, Weekly and Monthly Charts you will soon see how well it works and will learn to get trend indications very quickly.

March 6, 1955

CHAPTER 4

MASTER CALCULATOR FOR WEEKLY TIME PERIODS TO DETERMINE THE TREND OF STOCKS AND COMMODITIES

MASTER CALCULATOR FOR WEEKLY TIME PERIODS TO DETERMINE THE TREND OF STOCKS AND COMMODITIES

by W. D. GANN

This Master Calculator shows Weekly Time Periods of 7 days each or a total of 52 weeks in one year. This represents 364 calendar days, therefore at the end of each year there is a gain of one day and at the end of 7 years a gain of 7 days, the time period coming out one week before the date of the important high and low prices. You must also add one day for each leap year. Suppose you want to get the time period for 15 years, you multiply 365 by 15, add the number of leap years and then divide the total days by 7 to get the weekly periods of 7 days each in order to use the Calculator. 'See Tables for Price and Time Periods.)

The total square of 52 is 2704, which we can use to measure weeks, days, months, years or hours. In using days, it would, of course, require 2704 days to pass thru the square of 52. This would give 386 weeks and 2 days or approximately 7 years and 5 months, very close to the important cycle of 7½ years, which is 90 months.

If we use hours to balance or square 2704, we get 112-2/3 days by dividing 2704 by 24, the total number of hours in a day during which time the earth makes one complete revolution on its axis.

The Square of 52, which is composed of 7-day periods, is one of the most important for measuring Price and Time. The number 7 is referred to in the Bible more times than any other number, except the number 3. Both of these numbers are very important to use in connection with price and time changes.

You start time periods from the actual dates of important high and important low prices and not from the first day of each month or the first day of each year.

The Calculator is 104 weeks wide, which equals 2 years. The time periods run across the bottom of the Calculator from left to right to 104, which completes 2 years, and to 208, which completes 4 years. At the top of the Calculator, running across to the left, the time periods run to 312 which ends 6 years, and to 416, which ends 8 years, and to 520, which completes a 10-year cycle.

DIVISIONS OF TIME PERIODS

The year is divided by					
1/8,	which	equals	6½	weeks	
1/4,	"	"	13	"	
1/3,	"	"	17	"	
3/8,	"	"	19½	"	
1/2,	"	"	26	"	a most important time and resistance level
5/8	"	"	32½	"	
2/3	"	"	35	"	
3/4	"	"	39	"	very important for change in trend.
7/8	"	"	45½	"	
1	year, which is 52 weeks.				

The angles run from each of the time periods for Price and Time in order to balance the Square and show resistance levels where price and time periods indicate a change in trend.

THIRD AND FOURTH DIMENSIONS
OF TIME AND PRICE

We know of three dimensions--height, width and length--but there is a fourth dimension or element in market movements. We prove the fourth dimension with the Master Calculator or Square of 52 in Time Periods of 7 days each for 7 weeks or more and the same price relation. 7 x 52 equals 364 or 7 years.

THE CIRCLE, TRIANGLE AND SQUARE

The circle of 360° and the nine digits are the basis of all mathematical calculations. The Square and the Triangle form within the circle but there is an inner circle and an inner square, as well as an outer square and an outer circle which prove the fourth dimension in working out market movements.

PRICE

The most important points to consider are:

1. Lowest price.
2. Highest price.
3. The 1/2 point, mean or average between the extreme high and the extreme low. We get the fourth dimension, as shown on the Master Calculator, by drawing 45° angles from the 1/2 point or gravity center, which is the most important for price resistance.
4. Volume of Sales. This is the power which drives the market up or down but remember that TIME is the most essential element and when Time is completed, the volume of sales starts to move the market up or down.

TIME

Time is divided into sections or cycles by which we determine the change in trend.

1. Daily high and low prices
2. Weekly high and low prices
3. Monthly high and low prices
4. Yearly high and low prices

The Weekly and the Yearly Time Periods are most important for trend indications and for changes in trend.

The day is divided into hours, minutes and seconds. The 4 divisions of the day are: Sunrise, Noon, Sunset and Midnight. Of these the most important are: Noon, when the Sun is straight overhead or on a 90° angle, and Midnight, the opposite point or 180° from Noon and 90° from Sunset.

Because we are using 7-day Time Periods with the Calculator, 1/2 of 7 days or 3½ days is important to watch for change in trend. Always watch the 3rd and 4th day from any important high or low level for a minor change in trend which later may become a major change.

<u>7-day Periods</u> -- The time periods of 7 calendar days from any important high or low level is of great importance. 14 days is the most important and 21 days or 3 weeks is next in importance. Reactions will often run 2 weeks and sometimes 3 weeks and then resume the main trend. Rallies in a Bear Market often run 14 days and sometimes 21 days and then resume the downward or main trend.

<u>Multiples of 7 days</u> -- The square of 7 or 49 days is very important for change in trend. You can start to watch for this change after the 42nd day but the first indication of a change may not occur until the 45th or 46th day, which is 1/8 of a year or 365 days. 1/16 of a year is 23 days. Therefore, both the 46-day and 23-day periods are important to watch for change in trend.

Next in importance is 63 to 65 days because 7 x 9 is 63 and the square of 8 is 64. 81 days or the square of 9 is also of great importance. 90 to 91 days is 1/4 of a year or 7 x 13. This is of very great importance to watch for change in trend. Of course, of next importance is around 182 days or 1/2 of the year.

YEARS

Later we will refer to the four seasons or the divisions of the year, which are Spring, Summer, Fall and Winter and important to watch for change in trend. However, the divisions of Time are from the date of the actual important high and low prices.

The important yearly cycles are 1, 2, 3, 5, 7, 9, 10, 12, 14, 15, 18, 20, 21, 22½, 24, 25, 27, 28, 30, 40, 45, 49, 56, 60, 84, and 90 which is the Great Cycle. We divide the cycles into 1/2, which is the most important, and also into the periods of 1/8, 1/3 and 2/3, and watch these proportionate parts of the cycles for changes in trend. For example:

The Great Cycle of 90 years equals 1080 months;
1/2 is 45 years or 540 months
1/4 is 22½ years or 270 months
1/8 is 11¼ years or 135 months
1/16 is 5-5/8 years or 67½ months
The 30-year Cycle or any other cycle is divided up in the same way.

<u>Multiples of 7 Years</u> -- The multiples of 7 years or 84 months are all important to watch for change in trend. These are 7 years, 14, 21, 28, 35, 42, and 49, which is most important because it is the square of 7. Next 56 and 63 are very important, 63 because it is 7 x 9. 81, the square of 9, is very important.

Prices can also be used in sevens. Example: 98, 2 x 49. 126, 2 x 63. 162, 2 x 81, etc.

<u>Yearly Time Periods - Triangles and Squares</u> -- When 1/3 of a year from any important low comes out at the same time that 1/4 or 1/2 of a year from another important top or bottom comes out, it is of great importance for a change in trend. 1/2 of a yearly time period is always the most important, just the same as 1/2 of the highest selling price and 1/2 of the range of the price is important for resistance levels. By practice, study and comparison and by placing the Calculator over the Weekly high and low Chart, you will see how all these Price and Time Periods work out.

TIME, PRICE, VOLUME, VELOCITY, PITCH OR TREND

When a Time Cycle is completed, Volume increases and the market begins to move up faster or move down faster.

The pitch or trend is determined mostly by the 45° angle, which is the most important, but other angles can be used to determine the trend. The pitch or trend is the 4th dimension and shows whether the market is slow or fast by the angles, whether very acute or above the 45° angle or flat and slow, below the 45° angle, which causes a slow creeping market that may later regain important angles and increase the pitch of the angle and start moving up faster.

All of this is shown on the Master Calculator or Square of 52.

3 WAYS TO SQUARE OR BALANCE TIME AND PRICE

(1) Balance the lowest price with time measured in weeks and balance the highest price with time.
(2) Balance the range, which is the total between the extreme high and extreme low.
(3) Get the 4th dimension by balancing Price and Time in weekly time periods as shown on the Master Square of 52.

PRICE SCALE

The price scale runs up and down to 104, 208, 312, 416, and 520, which balances out with the Time Periods. For GRAINS, this scale is for cents per bushel. For STOCKS, it is $1.00 per share. The Price Periods are divided up into 1/8 and 1/3, the same as the Time Periods.

Scale for COTTON, COFFEE, COCOA and EGGS -- Each 1/8 cent equals 10 points. Therefore 52 would indicate 520 in price and 104 would indicate 1040 for Cotton or any other commodity trading in 100 points to 1¢.

EGGS--Weekly high and low chart -- Eggs trade at a minimum of 5 points. We use 10 points to 1/8 inch on the daily high and low chart. Experience has proven that a scale of 25 points to 1/8 inch, which represents one week in Time, works best. Therefore, 52 spaces on the Calculator would indicate 1300 or 13¢ for Eggs; 104 would represent 2600; 156 would represent 3900; 208 would represent 5200 or 52¢ per dozen for Eggs, etc. One year Time Period would give a range of 13¢, 1/2 of this would be 6½¢, 1/4 would be 325 and 1/8 would be 162. Therefore, if you want to get resistance levels for prices above 26¢, you would add 6½ which would give 32½, etc.

All of these are shown on the Table enclosed for prices which run up to the equivalent of 40 years calculated. All you have to do is run across the period marked "1/2" and get the exact date during each year
when the Time is at 1/2 or 182 days from an important high or low, and in the same way from the Table you get the price resistance levels based on the Square of 52.

HOW TO USE THE MASTER CALCULATOR

One column on the Calculator can be used for one month or one year but the Calculator is designed to be used on the Weekly high and low Chart for determining the important changes in trend.

HOW TO USE CALCULATOR ON WEEKLY CHART

Place the bottom or "0" of the Calculator on "0" below any price or place it on the low price, then you will see where the angles cross and resistance levels are indicated.

Place the Calculator marked "Top" at the high price on the exact date the important price is made, then you can see the important angles for resistance from the top down.

THE INNER SQUARE OR 1/2 POINT

Place the Calculator on 1/2 of the highest selling price or 1/2 of the range. Place the Calculator where it is marked 1/2 or 26 weeks over the chart on the same line that low or high is made. Placing the Calculator on 26 over the 1/2 point will show the resistance and whether the price is in strong or weak position.

THE INNER SQUARE OF 45° ANGLES

The Inner Square of 45° Angles starts from 26, which is 1/2 of 52, and moves up or down. It crosses at 26, which is 1/2 of 52. The 45° angle moving up from "0" crosses at 52 and 104 and the 45° angle moving down from a top or high level crosses at 52 and terminates at "0". All of these important 45° angles from any important high or low cross on 1/4, 1/2, 3/4, etc., as you can see, and balance out Time and Price.

MOST IMPORTANT TIME PERIODS

The most important Time Periods are the anniversary date of 1, 2, 3 years or more from the dates of the important highs and important lows. Second in importance is 1/2 of the Yearly Time Period; third in importance is 3/4 or 39 weeks in each year; fourth, the 1/3 point or 17 weeks and the 2/3 point or 35 weeks are also very important Time Periods for change in trend.

When you are working out Weekly Time Periods, you must also consider the importance of the 3-year cycle, the 5-year cycle, 7-year cycle, 10-year cycle, 15 years which is 1/2 of the 30--year cycle, and 20 years which is 1/3 of the 60-year cycle, and 30 years which is a complete cycle of 360 months. The longer the Time Period from an important top or bottom, the greater the variation because each year of the time period gains at least one day and in leap years gains an additional day before the end of the complete cycle.

The Table for Time and Price Periods shows the exact time in 52 weeks to a year or 364 calendar days. By figuring the leap years and the time gained at the rate of one day per year, you know how much time to subtract and can make the adjustment for the full period.

SEASONAL TIME PERIODS

In figuring Seasonal Time Periods, we do not start to calculate Time from January 1st but calculate the Time Periods from the date when the Spring Season starts on March 21. These periods are marked on the Table in 1/8, 1/3, etc. They are as follows:

May 5 ends	1/8 or $6\frac{1}{2}$	weeks from March 21
Jun. 21 "	1/4 or 13	"
Jul. 23 "	1/3 or 17	"
Aug. 5 "	3/8 or $19\frac{1}{2}$	"
Sep. 22 "	1/2 or 26	"
Nov. 8 "	5/8 or $32\frac{1}{2}$	"
Nov. 22 "	2/3 or 35	"
Dec. 21 "	3/4 or 39	"
Feb. 4 "	7/8 or $45\frac{1}{2}$	"
Mar. 20 "	1 year or 52	"

MIDSEASON TIME PERIODS

These are May 5, August 5, November 8, February 4. Important changes in trend occur around these midseason dates but all of the above Time Periods should be watched for important changes in trend.

The Table for Time Periods and important high and low prices is shown with figures at the top running from 1 to 36. The important Time Periods are shown with exact dates and if you want to look up something in the 7th year, you move over to the column marked "7" and move down to the 1/2 point. You will find that $7\frac{1}{2}$ years is 390 weeks, etc. and any price on this same line would be an important resistance level.

By studying, practicing and experimenting with the Master Calculator, you will learn how valuable these Time and Price Periods in multiples of 7 are.

W. D. GANN

January 10, 1955

Chapter 5

May Soy Beans
Square Of 67
Time Periods

MAY SOY BEANS SQUARE OF 67
TIME PERIODS FOR DAYS, WEEKS, AND MONTHS.

July 27, 1939 May Soy Beans Futures sold at the lowest price in history, 67¢ per bushel, therefore, the square or balancing of this price is 67 days, 67 weeks or 67 months. The square of 67 is enclosed made up on tracing cloth so that you can lay it over the Daily, Weekly or Monthly High or Low Chart and see the position in the square and the resistance based on time and price. This square shows the resistance levels in price of 1/8, 1/4, 1/3, 3/8, 1/2, 5/8, 2/3, 3/4, 7/8 and 67 the complete square. The time periods moving across the bottom and top of the chart from left to right are also divided up into periods fo 1/8, 1/3 and 2/3. The first complete time cycle of 67 or the first square is marked 1 with a ring around it and on up to the 12th square in time. The price periods are marked the same way. You will note that 436-3/4, the highest price that May Beans ever sold, was at 1/2 of the square. It was in the 7th square and was 6½ squares up in price. This was from 0 but the total gain from 67 to 436-3/4 was 369-3/4 and 5½ x 67 is 368½. When an extreme high or an extreme low price is reached it is important to check the time periods to see how the price and time works out on the angles and in the square.

1948, January 27th, was 102 months from July 27, 1939. This was 1 square of 67 and 35 in the second square. You move over to 35 and up to the price of 436 and you find it is just 1½ time periods over thehalf of the square but at the 45 degree angle moving up from 0 making this a resistance and selling level based on both time and price.

1948, January 15th, was 3095 days from July 27, 1939 which was 442 weeks and 1 day. 402 is 6 squares of 67 and this gives 42 in the 7th square and 42 is 5/8 of 67 and the price was at 6½ squares of 67. The price equalled 180 degrees, a strong resistance level and the time period equals 225 degrees, a strong resistance level and a price to sell short with a stop-loss order at 440.

It requires 4489 days to square 67 in time. This period expired 1951 November 10th. Note the position of May Beans and other beans at that time and you will see how well the time periods correspond with the price.

4489 days gives 641 weeks and 2 days. Note that 637 is 9½ x 67 and 641 is 4 weeks beyond the half of the square.

1953, February 5th, is 706 weeks from July 7th, 1939. Note that 670 is 11 squares of 67. This gives 36 weeks in the 12th square Follow line 36 up till you reach the price scale. This comes out on a 45 degree angle at a price of 304. May Beans were selling at 292. Note that 292 is at the 3/8 resistance level in the 5th square of 67. Therefore, they were in a weak position because they were below the time period.

The time period was just beyond the ⅝ of the square. Note that 10⅝ squares of 67 is 705⅛ weeks and for the price to be strong it would have to be above 304.

Feb. 6th May Beans declined to 285½. Note that this is ½ of the square of 67 and a minor resistance level but the end of the 4th square of 67 is 268.

1953, Feb. 5th, was 4942 days from July 27, 1939. This was 73 squares of 67 and 51 days over. In other words, the calendar time period was 51 days in the 74th square. Note that 50 days is 3/4 of the square of 67 and, of course, Feb. 4th was 50 days in the square or at the 3/4 point. The price closed at 292 on Feb. 4th which was at the 3/8 point. This showed on the daily that the price was in a weak position and the main trend was down. Therefore, on monthly, weekly and daily the main trend was plainly down based on the position in the square of 67. Note that Feb. 21st on the daily chart will be at the end of the 74th square from July 27, 1939, therefore, this is an important date to watch for a minor change in trend. Suppose the price should be at 276, which is 1/8 of the square, or at 268 which is the end of the 4th square, it would be important for support and a rally.

1920, Feb. 15, cash beans high 405. Feb. 15, 1953 will be 396 months. Note that 395 is 7/8 of 67, that is, it is in the 6th square. The square of 20 is always very important and this is 400 months, therefore, June 15, 1953 will end the square of 20 and be important for a change in trend on July or November Beans.

1932, Dec. 28th, cash beans low 44¢, for this we use the square of 44. 1952 Dec. 28th was 240 months, a 20 year cycle. Feb. 28, 1953 is the 242 month from the extreme low. Note that 242 is 4½ squares of 44 showing this to be a strong resistance in time and 286 is 6½ squares of 44. Therefore, when the price sold at 285¼ on Feb. 6th it was at the halfway point in price and the time is at a halfway point which is what caused the fast break. The ¼ point in the 7th square of 44 is 275 and the end of the 6th square is 264. 2/3 of 44 is 293 and 3/4 of 44 is 296 in the 7th square of 44 which is always important and when the price goes back below 3/4 it never recovers above it after it reached the month of February which was ½ from the square of 44 in time and in the 5th square. Both the square of 44 and the square of 67 can be used to determine time and price resistance. Also use the Master Calculator and square of 144.

You can lay the chart on tracing cloth over your daily, weekly, or monthly chart and get the correct position on time in the square and will be able to see when prices are in a strong or weak position.

Long years of research and working out the natural squares and the square of the high, low price and range are very important in determining the major and minor change in trend.

You must continue to check these time periods with price resistance levels and you will learn more about how to use the square of 44 and 67 for Soy Beans and the square of 144.

You can also use the Master Square of 144 for time and price periods because by laying it over the charts you can get any square from 1 to 144. The Master Square of 144 gives the price and trend calculation, and you should always use the Master Calculator from all important highs and lows.

W. D. GANN

February 7, 1953.

Chapter 6

The Basis Of My Forecasting Method
Geometrical Angles
A. For Stocks

TRUTH OF THE STOCK TAPE
WALL STREET STOCK SELECTOR
NEW STOCK TREND DETECTOR
HOW TO MAKE PROFITS IN COMMODITIES

W. D. GANN
82 WALL STREET
NEW YORK 5, N. Y.

AMERICAN ECONOMIC ASS'N
ROYAL ECONOMIC SOCIETY

THE BASIS OF MY FORECASTING METHOD

Mathematics is the only exact science. All power under heaven and on earth is given unto the man who masters the simple science of mathematics. Emerson said: "God does indeed geometrize." Another wise man said: "There is nothing in the universe but mathematical points." Pythagoras, one of the greatest mathematicians that ever lived, after experimenting with numbers and finding the proofs of all natural laws, said: "Before God was numbers." He believed that the vibration of numbers created God and the Diety. It has been said, "Figures don't lie." Men have been convinced that numbers tell the truth and that all problems can be solved by them. The chemist, engineer, astronomer would be lost without the science of mathematics.

It is so simple and easy to solve problems and get correct answers and results with figures that it seems strange so few people rely on them to forecast the future of business, stocks and commodity markets. The basic principles are easy to learn and understand. No matter whether you use geometry, trigonometry, or calculus, you use the simple rules of arithmetic. You do only two things: You increase or decrease.

There are two kinds of numbers, odd and even. We add numbers together, which is increasing. We multiply, which is a shorter way to increase. We subtract, which decreases, and we divide, which also decreases. With the use of higher mathematics, we find a quicker and easier way to divide, subtract, add and multiply, yet very simple when you understand it.

Everything in nature is male and female, white and black, harmony or inharmony, right and left. The market moves only two ways, up and down. There are three dimensions which we know how to prove--width, length and height. We use three figures in geometry--the circle, the square, and the triangle. We get the square and triangle points of a circle to determine points of time, price and space resistance. We use the circle of 360 degrees to measure Time and Price.

There are three kinds of angles--the vertical, the horizontal, and the diagonal, which we use for measuring time and price movements. We use the square of odd and even numbers to get not only the proof of market movements, but the cause.

HOW TO MAKE CHARTS

Charts are records of past market movements. The future is but a repetition of the past. There is nothing new. As the Bible says--"The thing that hath been, it is that which shall be." History repeats and with charts and rules we determine when and how it is going to repeat. Therefore, the first and most important point to learn is how to make charts correctly because if you make an error in the chart, you will make an error in applying the rules to your trading.

YEARLY CHART: You should keep a yearly high and low chart, that is, recording the extreme low and the extreme high price made during the calendar year on one line. The spacing for the price can be used one point to each 1/8 inch or two points or more, according to the activity and range of the stock.

MONTHLY CHART: You must always keep up a monthly high and low chart, which is the most important chart of all in determining the main trend. This chart records the extreme high and extreme low price for the calendar month on one line, and each space or 1/8 inch on the cross-section chart paper should represent one point or $1 per share.

WEEKLY CHART: The next and one of the very important charts to keep is a weekly high and low chart. Where stocks are selling below 50, it usually pays to make this chart up using each 1/8 inch to represent one-half point, or two spaces to represent one full point, or four points for each one-inch space. When stocks become very active, especially when they are selling above $100 per share, then you can make up the weekly chart using each space or 1/8 inch on the chart paper to represent one point or $1 per share.

SEMI-WEEKLY OR 3-DAY CHART: The next chart of importance to the Weekly Chart is a 3-day chart, that is, taking the extreme high and extreme low price made from the opening of the market on Monday morning until the close on Wednesday night, closing the chart on Wednesday night- then from the opening on Thursday to the close on Saturday, taking the extreme high and low and closing the chart on Saturday. This gives you a time period showing one-half of the week. This chart is very important as will be explained later on in the instructions. The spacing for this chart can be the same as for the weekly high and low chart.

WEEKLY MOVING-AVERAGE OR MEAN POINT: To get a Weekly Moving-Average, we take the extreme low for the week and the extreme high for the week and divide by 2, getting the half-way or mean point for the week. This can be recorded on the weekly high and low chart or on a separate chart, recording the Weekly Moving-Average with a dot and using one line on the chart for each week. Importance of this Weekly Mean Point will be explained later

DAILY CHART: When you are trading in a stock that is active, you should always keep up a daily high and low chart, but for study purposes it is enough to keep up the Weekly and Monthly Charts, which give you the main trend. The Daily Chart shows the minor trend and shows a change in trend much oftener than any of the other charts, but the indication does not last as long or run so far. This chart should be kept up the same as the others, except when stocks are selling below 50 or when they are in an inactive trading range- then the spacing should be 1/2-point to each 1/8-inch on the chart paper, allowing two spaces to represent one full point or $1 per share. When stocks are active and advancing very fast, making a wide range each day, then you can make the Daily Chart the same as the Weekly or Monthly, that is, using one point for each 1/8-inch on the chart paper. This spacing cuts the chart down and keeps it in a range where it is easy to see and read when fluctuations are wide.

No spaces are skipped on the Daily Chart for holidays or Sundays, therefore the time period is for actual market days and not calendar days. However, you should carry the calendar days along at least every two weeks, as later, under rules for Time Periods for change in trend, you will find that it is necessary to check up and know when the stock is 30, 60, 80, 120, 135, etc. days from a top or a bottom, which means calendar days, the exact measurement of Time for the daily chart. Often the Daily Chart on actual daily movements comes out on an exact mathematical angle of time measurement at the same time the calendar days come out on exact time measurement, making it a doubly important point for change in trend.

GEOMETRICAL ANGLES

After long years of practical experience, I have discovered that Geometrical Angles measure accurately Space, Time, Volume and Price.

Mathematics is the only exact science, as I have said before. Every nation on the face of the earth agrees that 2 and 2 make 4, no matter what language it speaks. Yet all other sciences are not in accord as mathematical science. We find different men in different professions along scientific lines disagreeing on problems, but there can be no disagreement in mathematical calculation.

There are 360 degrees in a circle, no matter how large or how small the circle may be. Certain numbers of these degrees and angles are of vast importance and indicate when important tops and bottoms occur on stocks, as well as denote important Resistance Levels. When once you have thoroughly mastered the Geometrical Angles, you will be able to solve any problem and determine the trend of any stock.

After 35 years of research, tests and practical applications, I have perfected and proved the most important angles to be used in determining the trend of the stock market. Therefore, concentrate on those angles until you thoroughly understand them. Study and experiment with each rule I give you, and you will make a success.

We use geometrical angles to measure Space and Time periods because it is a shorter and quicker method than addition or multiplication, provided you follow the rules and draw the angles or lines accurately from tops and bottoms or extreme highs and lows. You may make a mistake in addition or multiplication, but the geometrical angles accurately drawn will correct this mistake. For example: If you should count across the bottom of your chart 120 spaces, which represents 120 days, weeks, or months, then you begin at "O" and number vertically on your chart up to 120- then from this top point at 120 draw a 45-degree angle moving down, this will come out at "O" on 120 points over from the beginning. If you have made a mistake in numbering, this will correct it.

Angles drawn on a chart always keep before you the position of the stock and its trend whereas if you had a resistance point on time written down, you might mislay it or forget it but these angles are always on the chart in front of you.

These angles or moving-average trend lines correctly drawn will keep you from making mistakes or misjudging the trend. If you wait and follow your rules, these angles will show you when the trend changes.

The moving-average as commonly used is obtained by taking the extreme low price and the extreme high price of the calendar day, week or month, and dividing it by two to get the mean or average price for the day, week or month, and continuing this at the end of each time period. This is an irregular movement in spaces or points per week because at one time it may move up 2 points per week and at another 5 points per week, while the time period is a regular unit. Therefore geometrical angles, which are really moving-averages, move up or down at an uniform rate from any bottom or top on a daily, weekly or monthly chart.

HOW TO DRAW GEOMETRICAL ANGLES

There are three important points that we can prove with mathematics or geometry: the Circle, the Square, and the Triangle. After I have made the Square, I can draw a Circle in it using the same diameter, and thereby produce the Triangle, the Square and the Circle.

The Angles or moving-trend-line averages measure and divide Time and Price into proportionate parts. Refer to Form "1", where I have drawn the square of 28. You will note that this is 28 high and 28 wide--in other words, 28 up and 28 across. It is the same as a square room which has a bottom or floor, a top or ceiling, and side walls. Everything has width, length, and height.

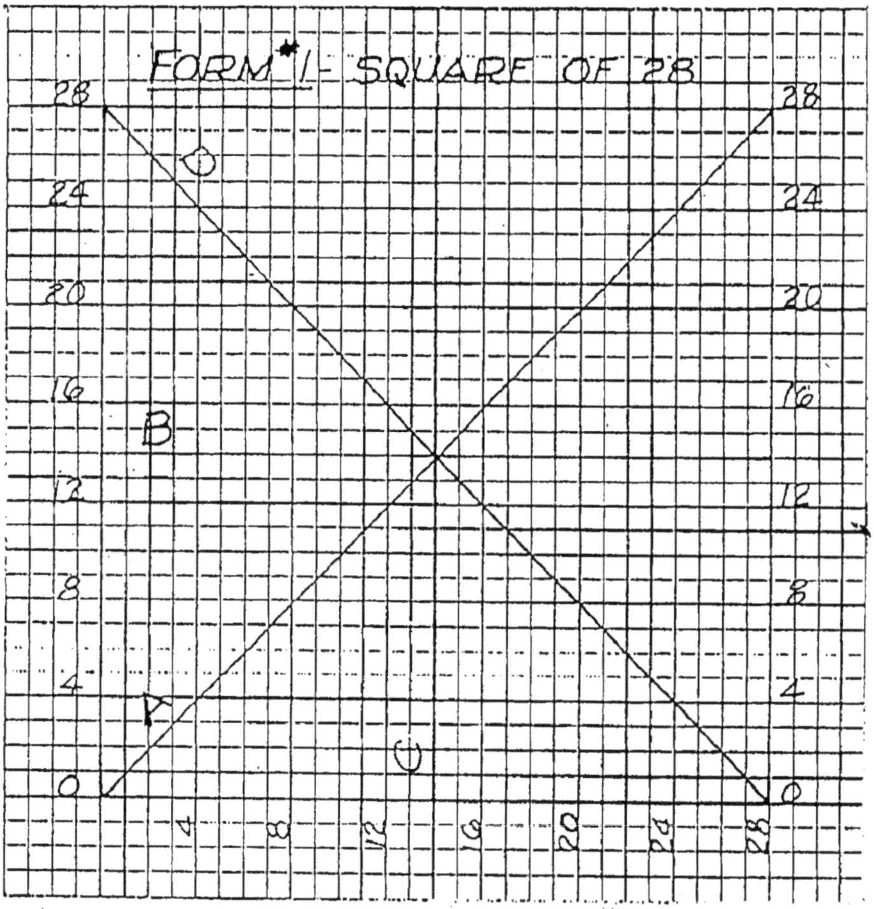

To get the strongest and most important points in this Square, I divide it into two equal parts by drawing a horizontal and a vertical line. Note angle marked "A", which divides each of the smaller squares into two equal parts and runs from "0" to "28" diagonally. This is a diagonal line moving on a 45° angle and divides the large Square into two equal parts. Then note angle "B" at "14" running horizontally across. This divides the Square into two equal parts. Note angle "C", which is a vertical line, running up from "14", which is one-half of "28". This crosses at the center or half-way point at 14, where the other angles cross, dividing the Square into two equal parts. Then note angle "D", which forms another 45° angle moving from the N. W. corner to the S. E. corner, crossing "14" at the exact half-way point. You see by this that if we draw the first line thru the center of the square, we divide it into two equal parts- then when we draw lines from the other directions, we divide it into four equal parts-then by drawing the two lines from each corner, we divide the square into 8 equal parts and produce 8 triangles.

As you look at this Square, it should be easy for you to tell with your eye where the strongest support point is or resistance point is. It is at the center where all the angles cross. Four angles cross at this point, so naturally this would be a stronger support point than a place where only one angle crosses. I could divide each one of these smaller squares into four or eight equal parts by drawing angles in the same way. Later, when I give you the rules and examples, I will explain how to square the Range of a stock, that is, the difference between the extreme low and the extreme high prices, or the difference between any low point and any high point, and also how to square the bottom price. For example: If the top of a stock is 28, this Square of 28 x 28 would represent squaring the Price by Time, because if we have 28 points up in Price, and we move over 28 spaces in Time, we square the Price with Time. Therefore, when the stock has moved over 28 days, 28 weeks, or 28 months, it will be squaring its price range of 28.

PATTERN CHART FOR GEOMETRICAL ANGLES

The Square of 90, or the Pattern Chart, shows all the measured angles that are important to use in determining the position of a stock. These angles are as follows: 3¾, 7½, 15, 18¾, 26¼, 30, 33¾, 37½, 45, 52½, 56¼, 60, 63¾, 71¼, 75, 82½, 86¼, and 90 degrees.

It is not necessary to measure these angles with a protractor. All you have to do to get the angles correct is to count the spaces on the chart paper, using 8 x 8 to the inch, and draw the lines or angles accordingly.

On the square of 90, which you will receive with these instructions, note how equal angles drawn from the top and from the bottom prove themselves by the point at which they cross. For example:

The angle of 8 x 1 drawn from "0" and the angle of 8 x 1 drawn from "90" down both cross at 45, 5-5/8 points over from "0" counting to the right. Then, the angle of 4 x 1 from "0" and the angle of 4 x 1 down from "90", you will notice, cross at 11¼ on 45, equidistant from the other angle and twice the measure. The reason why these angles prove this way is because the 45° angle or 45 points or degrees from "0" to 45 is one-half of 90. Therefore, parallel angles beginning at "0" going up and at 90 coming down, must cross on a 45° angle or at the gravity center.

HOW TO DRAW ANGLES FROM A LOW POINT RECORDED BY A STOCK

An example marked "Form 2" shows you the most important angles to use when a stock is working higher and advancing. (See page 6)

FIRST IMPORTANT GEOMETRICAL ANGLE: 45° or 1 x 1 The first and always most important angle to draw is a 45-degree angle or a moving-average that moves up one point per day, one point per week or one point per month. This is a 45° angle because it divides the Space and Time Periods into two equal parts. As long as the market or a stock stays above the 45° angle, it is in a strong position and indicates higher prices. You can buy every time a stock rests on the 45° angle with a stop loss order one, two or three points under the 45° angle, but remember the rule— never use a stop loss order more than 3 points away. Unless stocks are near the low levels or just starting in a bull market or selling at very low prices, I always use a stop loss order one point under the 45° angle. If this angle is broken by one point, you will usually find that the trend has changed at least temporarily and the stock will go lower.

An easy way to calculate accurately how to put on this 45° angle is: For example: If the time is 28 days, 28 weeks, or 28 months from the point where the stock was bottom, then the angle of 45° must be 28 points up from the bottom and would cross at 28. This is one of the easiest angles to put on and one of the simplest to learn. You can beat the market by trading against the 45° angle alone if you stick to the rule-- wait to buy a stock on the 45° angle or wait to sell it against the 45° angle.

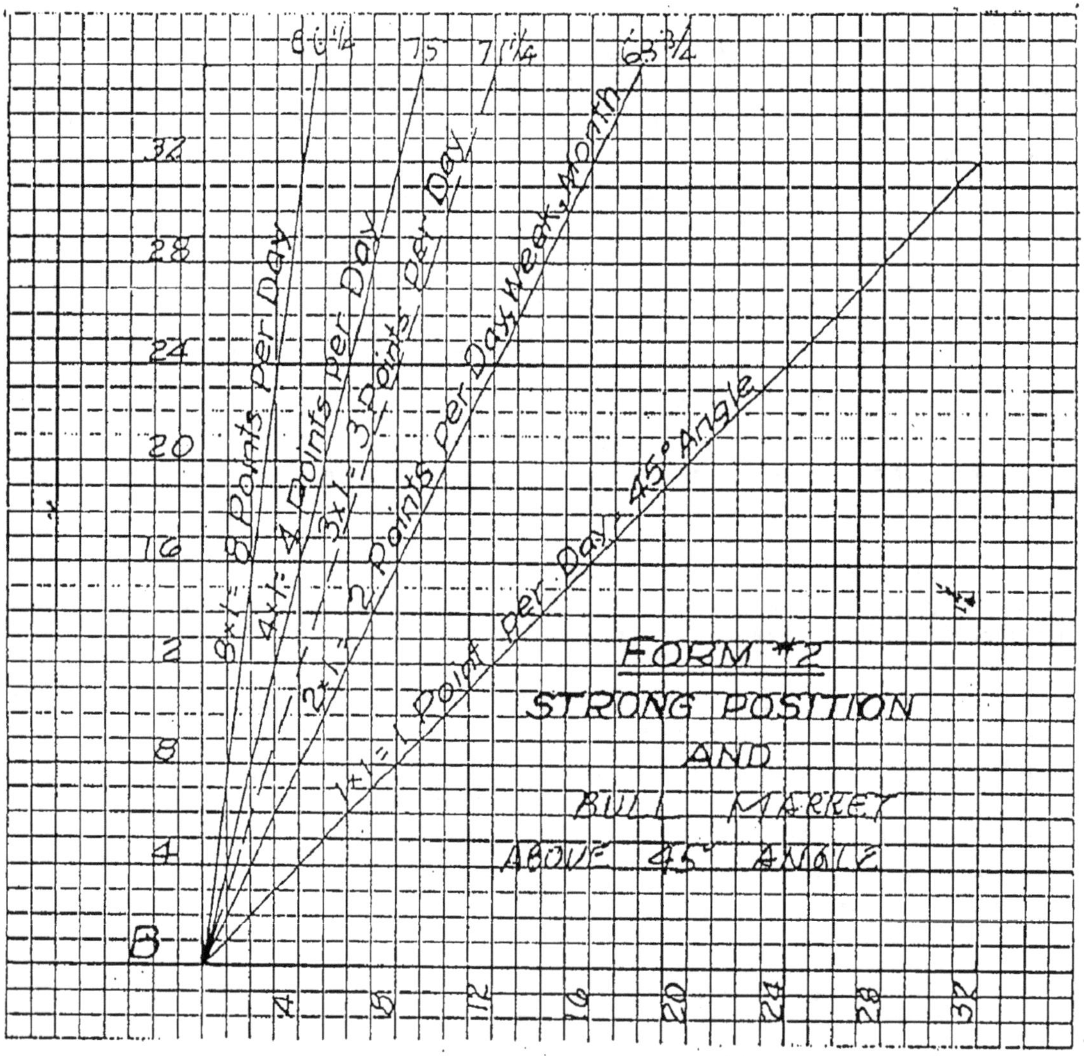

NEXT IMPORTANT ANGLE
2 x 1

is the angle of 2 x 1, or the moving-average which moves up at the rate of 2 points per day, week or month. It divides the space between the 45-degree angle and the vertical angle into two equal parts and measures $63\frac{3}{4}$°. That is why it is the next strongest and most important angle. As long as a stock holds above this angle, it is in a stronger position than when it is resting on a 45° angle because it is a more acute angle. When a stock breaks under this angle of 2 x 1, or two points for each time period, then it indicates that it will go lower and reach the 45° angle. Remember the rule of all angles: No matter what angle the stock breaks under, it indicates a decline to the next angle below it.

THIRD IMPORTANT ANGLE, which is still stronger as long as a stock holds above it, 4 x 1 is the angle which moves up 4 points per day, week, or month. This angle is 4 x 1, or 4 points of Space equal one period of Time. It measures 75° and divides the space between the angle of 2 x 1 and the 90° angle into two equal parts. Any stock that continues to advance 4 points per day, 4 points per week, or 4 points per month, and remains above this angle is in a very strong position as long as it stays above it, but when it breaks under, it indicates the next angle or next support point according to the position of the stock on Time.

FOURTH IMPORTANT ANGLE 8 x 1 is the angle of 8 x 1 or the one that moves up 8 points per day, week or month. This angle measures $82\frac{1}{2}°$. As long as a stock can hold above this angle on daily, weekly or monthly chart, it is in the strongest possible position, but when it reverses trend and declines below this angle, then it indicates a decline to the next angle.

NEXT ANGLE: 16 x 1 It is possible to use an angle of 16 x 1, or 16 points of Price to one period of Time, which measures $86\frac{1}{4}°$, but this angle is only used in fast, advancing markets, like 1929, when stocks are moving up or down 16 points or more per week or per month. There are very few stocks that will move up 16 points per day, week or month, and very seldom.

You will note that with these four important angles we show the strong or bullish side of the market. All the time by dividing the Space with angles we are getting the half-way point or the gravity center of Time and Price.

3 x 1 ANGLE: Note the angle drawn in Green, marked "3 x 1", which moves up at the rate of 3 points per day, week or month, measuring $71\frac{1}{4}°$. This angle is important at times after markets have had a prolonged advance and are a long distance up from the bottom. It is an important angle to use on Monthly and Weekly charts.

These are all the angles you need as long as a stock continues to advance and work up and stays above the angle of 45° or the moving-average of one point per day, week or month.

While there are 360 degrees in a circle and angles can form at any of these degrees, all of the important angles form between "0" and "90" because 90 is straight up and down and the most acute angle on which a stock can rise. For example: The 45° angle divides the space from "0" to "90" in half. The angle of 135° is simply another angle of 45° because it is one-half of the next quadrant between 90 and 180. 225 and 315 in a circle are also 45° angles. Therefore all of the angles valuable in determining the trend of a stock are found between "0" and "90" degrees. When we divide 90° by 8 we get the most important angles to use- then divide it by 3 we get 30 and 60° angles, which are important to use for Time and Resistance Points.

WHAT KIND OF BOTTOMS TO DRAW ANGLES OR MOVING-AVERAGE LINES FROM

DAILY CHART: If a stock has been declining for some time- then starts to rally (by rallying from a bottom it must make higher bottoms every day and higher tops)- then after a 3-day rally on the daily high and low chart, you can put on the 45° angle and the angle of 2 x 1 from the bottom or low point. As a rule, it will only be necessary to put on these two angles at first. If this bottom holds and is not broken, then you can put on the other angles from the bottom.

WEEKLY CHART: If a stock is declining and reacts for more than one week and continues down, we will say, for three weeks or more, then starts to rally and advances two weeks or more, you would start to put the angles on from the low point of the decline, only using the angles above the 45° angle until the stock again breaks under the 45° angle- after that you would use the other angles on the lower or bearish side of the Square.

WHAT TO DO AFTER THE 45° ANGLE FROM BOTTOM IS BROKEN

After a stock makes top, either temporary or otherwise, and breaks under the 45° angle and starts moving down, then the first thing you do is to draw angles below the 45° angle, starting from the bottom or low point. Note example marked "Form #3":

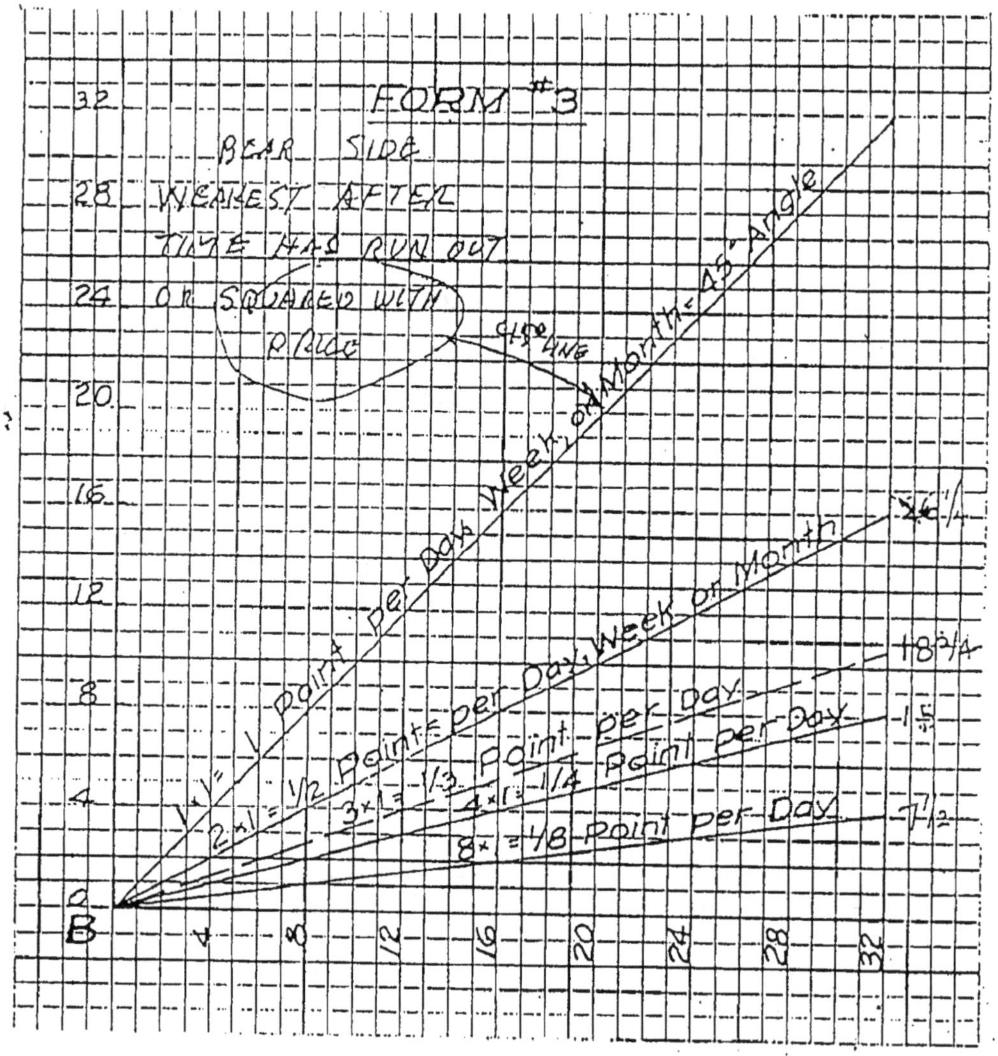

FIRST ANGLE ON BEAR SIDE OF THE SQUARE: 2 x 1 — The first angle that you draw on the bear side of the Square is the angle of 2 x 1 or 2 points over and one point up, which moves at the rate of one-half point per day, week or month and measures $26\frac{1}{4}$°. This is the first support angle which the stock should reach after it breaks under the 45° angle. As a general rule, when the stock reaches this angle, it will receive support and rally. Sometimes it will rest on it for a long period of time, holding on this angle and making higher bottoms. But when this angle of 2 x 1, or moving-average of one-half point per day, week or month is broken, then you must draw the next angle of 4 x 1.

NEXT IMPORTANT ANGLE: 4 x 1 The next important angle on the bear side of the Square, which moves up at the rate of 1/4-point per day, is the angle of 4 x 1, measuring 15°. It will be the next strong support angle which the stock should get support on and rally from.

NEXT ANGLE 8 x 1: Then after the 4 x 1 angle is broken, the next important angle that you will put on your chart is the angle of 8 x 1, which moves at the rate of 1/8-point per day, week or month and measures $7\frac{1}{2}°$. This is often a very strong support angle. After a stock has had a big decline, it will often rest on this angle several times or may make final bottom and start up from this angle, crossing other angles and getting back into a strong position again. Therefore this angle is important to use on a monthly or weekly chart after a prolonged decline.

ANGLE 16 x 1: This angle can be used on a monthly chart after a long period of time has elapsed from an important bottom. It moves at the rate of 1/16 point per month and measures $3\frac{3}{4}°$.

ANGLE OF 3 x 1: This angle, drawn in rek ink, is a very important angle, measuring $18\frac{3}{4}°$. I strongly advise using it at all times and keeping it up on monthly charts from any important bottom. It can also be used to advantage at times on weekly charts, but is seldom of much value on a daily chart. It moves at the rate of one-third point per day, week, or month. By drawing this on the monthly chart for a long period of years, you will soon be convinced of its value and also by testing it on a weekly chart, will find it valuable.

This completes all of the angles that you will need to use from any bottom at any time.

HOW TO DRAW ANGLES FROM TOPS ON DAILY, WEEKLY OR MONTHLY CHARTS

POSITION UNDER 45° ANGLE DRAWN FROM TOP: After a stock has made top and declined for a reasonable length of time, say, three days, three weeks or three months, breaking previous bottoms, then you start to draw angles down from the top. Note example marked "Form #4", which is the pattern for drawing angles from the top under the 45° angle. (see page 10)

45° ANGLE FROM TOP: The first angle you draw is the angle of 45° or a moving-average which indicates a decline of one point per day, week or month. As long as the stock is below this angle, it is in the weakest position and in a bear market.

OTHER ANGLES: In many cases a stock will start declining an average of 8 points per day, week or month, or 4 points per day, week or month, or 2 points per day, week or month, therefore you should put on all of these angles from the top, which move down faster than the angle of 45°.

WEAKEST POSITION: The stock is in the weakest possible position when it declines and keeps under the angle of 8 x 1. It is in the next weakest position when it is dropping down at the rate of 4 points per day, week or month, or under the angle of 4 x 1. It is in its next weakest position when it is dropping down under the angle of 2 x 1.

STRONGEST POSITION: The stock is in a stronger position and indicates a better rally when it crosses the angle of 2 x 1, but this depends on how far it is down from the top and how far the angles are apart, as will be explained later under the rules.

CHANGING TREND: As long as a stock is declining one point per day, week or month, or falling below or under the 45° angle, it is still in a bear market and in a very weak position. When a stock rallies and crosses the angle of 45° after a prolonged decline, then you are ready to put on the angles on the other side of the 45° angle, which shows that the stock is in a stronger position in a bear market and may be getting ready to change into a bull market.

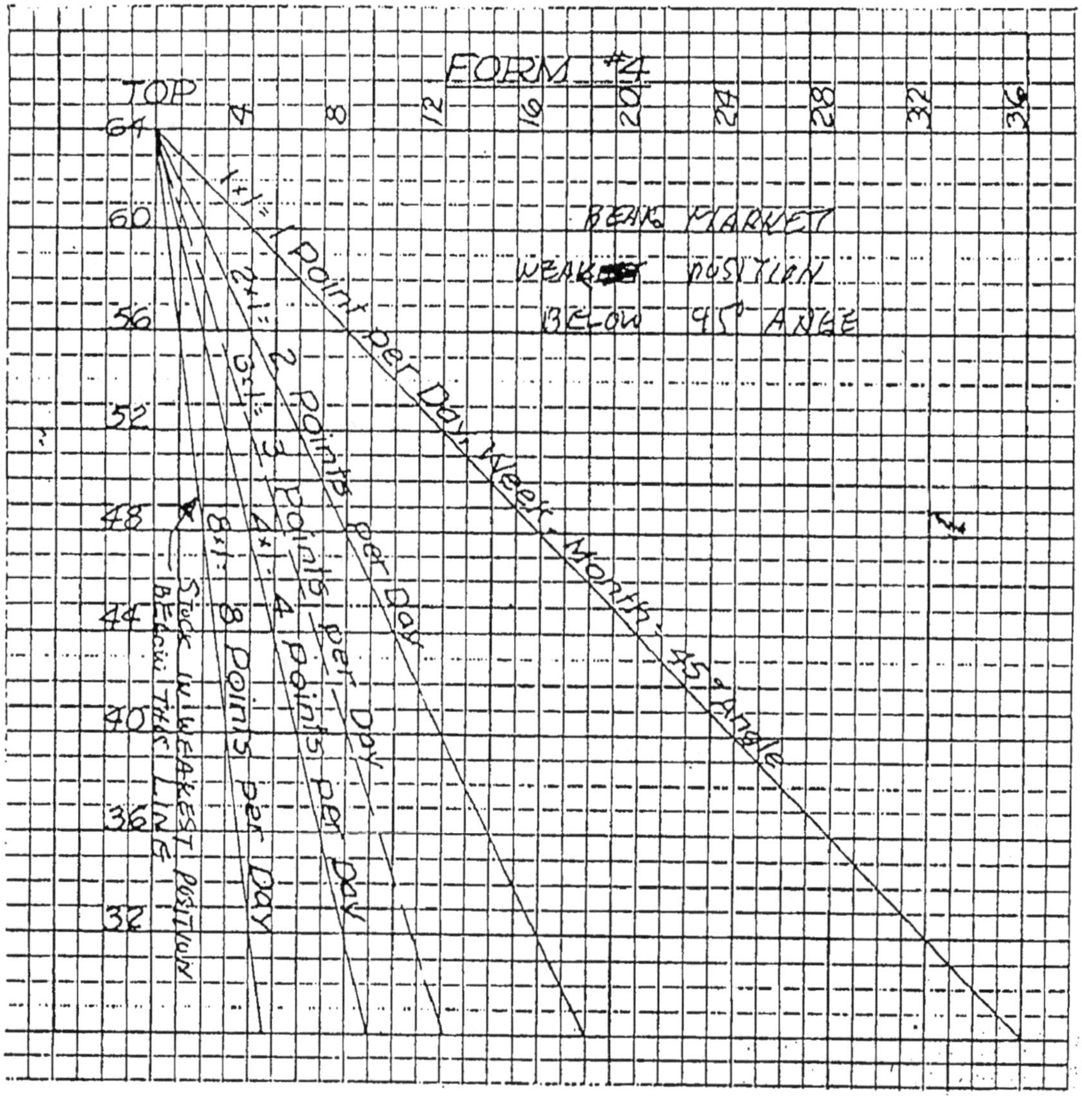

POSITION ABOVE 45° ANGLE DRAWN FROM TOP

Refer to Form #5, which is the pattern for drawing angles above the 45° angle from the top. (See page 11)

2 x 1 ANGLE FROM TOP: The first angle or moving-average you draw after the 45° angle from the top is crossed and after the stock indi-

cates that it has made a temporary bottom is the angle of 2 x 1, moving over 2 points and down one point, or 1/2-point per unit of Time. This is moving down at the rate of 1/2-point per month, week or day.

4 x 1 ANGLE: The next is the angle of 4 x 1 which moves down at the rate of 1/4-point per day, week or month.

8 x 1 ANGLE: The next angle is the angle of 8 x 1, which moves down at the rate of one point every 8 days, 8 weeks or 8 months, or 1/8-point per time period.

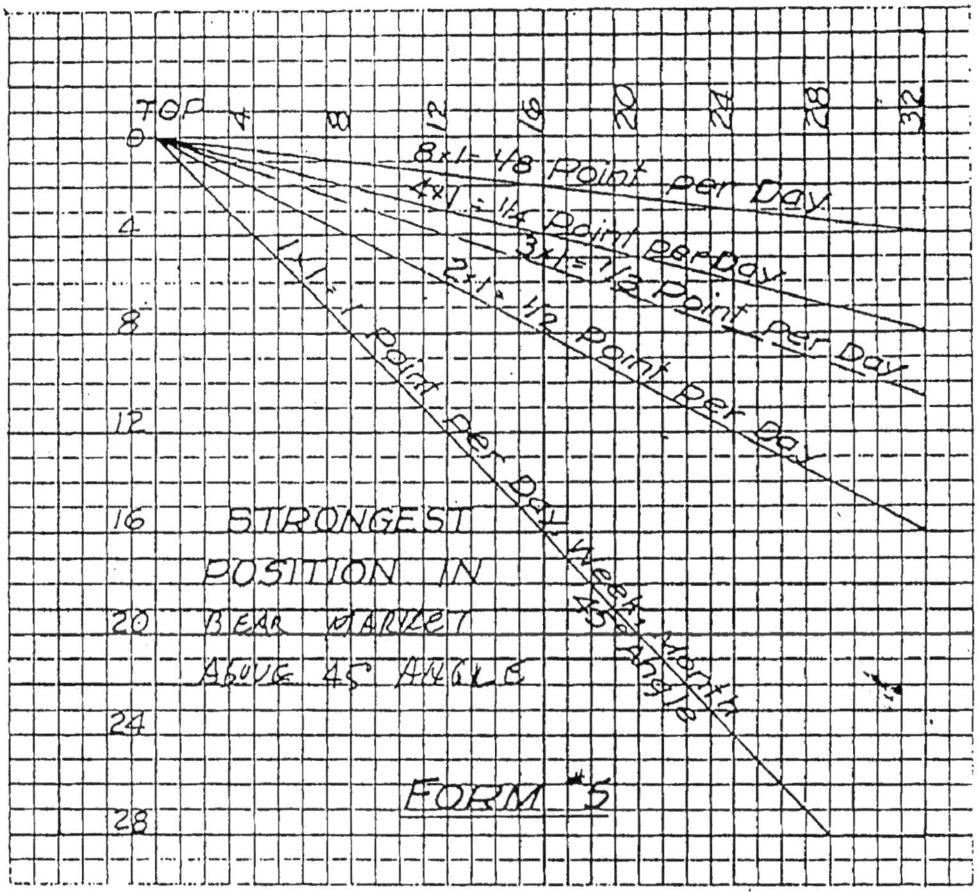

STRONG POSITION: After the stock has crossed the angle of 45° and rallied up to the angle of 2 x 1, it will meet selling and react to some angle coming up from the bottom of the last move, but it is in a stronger position when it holds above this angle of 2 x 1 and is in the next strongest position when it crosses the angle of 4 x 1. Crossing the angle of 8 x 1, which is of least importance, it indicates that it is in a very strong position again from the top. You must always consider a movement coming up from bottom and its position on angles from the bottom to determine its strength. It is important to consider the number of points it has moved up from the bottom and how many points it is down from the top.

3 x 1 ANGLE: The angle of 3 x 1 drawn in red on Form #5 moves down at the rate of one point every three days, three weeks or three months, or one-third point per day, week or month. This angle is important to use after prolonged declines.

This completes the forms of all the angles that you will need to use at any time from tops or bottoms. Practice putting these angles on tops and bottoms until you thoroughly understand how to do them and know that you are getting them absolutely accurate. Then you can begin to study the rules for determining the trend according to the position of the stock on angles.

DOUBLE AND TRIPLE TOPS OR BOTTOMS

ANGLES CROSSING EACH OTHER: When there is a double bottom several days, weeks or months apart, you draw angles from these bottoms, which are near the same price levels. For example: From the first bottom draw a 45° angle and from the second bottom draw an angle of 2 x 1- then when these angles cross each other, it will be an important point for a change in trend. Note on chart marked Form #6 that I have drawn the 45° angle from the first bottom "1B" and the angle of 2 x 1 on the right hand side of the 45° angle. Then, from the second bottom "2B" I have drawn a 45° angle and the angle of 2 x 1, which gains 2 points per day, week or month, on the left hand or bull side of the 45° angle. You will note that the angle of 2 x 1 from the second bottom crosses the angle of 2 x 1 on the bear side from the first bottom at 48, and that when the stock breaks under these angles, a change in trend takes place and it goes lower.

Note that the angle of 2 x 1 from the third bottom "3B" crosses the angle of 2 x 1 on the bear side from the first bottom at 53½ and crosses the 45° angle from the second bottom at 58. This would be a point to watch for change in trend. I have placed a circle where those angles from the different bottoms come together.

Apply this rule to double tops and triple tops in the same way. It is not necessary for the tops or bottoms to be exactly at the same price level, but near the same level. Remember, always draw 45° angles from all important tops and bottoms.

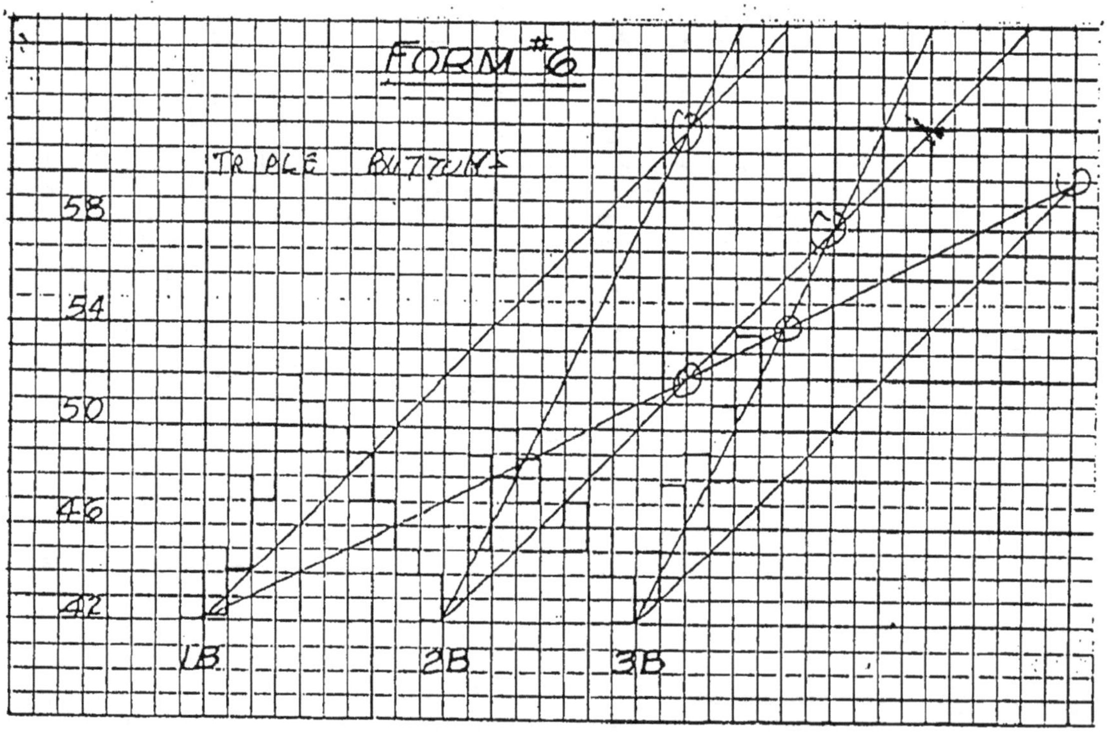

PARALLEL ANGLES

Parallel angles or lines run from important tops and bottoms. As previously explained, the 45° angle is the most important and should be drawn from all important tops and bottoms. If a stock starts advancing, we draw a 45° angle from the bottom- then if the stock makes top, declines and makes a higher bottom- then advances and makes a higher top, we draw a 45° angle from the first top, running the line up. This will give the oscillation or width of fluctuation in a parallel between the 45° angle from the bottom and the 45° angle running up from the top. Often a stock will advance to the 45° angle from the first top, fail to cross it, then decline and rest on the 45° angle from the first bottom- then advance again, working up for a prolonged bull campaign between these parallel angles.

When the angles are very far apart, you can draw another 45° angle equidistant between them, which is often a strong support angle from which a stock will rally, but when it breaks under, it declines to the bottom parallel.

Parallels can form between the angles of 2 x 1 or 4 x 1 just the same as between 45° angles, which often occurs in slow-moving stocks.

GEOMETRICAL ANGLES OR MOVING-AVERAGE LINES DRAWN FROM "0"

When a stock reaches bottom and starts up, you have been instructed to draw angles from this exact low point, which shows the support in time periods, but there are other angles that later on will be just as important and sometimes more important than the angles drawn from the bottom of a stock. These are the angles that begin at "0" or zero and move up at the same rate that they move up from the bottom. The starting point must be on the same line that the bottom is made on as the time period begins from this bottom, but the angles move up from "0". These angles should be started every time a stock makes a bottom, especially on weekly and monthly charts, and should also be carried up on important movements on the daily chart. Example: See chart marked Form #7 on page 14.

If a stock makes low at 20, as shown on the chart, starting the 45° angle from "0", when will this angle reach 20? Answer: It will reach 20 in 20 days, 20 weeks or 20 months from the bottom or its starting point. In other words, in 20 days, 20 weeks, or 20 months, it will be up 20 from "0" and at the price where the stock made bottom. Then the angle will continue on up at the same rate, and later, when the stock breaks under the 45° angle from the actual bottom made at 20 and breaks the other support angles drawn from the actual bottom at 20, the next important point for support will be the angle of 45° moving up from "0". When this angle is broken, it is in the weakest possible position and indicates much lower prices, but this depends on how high the stock is selling and how much it has declined at the time it breaks the 45° angle from "0". These angles drawn from "0", especially the 45° angle, proves when Price and Time are balancing or when the stock is squaring out from its bottom.

"0" ANGLES STARTING AT THE TIME TOP IS MADE

When a stock reaches extreme top on a daily, weekly or monthly chart and the trend turns down, you should start an angle of 45° from "0" moving up from the exact space and date that the top is made. This will prove the square of the time period. It is very important when this angle is reached and indicates a change in trend. It is the last strong support and when broken, it will indicate much lower prices.

I have instructed you in each case to first draw the 45° angle from bottom, top and from "0" at bottom and top, but this does not mean that you must not use the other angles. All of the other angles can be used from "0", but the 45° angle is the first and most important. After this angle is broken, then you can use the other angles. It is not necessary to carry all of them along until you need them, but on the monthly chart, after a long series of years, those other angles should be carried along when the stock begins to approach the levels where they would be broken or where the stock would rest on them and receive support.

45° ANGLE FROM "O" TO TOP AND BOTTOM: When a 45° angle moving up from "O" reaches the line or price of the bottom, it is very important- then again when it reaches the point of the extreme high price, it is very important for a change in trend.

You should carry 45° angles and other angles up from "O" from all important first, second, and third higher bottoms, especially those where very much time has elapsed between those bottoms. You should also start the angle of 45° up from "O" from the first, second, and third lower tops, especially those which show much time period elapsed. These angles are the most important to be carried on the weekly and monthly charts.

Never overlook keeping up the angles from "O" because they will tell you when Time is squaring out with Price from tops and bottoms and will locate support angles or moving-average lines at a point on the bear side after the first 45° angle from a bottom is broken. You could not locate this support point in any other way except by the angles from "O".

You should go back over past records and bring up these angles and square out different tops and bottoms so that you can prove to yourself the great value of using these angles.

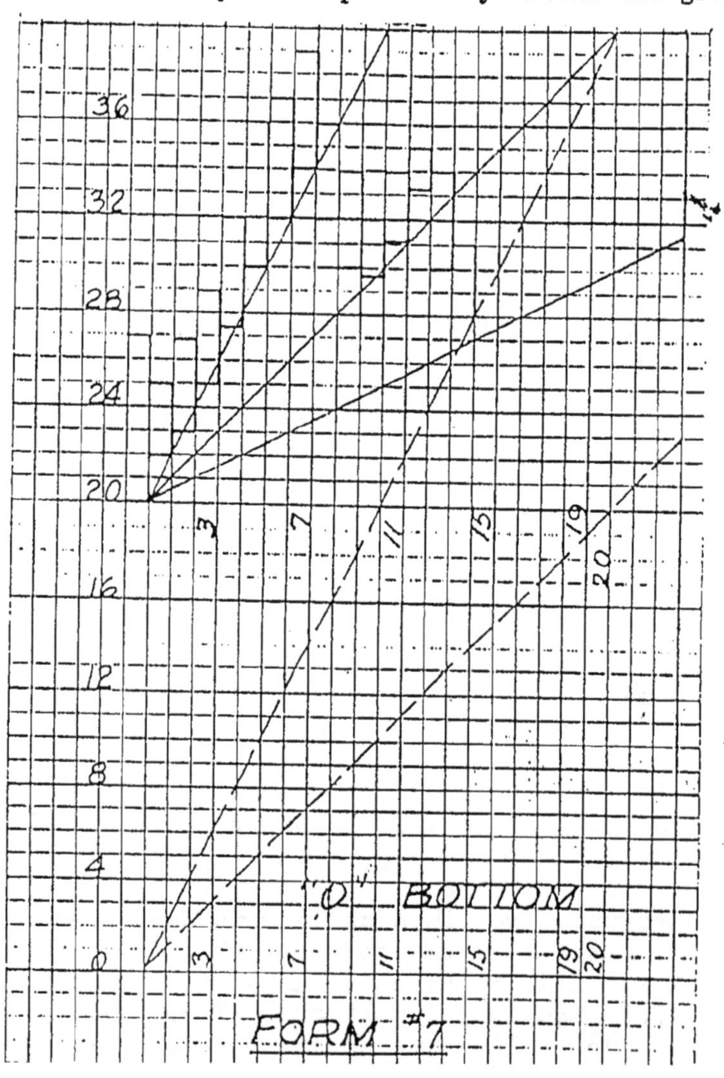

ANGLES FROM TOPS DOWN TO "O" AND UP AGAIN

A 45° angle starting down from any important top on a monthly or weekly chart should be continued down until it reaches "O" and then started up again at the same rate. After a long number of years between important tops and bottoms, this angle coming down and going up again is important. A 45° angle can also be continued down from any important bottom to "O" and then started up again. This will show the squaring of Price with Time from either top or bottom.

Angles can be started from "O" at the time any important time cycle runs out. For example: U. S. Steel made extreme low in 1904. May, 1924 would be the end of a 20-year cycle or 120 months. In May, 1924 Steel made top at 109 against a 45° angle beginning at "O" at the time bottom was made at 38 in February, 1915. On account of the importance of this top and a 20-year cycle running out here, we would start a 45° angle and other angles, if we need them, from "O" in May, 1924.

May, 1931 would end a 7-year cycle of 84 months from 1924. The 45° angle running up from "O" in May, 1924 crossed at 84 in May, 1931. Note that Steel made low at $83\frac{1}{8}$ in June, 1931. In June, 1924 Steel made the last low at $94\frac{1}{4}$, showing the importance of the end of the 20-year cycle. The 45° angle moving up from "O" in June, 1924 crossed at 84 in June, 1931, and Steel declined and rested on this angle.

TWO 45° ANGLES FROM THE SAME BOTTOM

As we have previously explained, the 45° angle moves up at the rate of one point per month and moves down at the rate of one point per month.

Refer to example on Chart #8:

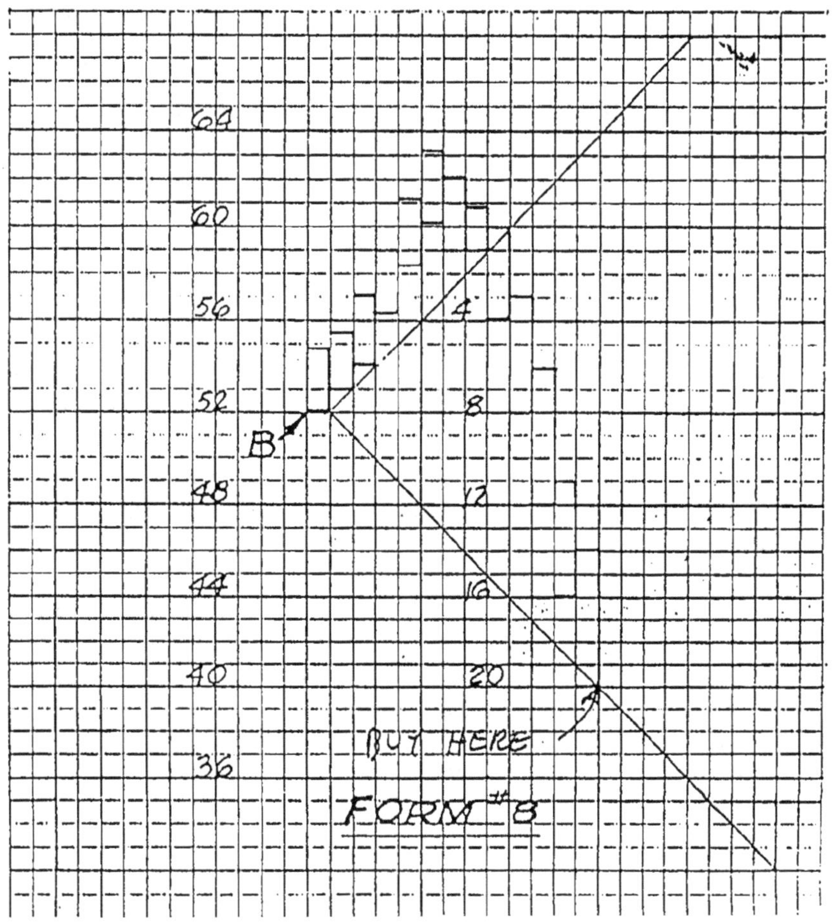

You will note that the low on this chart is shown as 52 and the stock moves up to a high of 63. A 45° angle is drawn up from the bottom, and after the stock reaches top and starts to work down, it breaks the 45° angle, getting under it at a price of 59. You will note that I have drawn another 45° angle down from the bottom at 52. At the point where the stock breaks under the 45° angle moving up from 52 to the 45° angle moving down from 52, the distance in points is 16, therefore the angles have widened until the stock could decline 16 points, if it went straight down, before it reached the 45° angle moving down from the bottom.

Note that I have shown on the chart that the stock continues down until it reaches 40, where it rests on the 45° angle from the bottom at 52. This would indicate the strongest support point and at least a temporary rally, especially as the stock is down 23 points from the top. Later you will find under "Resistance Levels" that $22\frac{1}{2}$ to 24 points is a strong support point.

U. S. STEEL: Take the extreme low point of U. S. Steel at $111\frac{1}{4}$ in January, 1927. Start a 45° angle on the monthly chart moving up at the rate of one point per month- then start a 45° angle moving down at the same rate. This shows the spreading of the angles and what can happen when Steel breaks under the 45° angle coming up from that bottom and the point where it can decline in extreme panicky markets, like 1931 and 1932.

The 45° angle coming up from the low of January, 1927 crossed at 156 in October, 1930. When U. S. Steel broke this angle it went right on down to $134\frac{3}{8}$ in December, 1930, where it rested on the angle of 2 x 1 from this bottom of January, 1927- then rallied to February, 1931, and at the time it broke under the angle of 45° from $111\frac{1}{4}$, it was on the 45th month, another indication of a sharp, severe decline. Here we look at the 45° angle moving down from $111\frac{1}{4}$ and find it is 90 points down from the 45° angle moving up from $111\frac{1}{4}$. These angles separate at the rate of two points per month and being 45 months from the bottom, the stock would have to decline 90 points to strike the 45° angle moving down from the bottom. The angles being so wide apart indicated that the stock could have a wide-open break. This happened in December, 1931, when Steel broke under the 45° angle moving down from $111\frac{1}{4}$, putting it into a very weak position- in fact, in the weakest position that a stock can get in until it can recover this angle. In June, 1932, when U. S. Steel declined to $21\frac{1}{4}$, it had dropped under the 45° angle moving down from the last low of $113\frac{3}{8}$ made in March, 1925, and closed two months below this angle before it started to recover angles.

This shows that when a stock gets into a very weak position by dropping under important angles moving down from bottoms, after having broken strong angles moving up from bottoms, it can decline to very low levels. These extreme fluctuations and declines have happened in the past and will happen again in the future. This proves the squaring out of Time on the down side or the balancing up of Price and Time.

Here is another illustration of the balancing of Price with Time: The angle of 45° moving up from "0" from the bottom at $21\frac{7}{8}$ from October, 1907 crossed at 262 in September, 1929 and Steel advanced to $261\frac{3}{4}$, which shows that in 262 months from the bottom in 1907 Steel had advanced an equivalent of one point per month. By striking the 45° angle and failing to cross it, it indicated that the Time was up and that the stock was turning downtrend for a prolonged bear market.

ANGLES OR MOVING-AVERAGE LINES FROM ONE TOP TO THE NEXT TOP

Refer to example on Chart #9 on page 17.

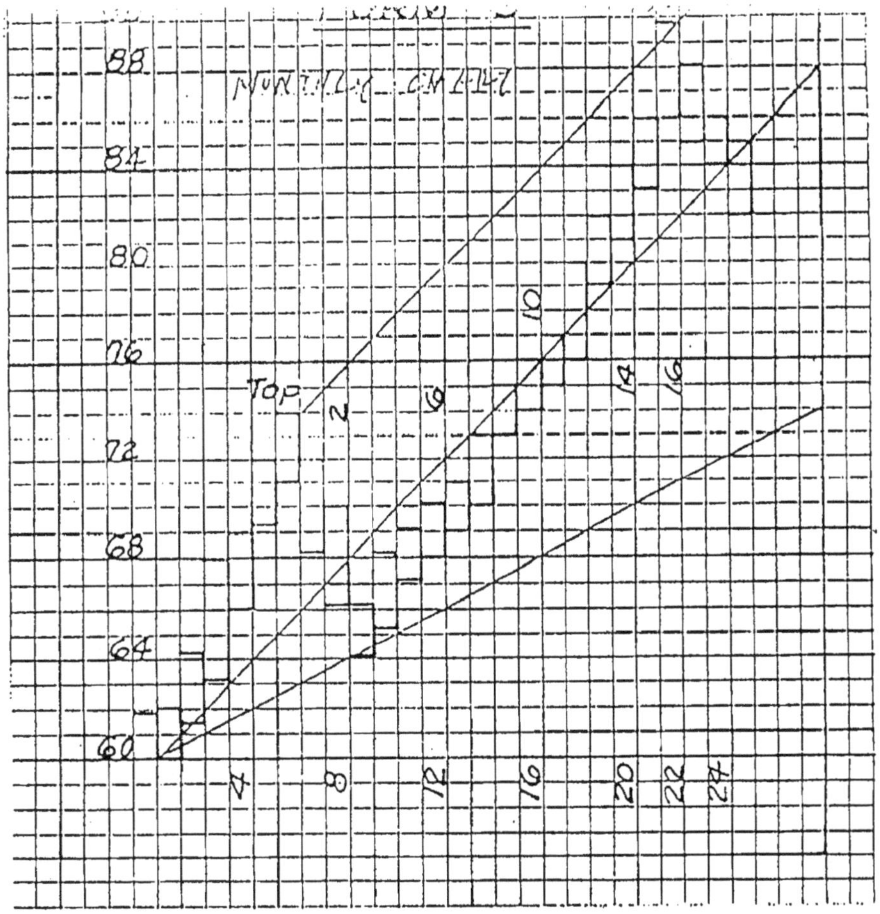

You will see that we have started the bottom at 60. The stock advances six months to 74, to a point marked "T" and makes top--reacts for three months to 64, breaking the 45° angle but resting on the angle of 2 x 1 from the bottom--then starts advancing and finally crosses again the 45° angle from 60, getting into a stronger position, having regained this angle. In order to determine where it might meet resistance, as it is in new high territory, we draw a 45° angle from the top at 74. The stock advances to 90 on the 22nd month from the bottom, striking the 45° angle from the first top at 74, on the 16th month from the first top. Being 16 points up above the first top, the Time equals the advance in the Price above the first top. The 45° angle shows that this is a strong Resistance point and a place to go short with stop one to three points above the 45° angle. A decline starts and in the third month the stock again breaks under the 45° angle from the bottom (at 60) at a very high level. In other words, it is 24 points up from the bottom and is now in a much weaker position, because it is so far from the base of support, and indicates a decline again to the angle of 2 x 1 (marked in green).

Don't overlook this rule: After a stock has advanced to a new high level, then declines to the old top at 74, this may be a support point unless it breaks 3 points under it. If it does and also breaks the angle of 2 x 1, it will be in a weaker position and the next point to watch for support and a rally would be the next bottom at 64.

ANGLES FROM BOTTOM OF FIRST SHARP DECLINE

When a stock that has been advancing for some time, makes top and holds for several days, several weeks or several months, then turns the trend down and has a sharp, severe decline, there is always a rally after this first decline. It usually makes a lower top on this secondary rally and then starts to work lower again. The bottom of the first decline is a very important point to draw angles from, especially the 45° angle moving down, as I have done on the chart marked Form #10.

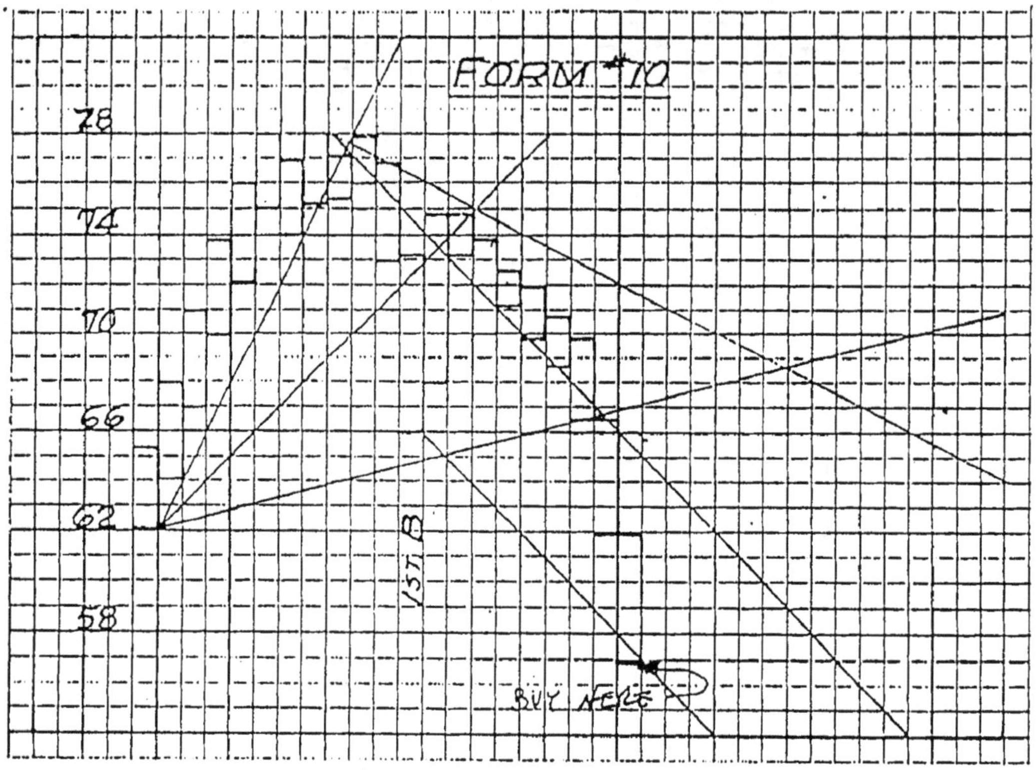

This chart shows the stock rallying up to around 75, where the 45° angle coming up from the last bottom crosses the angle of 2 x 1 coming down from the top. Then the decline started and at 66 the stock broke back under the angle of 45° from the top, which put it in a very weak position. It declined to the angle of 45° coming down from the bottom of the first sharp decline. This would be the squaring out of time from the bottom and would be a place to buy for a rally. A stock will often decline and drop a little below this angle from the bottom--then if it holds for several days or weeks under this angle or on it, it is a place to buy for a rally.

On a Monthly Chart always carry this angle down from the bottom of the first sharp decline, as it often becomes very important later on in a campaign.

After a stock has been advancing for some time and then has a sharp break lasting 2 to 3 days, 2 to 3 weeks, or 2 to 3 months--then rallies and afterward breaks under the lows of this first sharp break, it indicates that the main trend has turned down and that it is going lower.

Apply the same rule when a stock has been declining for a long time and then makes a sharp, quick recovery for 2 to 3 days, 2 to 3 weeks, or 2 to 3 months, then reacts and then crosses this first rally point that it made, an indication of higher prices.

LAST SWING IN A BULL OR BEAR MARKET

It is important to draw angles from the point where the market starts up and makes its last run in a bull market. Refer to Chart #11 on page 19.

In this example note point marked "last bottom". In the last stage of the bull market a fast advance follows to a price of 84. We have drawn the angle of 2 x 1 (a gain of 2 points per day, week or month) and the 45° angle from this bottom. When the angle of 2 x 1 was broken, it indicated that the trend had turned down. The stock declined and rested on the 45° angle--then rallied and made a second lower top-- then broke the 45° angle-- declined sharply and rested on the 45° angle drawn from the top at 84, which indicated that Time and Price had squared out or were equal. This would be a point to buy, with a stop loss order 2 to 3 points under this angle, for a rally back to the angle of 2 x 1 from the top, as shown on the chart.

In very active fast-moving markets a stock may stay above the angle of 4 x 1 or the angle of 8 x 1 from the "last bottom," but on the daily or weekly chart after this first acute angle is broken, it indicates that the trend has turned down.

Always remember that after a prolonged advance, when the main trend turns down, it is safer to wait for rallies and sell short than to buy against the trend.

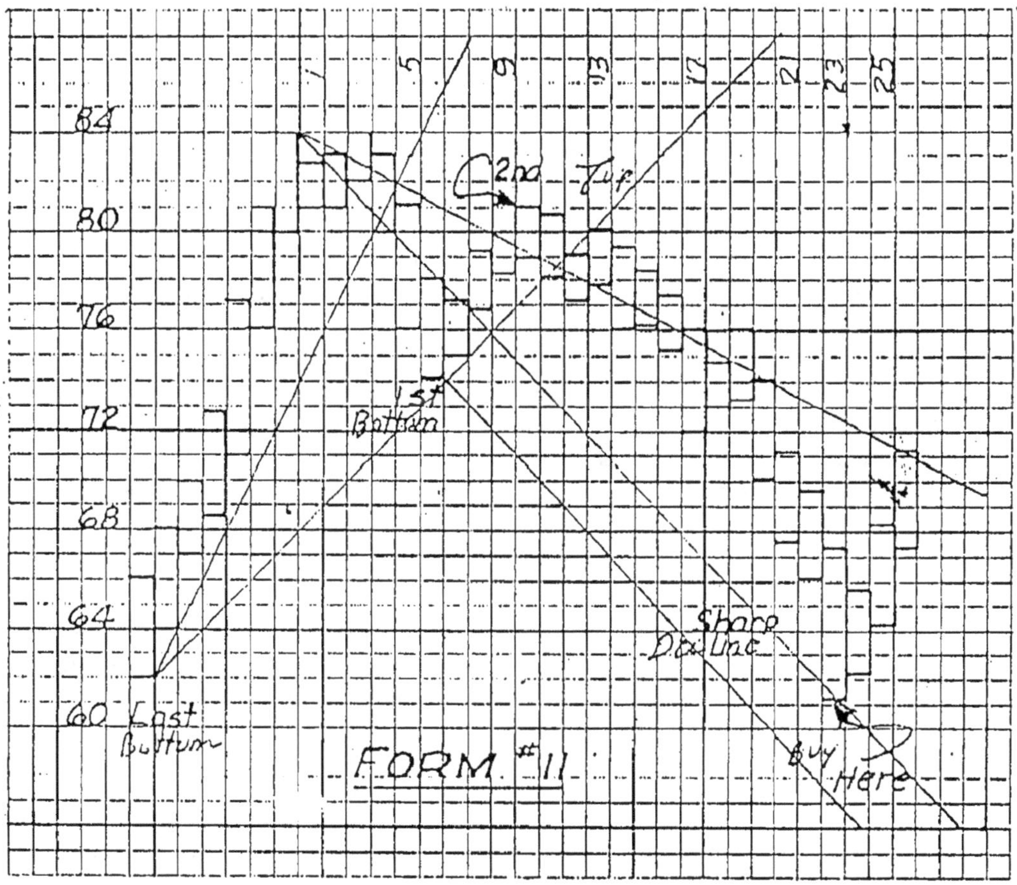

All of these rules are reversed at the end of a bear market or sharp decline. It is important to note when the market starts down from the last top or rally and makes its last run to bottom. Draw angles from this last top and watch when the market reaches these important angles and crosses them. For example:

On March 9, 1932 the Dow-Jones 30 Industrial Averages made last top at 90, from which a decline followed, with very small rallies, reaching bottom at 41 on July 8, 1932. Note on the weekly chart that the angle of 2 x 1 from the top at 90 crossed at 50 in the week ending July 30, 1932 and after they crossed this level they never declined to 50 again, and advanced to 81 in September, 1932. The crossing of this angle was the first definite indication that the main trend had turned up.

It is also important to review the major swing from November 9, 1931, when the Averages reached a high of 119½, to the low at 40½ in July, 1932. This was the last big swing of the bear market, a decline of 79 points. The half-way point of this was at 80. In September, 1932 the Averages rallied to 81-- then after they reacted to 50 and advanced, getting above the half-way point, and crossed 81, they indicated an advance to 119 anyway. After they crossed the half-way point the second time and advanced above 81, they never sold down to it again until they advanced to 149½ in November, 1935.

After a stock has been advancing for a long time, in the last run when there is a lot of momentum, it may cross angles from previous tops or bottoms, then fall back under them, which is an indication of weakness. When a stock has a sharp decline and is making bottom, it will drop under important angles and then recover quickly, getting above them, which shows that it is getting into a strong position and changing trend.

ANGLES FROM HIGHER BOTTOMS AND LOWER TOPS

What rule should be followed when stocks make higher bottoms and lower tops?

As stocks advance and make higher bottoms on the monthly, weekly or daily chart, you should always draw angles from higher bottoms. Then, in the last section of a bull market, if these important angles are broken from the last bottom, you know that the trend has turned down.

Apply this same rule as a market declines. Draw the angles from each lower top and watch the angles until the stocks again cross the 45° angle from a second, third, or fourth lower top. The second lower top or second higher bottom is always very important to draw angles from and to measure Time from as well.

Example: Dow-Jones Industrial Averages—

September 3, 1929 - Extreme high-
November 13, 1929 - Bottom of first sharp decline-
April 17, 1930 - Big rally in bear market, second lower top-
July 8, 1932 - Extreme low, final bottom-
September 8, 1932 - Top of first sharp advance after bear market ended-
February and March, 1933 - Second higher bottom from which bull market was resumed.

These are the most important tops and bottoms to draw angles from.

SECTIONS OF MARKET CAMPAIGNS:

All market campaigns, up or down, move in 3 to 4 sections. When an advance starts, the market runs for several weeks or several months and then halts for several weeks or months, moving up and down over a range of 5 to 20 points, according to the price of the stock--then the advance is resumed and the stock crosses the high level of the first section, moves higher, halts again, and reacts for a period of time-- then crosses the top of the second section and moves up again for another period of time and halts for the third time, which is a very important point to watch as markets often culminate at the end of the third section and a bigger decline follows,

Most markets run out in three important sections or campaigns. However, after resting and reacting, if a stock crosses the third top, it will then move up to the top of the fourth section. This fourth advance may be a shorter period of time than the previous sections, or in some cases may consume a greater period of time, especially if the stock is very active and high-priced. This fourth top is very important and generally marks a culmination and a reversal for a bigger decline.

For example: On March 12, 1935 CHRYSLER MOTORS declined and made low at 31--

FIRST SECTION of the advance carried the stock up to 49⅜ on May 16- then the stock declined to 41¼.

SECOND SECTION— On June 27 the advance started and the stock advanced to new high levels, reaching 62⅜ on August 10, which was top of the second section- then there was a reaction to 57½ and a resting period.

THIRD SECTION— Then there was another advance which started August 28. The stock crossed the top of the second section and reached high at 74 on September 11, top of the third section. Then followed a reaction to 68 on September 21.

FOURTH SECTION— In October the top of the third section was crossed and on November 18 Chrysler reached 90, top of the fourth section, where it held for 5 weeks in a 6-point range while distribution was taking place. This was a most important point to watch for a final top and a change in trend. Then the trend turned down.

Reverse this rule in a bear market. Watch the action of the market when it makes the third and fourth decline. But, remember, in a bear market when rallies come, they may make only one section or one move or in extreme cases only make the second section- then reverse and follow the main trend down.

You will find it very helpful to study and watch these various sections of a campaign and by applying the angles from tops and bottoms you can detect the first minor and major changes in trend.

STRENGTH OR WEAKNESS DENOTED BY POSITION ON ANGLES

The angles on the Monthly and Weekly Charts are of greater importance than those on the Daily Chart because the daily trend can change quite often, while only the major changes are shown according to the angles on the Monthly and Weekly Charts.

Always consider the distance a stock is from its beginning point when it breaks any important angle or crosses any important angle. The further away from the beginning point, the more important the change in trend, whether this is crossing an angle from the top or breaking under an angle from the bottom.

WHEN A STOCK IS IN THE WEAKEST POSITION:

A stock is in the weakest position when it has completed distribution and broken under a 45° angle from an important bottom on the weekly or monthly chart. It is also in the weakest position when it has broken under the half-way point between any important top or bottom. The longer the time period has run and the higher the price, the weaker the position. For example:

If a stock has advanced to 150 and has only moved down 25 points when the 45° angle from an extreme low on a weekly or a monthly chart is broken, then it is in a very weak position because it is so far above the half-way point on its price movement, already having squared out the time period with price.

Weakness in a stock develops when it breaks the 3/4-point, the 2/3-point, the 1/2-point, etc., but the position on the timing angles from the bottom tells you still more about the weak position. A stock shows its first weakness when it breaks the first important angle coming up from the last bottom in the final run in a bull market.

WHEN A STOCK IS IN THE STRONGEST POSITION:

A stock is always in the strongest position coming up from a bottom when it is holding above the very acute angles on the daily, weekly or monthly charts, especially on monthly and weekly charts.

As long as a stock holds above the angle of 2 x 1 (a gain of 2 points per day) on the daily chart, it is in a very strong position as far as the bottom is concerned. In fact, it is always in a strong position on the daily as long as it holds above the 45° angle. The same applies to weekly and monthly charts, which are the most important trend indicators.

I have found that the stocks which have the biggest advances are those that always hold above the angle of 2 x 1 on the monthly chart or gain 2 points per month for a long period of time. I have seen stocks rest 10 or 15 times on the angle of 2 x 1 and never break it until they have advanced 100 points or more. In this way a stock stays ahead of time and stays within the square of time by being far above the angle of 45°, and therefore is in a very strong position. But the time must come when the cycle has run out and the main trend begins to change from a bull market to a bear market---then the breaking of the angle from the last bottom shows a change in trend.

Another indication that a stock is in a strong position is when it advances and moves up above the half-way point of the previous price movement and then holds the half-way point, that is, advances above it and then reacts and fails to break under it. This is just the same as resting on a 45° angle and indicates a very strong position.

STRONGEST BUYING AND SELLING POINTS:

The cinch buying point is when a stock rests on a 45° angle, placing a stop loss order below it.

Another point to buy is on the half-way point of the price movement, placing a stop loss order under the half-way point.

When the main trend is up, it is also safe to buy when a stock reacts to the angle of 2 x 1 (a gain of 2 points per time period) on the weekly or monthly chart.

REGAINING ANGLES OR CROSSING LINES:

Remember, when any stock breaks under the 45° angle from the extreme low point of a move on the daily, weekly or monthly chart, it is then in a very weak position and indicates a decline to the next angle. However, when a stock can regain the 45° angle, it is in a stronger position.

The same rule applies to a 45° angle drawn up from any top. When a stock crosses the angle on the daily, weekly or monthly and stays above the 45° angle or any other angle to the left of the 45° angle, it is in a very strong position.

After a stock once drops below or gets above any important angle and then reverses its position by getting back above the angle or dropping back below it, it changes the trend again.

WHEN A STOCK IS IN STRONG POSITION FROM BOTTOM AND IN WEAK POSITION FROM TOP:

A stock is in a strong position from the bottom when it is keeping above the angle of 45° or the angle of 2 x 1, but at the same time it can be in a weak position when it rallies up and strikes against a 45° angle or the angle of 2 x 1 coming down from the top— then it is a short sale until it can cross these angles or cross previous tops. When it breaks the angles from the bottom, it is in a weak position and indicates lower.

A stock can be in a strong position from the top and in a weak position from the bottom, that is, it may cross some important angles from the top after a long period of time, but at the same time may break under the 2 x 1 angle or 45° angle from the bottom, which would indicate that it is in a weak position and getting ready to go lower.

WHEN ANGLES FROM EXTREME TOP ARE CROSSED:

The 45° angle drawn from the extreme high point of a stock is most important and when it is crossed, a major move may be expected. For example:

On the weekly chart of the Dow-Jones Industrial Averages, note the 45° angle moving down from 386, the high of September 3, 1929. January 12, 1935 was 279 weeks from the 1929 top. Taking 279 from 386, we get 107, the price at which the angle of 45° would cross. These Averages advanced to 106½ in the week ending January 12, 1935-- then reacted to 100 in the week ending February 9. This was the first time that they had held within one-half point of this angle and the first time that they had ever reached it since the top was made. During the week ending February 16, 1935, the Averages crossed the 45° angle at 103 for the first time, and during the week ending February 23, 1935 advanced to 108, where they hit the angle of 45° moving up from the low of 85½ in September, 1934, and also hit the angle of 2 x 1 coming up from the low of July 8, 1932. This was a strong resistance point and the Averages reacted to 96 in the week ending March 18, 1935, where they rested on the 45° angle from the 1929 top and also where the 3 x 1 angle (a gain of 1/3 point per week) from September, 1929 coming up from "0" crossed the angle of 45° coming down from the 1929 top. This was a strong support point for a change in trend. The advance started and the Averages moved up to new high levels. This proves the importance of angles, especially the 45° angle drawn from any extreme top, and the point at which any other angle crosses the 45° angle.

Watch the 45° angle from 1929 top when it reaches "0" or when it is 386 weeks down from the top. This will be in the latter part of January, 1937. Note what happens at that time.

ANGLES FOR SEMI-WEEKLY CHART

The semi-weekly chart is a great help at the end of extreme advances or extremes declines. By applying all of the rules and using the geometrical angles from tops and bottoms on the semi-weekly chart, you will often get an indication of a change in trend two to three days before a change in trend is shown on the weekly chart.

A change in trend on the semi-weekly chart is of greater importance than a change in trend on the daily chart. It is much better to rely upon this chart than on the daily chart when markets are in a narrow trading range.

ANGLES FOR NEW LISTED STOCKS

Years of experience and research, which has cost me a large amount of money have enabled me to develop a method that will account for all market movements and give rules to determine the trend from any top or bottom.

It is important to know how to determine the trend when a stock is first listed on any exchange. When a stock has never fluctuated before, we have no top or bottom to draw angles from. Therefore, in order to determine the trend, we use the square of 90, which is 90 up and 90 across, and put all the natural angles on, like the Pattern Chart. As we have said before, the square of 90 is very important because it is one-quarter of a circle of 360°, and as 90° or the vertical angle is the greatest angle that can be used, all of the other angles are found between "0" and "90".

If a new stock opens at 18 or any point below 22½, then you could make out a square of 22½ to determine the position of the stock on angles. If the stock opened at 36 or any point between 22½ and 45, you could make up a square of 45. If it opened at 50 or between 45 and 67, you could make up a square of 67½. However, you could place any stock opening at any price below 90 in the square of 90 and get its proper position and strength or weakness on angles. If the stock opened at 100 or above 90 and under 135, you could make up a square of 135, or could make another square of 90 numbering from 90 to 180.

You could start a monthly chart on a square of 90 at the price where the stock opens or trading begins, as shown on U. S. Steel. (Refer to Special Analysis of U. S. Steel.) After the stock breaks any of these natural angles drawn from "0", it is just the same as breaking under an angle drawn from a bottom. When it crosses any of the angles drawn down from "90", it is just the same as crossing an angle from a top, as you can see by experimenting with U. S. Steel or any other stock, but always consider price resistance levels and how much the stock is up or down from the bottom or top. You can determine the first change in trend by the 3-day or semi-weekly Chart, daily chart, and weekly chart by bringing up the important Geometrical Angles from any higher or lower bottom as the market movements develop.

QUICK CALCULATION OF ANGLES

It is not necessary to draw these angles from a point a long way back. You can make the calculation and determine where they cross. For example: Suppose in 1900, in the month of January, a stock made bottom at 15, and we wish to calculate where the 45° angle will cross 10 years later in January, 1910. The 45° angle rises at the rate of one point per month- then 10 years would be 120 points or months-- add this to 15 at the bottom-- then the 45° angle would cross at 135 in January, 1910. All of the other angles may be calculated a long period back in the same way.

ANGLES SELDOM USED

3 x 2 ANGLE: This angle of 3 x 2 on the left side of the 45° angle rises at the rate of 8 points in 12 months. A stock must show a gain of 3/4-point per month in order to keep above this angle. This angle can be used when other important angles from the bottom have spread far apart, as it will show the position and resistance or support point between the other angles.

LATITUDE AND LONGITUDE

On all charts--daily, weekly or monthly--the price must move up or down on the vertical angles. Therefore, the price movement is the same as latitude. You should begin with zero or "0" on any chart--daily, weekly or monthly--and draw the important angles and resistance levels across, which measure latitude.

Next, number the time points in days, weeks or months across, and draw the horizontal angle at each important natural angle, such as, $11\frac{1}{4}$, $22\frac{1}{2}$, $33\frac{3}{4}$, 45, $56\frac{1}{4}$, $67\frac{1}{2}$, $78\frac{3}{4}$, 90, $101\frac{1}{4}$, $112\frac{1}{2}$, 120, etc. Then you will know when price reaches these important angles and meets resistance.

Longitude measures the time running across the chart, as it moves over each day, week or month. Therefore, you must keep your chart numbered from each important top and bottom in order to get the time measurements according to angles. These important angles, such as, $11\frac{1}{4}$, $22\frac{1}{2}$, $33\frac{3}{4}$, 45, $56\frac{1}{4}$, 60, $67\frac{1}{2}$, $78\frac{3}{4}$, 90, etc. from each bottom and top will show you where the strongest resistance in price and time takes place. These angles prove the parallel or crossing point. Study past records and see what has happened when prices on monthly charts reached these important angles or time periods.

For example: 90 points up in price from "0" we draw an angle horizonally across the chart. Then 90 days, weeks or months, going to the right across the chart, we draw a vertical angle up, which will cross the horizontal angle at 90 and prove the square. By keeping all these angles up and understanding them on your charts, you will know when important time cycles are running out.

If the price of a stock at 60 comes out on the 60th day, week or month, it will meet strong resistance because it has reached the square of price with Time. It is at the same latitude or price and the same longitude or time period. You can always put the square of 90 on a chart--either daily, weekly or monthly--and use the natural angles, but I advise only using this on the weekly and monthly. You can begin this square of 90 from any bottom or top, that is, going up 90 points, or from the natural points, which are 90, 135, 180, but you must not fail to square the extreme low and high price as well as the second and third lower tops and higher bottoms with Time.

RULE FOR KEEPING TIME PERIODS ON CHARTS

It is very important that you keep the time periods on all of your charts, carrying them across from the bottom and top of each important move in order to check up and know that you have your angles or moving-averages at the correct point and to see where major and minor cycles indicate changes in trend.

TIME PERIODS FROM BOTTOMS: When a stock makes bottom one month and then the following month makes a higher bottom and a higher top, or anyway, after it makes a higher bottom and rallies for one month or more, you can start numbering from that bottom. The month that it makes the low belongs to the old or downward movement and is the last move down. You count the first month up as one and then number across on the 1/2-inch squares, running them across, adding four each time.

For example: If a stock has made bottom and advanced 50 points, you look down at the bottom of the chart and find that you are on the 25th month- then the angle of 2 x 1, moving up 2 points per month, would cross at 50, while the 45° angle, moving up one point per month, would be at 25, and if the stock broke back under 50 the following month, it would be falling under the angle of 2 x 1 and indicate a further decline. Now, if you had an error on the chart in the timing or numbering across from the bottom, then the moving-average line or angle would not come out correctly.

TIME PERIODS FROM TOPS:

After a stock has advanced and made an extreme high and reacted for a few days, a fewweeks, or a few months, and you start putting on the angles from the top down, you must then begin to number the time periods across from the top. Apply the same rule for the top: The month, week or day that a stock makes extreme high finishes the upward movement and is not to be counted. You can count the number of days, weeks or months moving across after that, allowing the top month to be "0", the next month, week or day over to be "1", adding 4 across on the squares to get the correct position. If this Time Period is carried across on all the charts correctly, then you can always check up and find out if you have made any mistake in bringing down the angles or moving-average lines.

For example: After a stock has declined 75 points, either on a weekly or monthly chart, the angles move down the same, except where the spacing is different. Assuming that the spacing is one point per one-eighth inch, after it has moved down 75 points and all the angles are drawn down from the top, there may be an error in the angle of 2 x 1 because your ruler may have slipped and you may not have placed it correctly after it is down a distance from the top. Now, in order to prove exactly where the angle of 2 x 1 comes out, you determine the number of time periods there are. If 40 days, weeks or months have been required to decline the 75 points, the angle of 2 x 1 moving down 2 points per unit of time, would be down 80 from the top. If you find that this angle does not cross at 80, then you know that you made an error and should correct it.

This is a simple way to always know when the angles or moving-lines are correct because you simply add the movement to the bottom and subtract it from the top. Suppose the price referred to above, when the stock has declined 75 points, was 150, then subtracting 80 from the top at 150, the angle would cross at 70, and the price of the stock down 75 points would be at 75, therefore it would be above the angle of 2 x 1 from the top and in position for a rally if the time cycle indicated it.

POINTS FROM WHICH TO NUMBER TIME PERIODS

The most important point on the monthly high and low chart to carry the time period from is from the extreme low of the life of a stock and also from the date of incorporation or from the date trading in the stock began on the New York Stock Exchange. From the extreme low point the time period should always be carried across on the chart just the same as the important angles should be continued right along for years.

The next important point to number from is a second or third higher bottom,

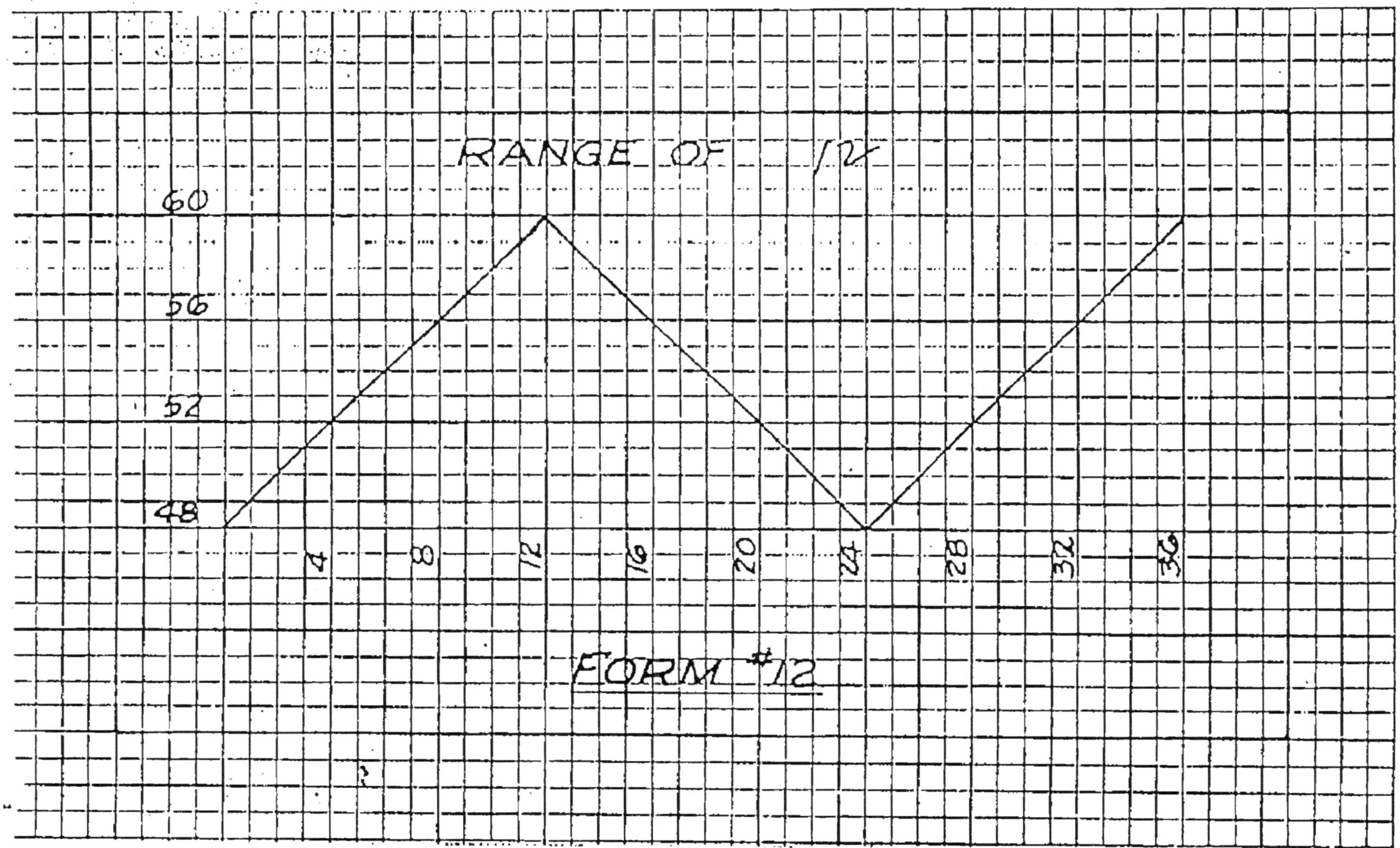
RANGE OF 12
60
56
52
48
4
8
12
16
20
24
28
32
36
FORM #12

but you should not consider a bottom established until the market has held up or advanced three to four months, then commence numbering from that bottom if it appears to be important. For example:

U. S. STEEL was incorporated February 25, 1901. Numbering the months across you will note that February, 1931, was 360 months, or 30 years, from the date of incorporation. Then start a new cycle and begin numbering across from "0". This will be working out the second cycle or circle of 360°.

The next important point is the extreme low of 8¾ made May 14, 1904. On the monthly chart carry the numbers across from this bottom, because it is the lowest bottom and therefore the most important. Note this 30-year cycle or 360 months ended May, 1934.

The next important point to number from and draw the angles from, is the low of 21⅞ in October, 1907, the first higher bottom. Then, the next important is the third higher bottom made in February, 1915. Always draw the angles and number the months across from any other important bottoms where campaigns start.

Use this same rule at tops. After top is reached and the trend turns down, then carry the time numbers across from the top, but after any top is crossed or bottom is broken that you are numbering from, then do not count that top or bottom of importance to number from, except to determine a time period on another cycle 3, 5, 7, 10 or 20 years ahead. Tops that stay for a long time without being crossed are always the most important to carry the Time Periods from. The extreme high reached by a stock is always most important until that high is crossed- then the next high point made on a secondary rally, which is always a lower top, is the next most important top to number from. For example:

On U. S. Steel you would carry the monthly measurement across first from the high in April 1901- then from the extreme high in October, 1909, and next from the high in May, 1917- then from the final high in September, 1929, being the most important to measure from, and also number from the April, 1930 top.

INDUSTRIAL AVERAGES: The Dow-Jones 30 Industrial Averages reached extreme high on September 3, 1929-- then declined sharply in the panic, reaching low in November 1929-- from this low there was a rally to April, 1930, which was the last high and very important to number from because it was a secondary top, the last rally in a bull market. After final low of the bear market was reached on July 8, 1932, a sharp rally followed to September, 1932, when top was reached-- then a slow decline followed, reaching bottom in late February and early 1933, making this a secondary higher bottom, from which stocks advanced to new high levels. The bottom in 1932 is the most important to number from and the next bottom of March, 1933 is next in importance.

Apply this same rule to weekly and daily bottoms and tops. Discontinue the time periods when any minor top or bottom is exceeded and carry only the main figures on time periods from important tops and bottoms as long as they remain unbroken.

The rule for discontinuing the use of tops and bottoms for Time Periods is: When a bottom or top is exceeded by three points, then discontinue the time period from that bottom or top.

Always note the number of months between extreme high and between extreme low points and note what angle the tops and bottoms come out on.

SQUARING THE PRICE RANGE WITH TIME

This is one of the most important and valuable discoveries that I have ever made, and if you stick strictly to the rule, and always watch a stock when Price is squared by Time, or when Time and Price come together, you will be able to forecast the important changes in trend with greater accuracy.

The squaring of Price with Time means as equal number of points up or down balancing an equal number of time periods--either days, weeks or months. For example: If a stock has advanced 24 points in 24 days, then moving the 45° angle or moving-average-line up at the rate of one point per day, the timing line or time period and the price of the stock are at the same level and the stock is resting on a 45° angle and you should watch for an important change in trend at this point. If a stock is to continue uptrend and remain in a strong position, it must continue to advance and keep above the angle of 45°. If it breaks back under this angle, then it is out of its square on the bear side of the 45° angle and in a weaker position. When you are squaring out Time on a daily chart, look at the weekly high and low chart and monthly high and low chart and see if the stock is in a strong position and has yet to run out the time periods, because on a daily chart it has to react and then recover a position, squaring its price many times, as long as the weekly and monthly point up. Market corrections or reactions are simply the squaring out of minor time periods and later the big declines or big advances are the squaring out of major time periods.

SQUARING THE RANGE: Refer to Form #12, where a range of 12 points is shown from 48 low to 60 high. Now, suppose a stock remains for several weeks or several months, moving up or down, in this range, never getting more than 12 points up from the bottom and not breaking the bottom: We start the 45° angle from the bottom of 48 and move it up to the top of the range to 60, then when we see the stock is holding this range and not going higher, we move the 45° angle back to the bottom; then back to the top of the range again, moving it up or down over this range until the stock breaks out into new low levels or new high levels. You will find that every time the 45° angle reaches the top of this range or the bottom of this range, there is some important change in trend of the stock.

You can also use the angles of 2 x 1 to the right of the 45° angle and the 2 x 1 to the left as they again divide the Time Period into two equal parts and are of some value.

If a stock finally moves out of this range on the up side, then the angles would begin at the new and higher bottom and move up, but from the point where the stock went into new high, or from any important bottom made while it was in the range, especially the last bottom that it made, which would be most important, you should then begin an angle at that bottom and continue on up again; watch when this angle is broken or when Time is squared out again with Price, which would be important for another change in trend, either major or minor.

THREE WAYS TO SQUARE TIME AND PRICE:

We can square the Range, that is, the number of points from extreme low to extreme high, with Time- then square the extreme low point with Time- and square the extreme high point with Time. When the market passes out of these squares and breaks important angles, the trend changes up or down.

1 - The range that a stock makes between extreme high and extreme low can be squared so long as it remains in the same price range. If the range is 25 points, it squares with 25 periods of Time-- days, weeks or months. Continue to use this time period as long as it stays in the same range.

2 - SQUARING TIME WITH BOTTOM OR EXTREME LOW PRICE:
The next important Price to square with Time is the lowest price or bottom of any important decline. For example: If the bottom of a stock is 25, then at the end of 25 days, 25 weeks or 25 months, Time and Price are equal. Then watch for a change in trend as based on its bottom or lowest selling price. As long as a stock continues to hold one bottom and advances, you can always use this time period running across and continuing the time period, noting every time it passes out of the squares. Watch especially when the stock reaches the third square, the fourth square, and again the seventh and ninth squares of its time period. These squares only occur frequently on the daily or weekly charts, as the monthly, in most cases, would move out of a range, up or down, before it squared a bottom as many as 7 or 9 times. However, this does sometimes happen when a stock is in a narrow range for many years.

3 - SQUARING TIME WITH TOP OR EXTREME HIGH PRICE:
The other important point to square Time with is the extreme high price of a stock. The Time period must be carried across from the high of the daily, weekly or monthly, and the square of the top price in Time must be noted and watched for a change in trend. If the top of a stock is 50, then when it has moved over 50 days, 50 weeks or 50 months, it has reached its square in Time and an important change is indicated. This can be determined by the position of the angles from top and bottom. For example:

Dow-Jones Industrial Averages-- The high of 386 on September 3, 1929 would require 386 calendar days to equal the Price in Time. This occurred on September 23, 1930. Look at the chart and note how the trend changed and turned down around that time. Then, on October 14, 1931, it run out this period again- and again November 4, 1932, November 25, 1933, December 16, 1934, and January 6, 1935. Look up those dates and you will see that important changes in trend occurred on the Daily Chart when this time period of 386 days balanced the price of 386.

Both major and minor tops and bottoms on all time periods must be watched as they square out right along. Most important of all is the extreme high point on the monthly high and low chart. This may be very high and work out a long time period before it squares the top, in which case you have to divide the price into 8 equal time periods and watch the most important points, like 1/4, 1/3, 1/2, 3/4, but most important of all is when Time equals Price.

When you are watching the position of a stock after it has squared out from a bottom or a top, always look up the time period and the angles from the opposite direction. If the market is nearing a low point, squaring out a top, see how its relation is to the bottom as it might be in the second or third square period from the bottom, which would be a double indication for a change in trend.

SQUARING WEEKLY TIME PERIODS:

The year contains 52 weeks and the square of this in Time and Price is 52 by 52. Therefore you can make up a square of 52 wide and 52 high; put on all of the angles from "O"; then chart the weekly high and low prices of any stock in this square. For example: If the low price of a stock is 50, then the top of this weekly square would be 52 added to 50, which makes 102 as top of the square. As long as the stock stays above 50 and moves up, it will be working in the weekly square of 52. On the other hand, if the stock makes top and works down, you would make up a weekly square 52 points down from the top and 52 over to get the time period.

You can take the past movement of any stock, put on a square of 52 by 52, and study the movement, noting 13 weeks or one-fourth, 26 weeks or one-half, and 39 weeks or three-fourths points on time, and the changes in trend which take place when the stock reaches these important Resistance Points in Time and Price. You would watch for a change in trend around these time periods.

SQUARING MONTHLY TIME PERIODS:

At the time a stock breaks a 45° angle, if it is selling at 135 on the 135th month, it is breaking a doubly strong Resistance Level-- a strong angle and a natural Resistance Level. This would be Time and Space balancing at Resistance Levels or geometrical angles and would indicate a big decline to follow. - Reverse this rule at the end of a bear campaign.

On a monthly chart twelve months completes a year, therefore the square of 12 is very important for working out time periods on the monthly chart. The square of 12 is 144 and important changes often occur on even 12 months' periods from a bottom or top of a stock. It will help you if you use the Resistance Levels on prices of the even 12's, noting 24, 36, 48, 60. 72, 84, 96, 108, etc. Watch how the stock acts on angles when it reaches these important Resistance points in Price.

PRICE AHEAD OF TIME

Why do stocks often cross the 45° angle on the daily, weekly or monthly chart, then have an advance for a short period of time, decline and rest on the same 45° angle? Because when the stock crosses the 45° angle the first time, it has not run out or overcome the square of Time with Price. Therefore, on the secondary reaction, when it rests on the 45° angle, it is at a time when the stock has reached the square of distance in Time. After that a greater advance follows.

Reverse this rule at the top of a bull market. When a stock breaks under the 45° angle a long distance from the base or bottom, it is most important. Many times a stock will rest on the 45° angle in the early stages of an advance, then later, on a reaction, rest on it again; then have a prolonged advance, re-act and rest on the 45° again, and then advance to a higher level; then break the 45° angle the next time, which places it in an extremely weak position because it is so far away from the base and so much time has elapsed since the stock made low. Don't forget--It is most important when angles are broken on the monthly and weekly charts.

This accounts for stocks that have a sharp, quick decline from the top and then advance and make a slightly higher top or a series of slightly lower tops, and work over until they overcome the square of the price range at a comparatively high level and break the 45° angle, then a fast decline follows.

STRONGEST ANGLES FOR MEASURING TIME AND PRICE

90° ANGLE: Why is the 90 degree angle the strongest angle of all? Because it is vertical or straight up and straight down.

180° ANGLE: What is the next strongest angle to the 90° angle? The 180° angle because it is square to the 90° angle, being 90° from the 90° angle.

270° ANGLE: What is the next strongest angle to the 180° angle? The 270° angle because it is in opposition to 90, or 180° from the 90° angle, which equals 1/2 of the circle, the strongest point. 270 months equals $22\frac{1}{2}$ years, which is 1/2 of 45.

360° ANGLE: What is the next strongest angle after 270? It is 360°, because it ends the circle and gets back to the beginning point and is opposite 180° or the half-way point, or the angle which equals 1/2 of the circle.

120° AND 240° ANGLES What angles are next strongest to 90, 180, 270, and 360°? Answer: 120° and 240° angles, because they are 1/3 and 2/3 of the circle. 120° is 90 plus 30, which is 1/3 of 90. 240 is 180 plus 1/3 or 60, which makes these strong angles, especially strong for measurements of time.

45° - 135° - 225° - 315°: What angles are next in strength?
Answer: 45° angle, because it is 1/2 of 90,
135° angle, because it is 90 plus 45,
225° angle, because it is 45 plus 180°, and
315° angle, because it is 45 from 270.
The angle of 225° is 180 from 45 and the angle of 315° is 180 from 135.

CARDINAL & FIXED CROSS: The angles of 90, 180, 270, and 360 form the first important cross, known as the Cardinal Cross. The angles of 45, 135, 225, and 315 for the next important cross, which is known as the Fixed Cross. These angles are very important for the measurements of time and space or price, and volume.

$22\frac{1}{2}$° - $67\frac{1}{2}$° - $78\frac{3}{4}$°: Why is the angle of $22\frac{1}{2}$° stronger than $11\frac{1}{4}$°? Because it is twice as much, being the same reason that a 45° angle is stronger than a $22\frac{1}{2}$° angle. Again, the angle of $67\frac{1}{2}$° is $1\frac{1}{2}$ times 45, therefore quite strong when anything is moving up toward 90°. $78\frac{3}{4}$° is stronger than $67\frac{1}{2}$°, because it is 7/8 of 90, and therefore one of the strongest points before 90 is reached--important to watch both on time, price, and volume. Many stocks have important moves and make tops or bottoms around the 78th to 80th day, week or month, but don't overlook 84 months or 7 years, a strong time cycle.

DIVISION OF $1: 1/8-POINTS Why are the angles of 1/8 of a circle most important for time and space measurement? Because we divide $1 into 1/2, 1/4, and

1/8 parts. We use 25 cents or one quarter, 50 cents or half dollar, and long years ago we had 12½ cent pieces. While the most important figures of our basis of money are the four quarters, we do use the 1/8 part or 12½ cents in all calculations. Stock fluctuations are based on 1/8, 1/4, 3/8, 1/2, 5/8, 3/4, 7/8 and the whole figure. Therefore, any price measurement as well as time will work out closer to these figures when changed into angles of time than 1/3 or 2/3 points for the simple reason that the fluctuations moving in 1/8 proportion must come out closer to these figures.

Figuring $100, or par, as a basis for stock prices and changing those prices to degrees, 12½ equals 45°, 25 equals 90°, 37½ equals 135°, 50 equals 180°, 62½ equals 225°, 75 equals 270°, 82½ equals 315°, and 100 equals 360°. For example:

When a stock sells at 50 on the 180th day, week or month, it is on the degree of its time angle.

On February 1, 1915, U. S. Steel made a low at 38, which is closest to a price of 37½, which is 3/8 of 100 and equals 135° angle. Steel was 14 years or 168 months old on February 25, 1915, and hit the angle of 135°, which showed that Steel was behind time, but that it was in a strong position, holding at 38 above the 135° angle or the price of 37½.

When Steel reached 200, it equalled 2 circles of 360°. When it advanced to 261¾, it was closest to 62½ in the third 100 or nearest the 225° angle or 5/8 point, which is the strongest angle after it crossed the half-way point at 250 or 180° angle.

W. D. Gann

November, 1935

Chapter 6

The Basis Of My Forecasting Method
Geometrical Angles
B. For Commodities

I N D E X

Page

THE BASIS OF MY FORECASTING METHOD FOR GRAINS

Mathematics is the only exact science. All power under heaven and on earth is given unto the man who masters the simple science of mathematics. Emerson said, "God does indeed geometricize." Another wise man said, "There is nothing in the universe but mathematical points." Pythagoras, one of the greatest mathematicians who ever lived, after experimenting with numbers and finding the proofs of all natural laws, said, "Before God, was numbers." He believed that the vibration of numbers created God and the Diety. If has been said, "Figures don't lie." Men have been convinced that numbers tell the truth and that all problems can be solved by them. The chemist, engineer and astronomer would be lost without the science of mathematics.

It is so simple and easy to solve problems and get correct answers and results with figures; it seems strange so few people rely upon them to forecast the future of business, stocks and commodity markets. The basic principles are easy to learn and understand. No matter whether you use geometry, trigonometry or calculus, you use the simple rules of arithmetic. You do only two things: increase or decrease.

There are two kinds of numbers, odd and even. We add numbers which is increasing; we multiply which is a shorter way to increase; we subtract which decreases; and we divide which also decreases. With the use of higher mathematics, we find a quicker and easier way to divide, subtract, add and multiply, yet very simple when you understand it.

Everything in nature is male or female, white or black, harmony or inharmony, right or left. The market moves only two ways: up or down. There are three dimensions which we know how to prove: width, length and height. We use three figures in geometry: the circle, the square and the triangle. We get the square and triangle points of a circle to determine points of time, price and space resistance; we use the circle of 360 degrees to measure time and price.

There are three kinds of angles: the VERTICLE, HORIZONTAL and DIAGONAL which we use for measuring Time and Price Movements. We use the square of odd and even numbers to get, not only the proof of market movements, but the cause.

HOW TO MAKE CHARTS

Charts are records of past market movements. The future is but a repetition of the past; there is nothing new. As the Bible says, "The thing that hath been, it is that which shall be." History repeats and with charts and rules we determine when and how it is going to repeat. Therefore, the first and most important point to learn is how to make charts correctly because, if you make an error on the chart, you will make an error in applying the rules to your trading.

Spacing: Use 1/8" for 1¢ per bushel on the daily, weekly or monthly charts except when the price is selling below $1 per bushel, then use 1/2¢ per bushel for each 1/8" space on the daily chart only.

No space is skipped on the daily chart for Sundays or holidays; therefore, the time period is for actual market days, but you should carry the calendar days across the top or bottom of the daily chart so that you will know when the price is 45, [illegible], 90, 120 or 180 days, etc., from an extreme low or high price.

Weekly Chart: When an option expires on May Wheat, or any other Grain, say, in the month of May for the May Option, and the new option does not start until August, you carry the time periods in weeks and begin the new option at the time period in the week in which it starts. This will enable you to always have the geometrical angles correct from any high or low, and to know the total time elapsed from any high or low price. This will make the geometrical angles correct for all past movements.

GEOMETRICAL ANGLES

After long years of practical experience, I have discovered that Geometrical Angles measure accurately Space, Time Volume and Price.

Mathematics is the only exact science, as I have said before. Every nation on the face of the earth agrees that 2 and 2 equals 4, no matter what language it speaks. Yet all other sciences are not in accord as mathematical science. We find different men in different professions along scientific lines disagreeing on problems, but there can be no disagreement in mathematical calculation.

There are 360 degrees in a circle, no matter how large or how small the circle may be. Certain numbers of these degrees and angles are of vast importance and indicate when important tops and bottoms occur in Grains, as well as denote important resistance levels. Once you have thoroughly mastered the geometrical angles, you will be able to solve any problem and determine the trend of any Grain.

GEOMETRICAL ANGLES (Contd.)

After 50 years of research, tests and practical applications, I have perfected and proved the most important angles to be used in determining the trend of the Grain Market. Therefore, concentrate on those angles until you thoroughly understand them. Study and experiment with each rule I give, and you will make a success.

We use geometrical angles to measure space and time periods because it is a shorter and quicker method than addition or multiplication, provided you follow the rules and draw the angles or lines accurately from tops and bottoms, or extreme highs and lows. You may make a mistake in addition, or multiplication, but the geometrical angles accurately drawn will correct this mistake. Example: If you should count across the bottom of your chart 120 spaces which represents 120 days weeks or months then you begin at "0" and number vertically on your chart up to 120 From this top point at 120, draw a 45 degree angle moving down. This will come out at 0 on 120 points over from the beginning. If you have made a mistake in numbering, this will correct it.

Angles drawn on a chart always keep before you the position of the option and its trend, whereas, if you had a resistance point on time written down, you might mislay it, or forget it, but these angles are always on the chart in front of you.

These angles or moving-average trend lines, correctly drawn, will keep you from making mistakes, or misjudging the trend. If you wait and follow the rules, these angles will show you when the trend changes.

The <u>mean-average</u>, as commonly used, is obtained by taking the extreme low price and the extreme high price of the calendar day, week or month, and dividing it by 2 to get the mean, or average price, for the day, week or month, and continuing this at the end of each time period. This is an irregular movement in spaces, or points, per week because at one time it may move up 2 points per week, and at another, 5 points per week, while the time period is a regular unit. Therefore, geometrical angles, which are really mean-averages, move up or down at a uniform rate from any bottom or top on a daily, weekly or monthly chart.

HOW TO DRAW GEOMETRICAL ANGLES

There are three important points which we can prove with mathematics or geometry: the Circle, the Square and the Triangle. After I have made the square, I can draw a circle in it using the same diameter, and thereby produce the triangle, the square in the circle.

HOW TO DRAW GEOMETRICAL ANGLES (Contd.

The angles, or moving trend line, measure and divide time and price into proportionate parts. Refer to Form 1, where I have drawn the square of 28. You will note that this is 28 high and 28 wide. In other words, 28 up and 28 across. It is the same as a square room which has a bottom or floor, a top or ceiling, and side walls. Everything has width, length and height. 28¢ was the low price for Cash Wheat in 1852.

To get the strongest and most important points in this square I divide it into 2 equal parts by drawing a horizontal and a vertical line. Note angle marked "A" which divides each of the smaller squares into 2 equal parts and runs from 0 to 28 diagonally. This is a diagonal line moving on a 45 degree angle and divides the large square into 2 equal parts. Then, note angle "B" at "14" running horizontally across. This divides the square into 2 equal parts. Note angle "C" which is a vertical line running up from 14, which is 1/2 of 28. This crosses at the center or 1/2 point at 14 where the other angles cross, dividing the square into 2 equal parts. Then, note angle "D" which forms another 45 degree angle moving from the N.W. corner to the S.E. corner, crossing 14 at the exact 1/2 point. You see by this that if we draw the first line through the center of the square, we divide it into 2 equal parts. When we draw the lines from the other directions, we divide it into 4 equal parts. Then, by drawing the 2 lines from each corner, we divide the square into 8 equal parts and produce 8 triangles. We use 28 because 28¢ was the <u>lowest price Cash Wheat ever sold</u>.

As you look at this square, it should be easy for you to tell with your eye where the strongest support point is, or resistance point. It is at the center where all the angles cross. 4 angles cross at this point so, naturally, this would be a stronger support point than a place where only 1 angle crosses. I could divide each one of these smaller squares into 4 or 8 equal parts by drawing angles in the same way. Later, when I give you the rules and examples, I will explain how to square the range of an option, that is, the difference between the extreme low and the extreme high prices, or the difference between any low point and any high point, and also how to square the bottom price.

Example: If the low of Wheat is 28, this square of 28 x 28 would represent squaring the Price by Time, because, if we have 28 points up in price, and we move over 28 spaces in time, we square the price with time. Therefore, when the option has moved over 28 days, 28 weeks or 28 months, it will be squaring its price range of 28.

PATTERN CHART FOR GEOMETRICAL ANGLES

The square of 90, or the Pattern Chart, shows all the measured angles that are important to use in determining the position of an option.

PATTERN CHART FOR GEOMETRICAL ANGLES (Contd.)

These angles are as follows: 3-3/4, 7-1/2, 15, 18-3/4, 26-1/4, 30, 33-3/4, 37-1/2, 45, 52-1/2, 56-1/4, 60, 63-3/4, 71-1/4, 75, 82-1/2, 86-1/4 and 90 degrees.

It is not necessary to measure these angles with a protractor. All you have to do to get the angles correct is count the spaces on the chart paper, using 8 x 8 to the inch, and draw the lines or angles accordingly.

On the square of 90, which you will receive with these instructions, note how equal angles drawn from the top and from the bottom prove themselves by the point at which they cross. Example: The angles of 8 x 1 from "90" down both cross at 45, 5-5/8 points over from 0 counting to the right. Then, the angle of 4 x 1 from 0 and the angle of 4 x 1 down from 90, you will notice, cross at 11-1/4 on 45, equal distance from the other angle and twice the measure. The reason these angles prove this way is because the 45 degree angle, or 45 points or degrees from 0 to 45 is 1/2 of 90. Therefore, parallel angles, beginning at 0 going up and at 90 coming down, must cross on a 45 degree angle or at the gravity center.

HOW TO DRAW ANGLES FROM A LOW POINT RECORDED ON GRAIN OPTIONS

An example marked "Form 2" shows you the most important angles to use when Grain is working higher and advancing.

First Important Geometrical Angle

45° or 1 x 1

The first and always most important angle to draw is a 45 degree angle or a moving trend line that moves up 1¢ per day, 1¢ per week or 1¢ per month. This is a 45 degree angle because it divides the space and time periods into 2 equal parts. As long as the market or an option stays above the 45 degree angle, it is in a strong position and indicates higher prices. You can buy every time it rests on the 45 degree angle with a stop-loss order 1¢, 2¢ or 3¢ under the 45 degree angle, but remember the rule: Never use a stop-loss order more than 3¢ away. Unless Grain options are near the low levels, or just starting in a bull market or selling at very low prices, I always use a stop-loss order 1¢ under the 45 degree angle. If this angle is broken by 1¢, you will usually find that the trend has changed, at least, temporarily and the option will go lower.

An easy way to calculate accurately how to put on this 45 degree angle is, for example: If the time is 28 days, 28 weeks or 28 months from the price where the option was bottom, then the angle of 45 degrees must be 28¢ up from the bottom and would cross at 28. This is one of the easiest angles to put on and one of the simplest to learn. You can beat the market by trading against the 45 degree angle alone, if you stick to the rule: Wait to buy an option on the 45 degree angle or wait to sell it against the 45 degree angle.

HOW TO DRAW ANGLES FROM A LOW POINT, etc. (Contd.)

Second Important Angle — 2 x 1 — This is the angle of 2 x 1, or the moving trend line which moves up at the rate of 2¢ per day, week or month. It divides the space between the 45 degree angle and the vertical angle into 2 equal parts and measures 63-3/4°. That is why it is the next strongest and most important angle. As long as Grain holds above this angle, it is in a stronger position than when it is resting on a 45 degree angle because it is a more acute angle. When an option breaks under this angle of 2 x 1, or 2¢ for each time period, then it indicates that it will go lower and reach the 45 degree angle. Remember the rule of all angles: No matter what angle the option breaks under, it indicates a decline to the next angle below it.

Third Important Angle — 4 x 1 — Still stronger as long as an option holds above it; the angle which moves up 4¢ per day, week or month. This angle is 4 x 1 or 4 points of space or price, equals 1 period of time. It measures 75 degrees and divides the space between the angle of 2 x 1 and the 90 degree angle into 2 equal parts. Any option that continues to advance 4¢ per day, 4¢ per week or 4¢ per month, and remains above this angle, is in a very strong position as long as it stays above it, but when it breaks under, it indicates the next angle or next support point according to the position of the option on time and resistance levels.

Fourth Important Angle — 8 x 1 — The angle of 8 x 1 or the one that moves up 8¢ per day, week or month. This angle measures 82-1/2°. As long as the option can hold above this angle on daily, weekly or monthly charts, it is in the strongest possible position, but, when it reverses trend and declines below this angle, then it indicates a decline to the next angle.

Fifth Angle — 16 x 1 — It is possible to use an angle of 16 x 1, or 16¢ of price to 1 period of time, which measures 86-1/4°, but this angle is only used in fast, advancing markets, like 1947-48, when Grains are moving up or down 16¢ or more per week, or month. There are very few options that will move up 16¢ per day, week or month, and very seldom.

You will note that with these 4 important angles we show the strong or bullish side of the market. All the time, by dividing the space with angles, we are getting the 1/2 point or the gravity center of time and price.

Sixth Angle — 3 x 1 — Note the angle drawn in green marked "3 x 1" which moves up at the rate of 3¢ per day, week or month measuring 71-1/4°. This angle is important at times, after markets have had a prolonged advance and are a long distance up from the bottom. It is an important angle to use on monthly and weekly charts.

These are all the angles you need as long as an option continues to advance and work up and stays above the angle of 45 degrees, or the trend line of 1¢ per day, week or month.

While there are 360 degrees in a circle, and angles can form at any of these degrees. All of the important angles form between 0 and 90 because 90 is straight up and down and the most acute angle on which price can rise.

Example: The 45 degree angle divides the space from 0 to 90 in half. The angle of 135 degrees is another angle of 45 degrees because it is 1/2 of the next quadrant between 90 and 180. 225 and 315 in a circle are also 45 degree angles. Therefore, all of the angles valuable in determining the trend of Grain are found between 0 and 90 degrees. When we divide 90 degrees by 8 we get the most important angles to use, then divide it by 3 and we get 30 and 60 degree angles, which are important to use for time and resistance points.

BOTTOMS FROM WHICH TO DRAW ANGLES OR MOVING TREND LINES

Daily Chart; If Grains have been declining for sometime, then start to rally by rallying from a bottom, it must make higher bottoms every day and higher tops. Then, after a 3-day rally on the daily high and low chart, you can put on the 45 degree angle and the angle of 2 x 1 from the bottom or low point. As a rule, it will only be necessary to put on these 2 angles, at first. If this bottom holds and is not broken, then you can put on the other angles from the bottom.

Weekly Chart: If any option is declining and reacts for more than one week and continues down, for 3 weeks or more, then starts to rally and advances 2 weeks or more, you would start to put the angles on from the low point of the decline, only using the angles above the 45 degree angle until the option again breaks under the 45 degree angle. After that, use the other angles on the lower or bearish side of the square.

WHAT TO DO AFTER THE 45 DEGREE ANGLE FROM BOTTOM IS BROKEN

After an option makes top, either temporary or otherwise, and breaks under the 45 degree angle, and starts moving down, then, the first thing to do is draw angles below the 45 degree angle, starting from the bottom or low point. Note example marked "Form #3."

First Angle on Bear Side of the Square 2 x 1 The first angle you draw on the bear side of the square is 2 x 1 or 2¢ over and 1¢ up which moves at the rate of 1/2¢ per day, week or month, and measures 26-1/4°. This is the first support angle the option should reach after it breaks under the 45 degree angle. As a general rule, when the price reaches this angle, it will receive support and rally. Sometimes, it will rest on it for along period of time, holding on this angle and making higher bottoms;

but when this angle of 2 x 1, or moving trend line of 1/2¢ per day, week or month is broken, then you must draw the next angle of 4 x 1.

Second Important Angle 4 x 1 The next important angle on the bear side of the square, which moves up at the rate of 1/4¢ per day, is the angle of 4 x 1, measuring 15°. It will be the next strong support angle from which the price should get support and rally.

Third Angle 8 x 1 After the 4 x 1 angle is broken, the next important angle you will put on your chart is the angle of 8 x 1 which moves at the rate of 1/8¢ per day, week or month and measures 7-1/2°. This is often a very strong support angle. After the option has had a big decline, it will often rest on this angle several times or may make final bottom and start up from this angle crossing other angles and getting back into a strong position again. Therefore, this angle is important to use on a monthly or weekly chart after a prolonged decline.

Fourth Angle 16 x 1 This angle can be used on a monthly chart after a long period of time has elapsed from an important bottom. It moves at the rate of 1/16¢ per month and measures 3-3/4°.

Fifth Angle 3 x 1 This angle, drawn in red ink, is a very important angle measuring 18-3/4°. I strongly advise using it at all times and keeping it up on monthly charts from any important bottom. It can also be used to advantage at times on weekly charts, but is seldom of much value on a daily chart. It moves at the rate of 1/3¢ per day, week or month. By drawing this on the monthly chart for a long period of year, you will soon be convinced of its value and also by testing it on a weekly chart, you will find it valuable.

This completes all of the angles you will need to use from any bottom, at any time.

HOW TO DRAW ANGLES FROM TOPS ON DAILY, WEEKLY OR MONTHLY CHARTS

Position under 45° Angle drawn from Top: After an option has made top and declined for a reasonable length of time, say, 3 days, 3 weeks or 3 months, breaking previous bottoms, then you start to draw angles down from the top. Note example marked "Form #4." which is the pattern for drawing angles from the top under the 45 degree angle.

45° Angle from Top: The first angle you draw is the angle of 45 degrees, or a moving trend line which indicates a decline of 1¢ per day, week or month. As long as the option is below this angle it is in the weakest position and in a bear market.

Other Angles: In many cases an option will start declining an

Other Angles (contd.): average of 8¢ per day, week or month; or 4¢ per day, week or month; 2¢ per day, week or month. Therefore, you should put on all of these angles from the top which moves down faster than the angle of 45 degrees.

Weakest Position: The price of any Grain is in the weakest possible position when it declines and keeps under the angle of 8 x 1. It is in the next weakest position when it is dropping down at the rate of 4¢ per day, week or month, or under the angle of 4 x 1. It is in its next weakest position when it is dropping down under the angle of 2 x 1.

Strongest Position: The price is in a stronger position and indicates a better rally when it crosses the angle of 2 x 1, but this depends on how far it is down from the top and how far the angles are apart, as will be explained later under the rules.

Changing Trend: As long as the price is declining 1¢ per day, week or month, or falling below or under the 45 degree angle, it is still in a bear market and in a very weak position. When the option rallies and crosses the angle of 45 degrees after a prolonged decline, then you are ready to put on the angles on the other side of the 45 degree angle which shows that the price is in a stronger position in a bear market, and may be getting ready to change into a bull market.

POSITION ABOVE THE 45° ANGLE DRAWN FROM TOP

(Refer to Form #5 which is the pattern for drawing angles above the 45 degree angle from the top.)

2 x 1 Angle from Top: The first angle or moving trend line to draw, after the 45 degree angle from the top is crossed, and after the option indicates that it has made a temporary bottom, is the angle of 2 x 1 moving over 2¢ and down 1¢, or 1/2¢ per unit of time. This is moving down at the rate of 1/2¢ per month, week or day.

4 x 1 Angle: The next is the angle of 4 x 1 which moves down at the rate of 1/4¢ per day, week or month.

8 x 1 Angle: The next angle is the angle of 8 x 1 which moves down at the rate of 1¢ every 8 days, 8 weeks or 8 months; or 1/8¢ per time period.

Strong Position: After the price has crossed the angle of 45 degrees and rallied up to the angle of 2 x 1, it will meet selling and react to some angle coming up from the bottom of the last move, but it is in a stronger position when it holds above this angle of 2 x 1 and is in the next strongest position when it crosses the angle of 4 x 1. Crossing the angle of 8 x 1, which is of least importance, it indicates it is in a very strong position again from the top. You must always consider a movement coming up from bottom and its position on angles from the

POSITION ABOVE THE 45° ANGLE DRAWN FROM TOP (Contd.)

8 x 1 Angle (contd.): bottom to determine its strength. It is important to consider the number of cents it has moved up from the bottom and how many cents it is down from the top.

3 x 1 Angle: The angle of 3 x 1, drawn in red ink on Form #5, moves down at the rate of 1¢ every 3 days, 3 weeks or 3 months; or 1/3¢ per day, week or month. This angle is important to use after prolonged declines.

This completes the forms of all the angles that you will need to use at any time from tops or bottoms. Practice putting these angles on tops and bottoms until you thoroughly understand how to do them, and know that you are getting them absolutely accurate. Then, you can begin to study the rules for determining the trend according to the position of the price on angles.

DOUBLE AND TRIPLE TOPS OR BOTTOMS

Angles Crossing Each Other: When there is a double bottom several days, weeks or months apart, you draw angles from these bottoms which are near the same price level. Example: From the first bottom draw a 45 degree angle and from the second bottom draw an angle of 2 x 1. When these angles cross each other it will be an important point for a change in trend. Note on chart marked "Form #6" that I have drawn the 45 degree angle from the first bottom "1B" and the angle of 2 x 1 on the right hand side of the 45 degree angle. Then, from the second bottom "2B", I have drawn a 45 degree angle and the angle of 2 x 1 which gains 2¢ per day, week or month, on the left hand side or bull side of the 45 degree angle. You will note that the angle of 2 x 1 from the second bottom crosses the angle of 2 x 1 on the bear side from the first bottom at 48, and that when the price breaks under these angles, a change in trend takes place and it goes lower.

Note that the angle of 2 x 1 from the third bottom "3B" crossed the angle of 2 x 1 on the bear side from the first bottom at 53-1/2, and crosses the 45 degree angle from the second bottom at 8. This would be a point to watch for change in trend. I have placed a circle where these angles from the different bottoms come together.

Apply this rule to double tops and triple tops in the same way. It is not necessary for the tops or bottoms to be exactly at the same price level, but near the same level. Remember, always draw 45 degree angles from all important tops and bottoms.

PARALLEL ANGLES

Parallel angles or lines run from important tops and bottoms. As previously explained, the 45 degree angle is the most important and should be drawn from all important tops and bottoms. If an option starts advancing, we draw a 45 degree angle

PARALLEL ANGLES (Contd.)

from the bottom. Then, if the option makes tops, declines and makes a higher bottom, advances and makes a higher top, draw a 45 degree angle from the first top, running the line up. This will give the oscillation or width of fluctuation in a parallel between the 45 degree angle from the bottom and the 45 degree angle running up from the top. Often an option will advance to the 45 degree angle from the first top, fail to cross it, then decline and rest on the 45 degree angle from the first bottom. Advance again working up for a prolonged bull campaign between these parallel angles.

When the angles are very far apart, you can draw another 45 degree angle equal distance between them which is often a strong support angle from which the option will rally, but when it breaks under, it declines to the bottom parallel.

Parallels can form between the angles of 2 x 1 or 4 x 1 just the same as between 45 degree angles, which often occurs in a slow moving market.

GEOMETRICAL ANGLES OF MOVING TREND LINES DRAWN FROM "O"

When the price reaches bottom and starts up, you have been instructed to draw angles from this exact low point which shows the support in time periods, but there are other angles that later on will be just as important and sometimes more important than the angles drawn from the bottom. These are the angles that begin at "O" or zero, and move up at the same rate they move up from the bottom. The starting point must be on the same line that the bottom is made on, as the time period begins from this bottom, but the angles move up from O. These angles should be started every time an option makes a bottom, especially on weekly and monthly charts, and should also be carried up on important movements on the daily chart. Example: See chart marked "Form #7."

If an option makes low at 20, as shown on the chart, starting the 45 degree angle from 0, when will this angle reach 20? Answer: It will reach 20 in 20 days, 20 weeks or 20 months from the bottom or its starting point. In other words, in 20 days, 20 weeks or 20 months, it will be up 20 from 0, and at the price where the option made bottom. Then, the angle will continue on up at the same rate, and later, when the price breaks under the 45 degree angle from the actual bottom made at 20, and breaks the other support angles drawn from the actual bottom at 20, the next important point for support will be the angle of 45 degrees moving up from 0. When this angle is broken, it is in the weakest possible position, and indicates much lower prices, but this depends on how high the option is selling and how much it has declined at the time it breaks the 45 degree angle from 0. These angles drawn from 0 especially the 45 degree angle, proves when price and time are balancing, or when the price is squaring out from its bottom.

"O" ANGLES STARTING AT THE TIME TOP IS MADE

When an option reaches extreme top on a daily, weekly or monthly chart, and the trend turns down, you should start an angle of 45 degrees from O moving up from the exact space and date that the top is made. This will prove the square of the time period. It is very important when this angle is reached and indicates a change in trend. It is the last strong support and when broken, it will indicate much lower prices.

I have instructed you in each case to first draw the 45 degree angle from the bottom, top and O at bottom and top, but this does not meanthat you must not use the other angles. All of the other angles can be used from O, but the 45 degree ANGLE IS THE FIRST AND MOST IMPORTANT. After this angle is broken, you can use the other angles. It is not necessary to carry all of them along until you need them, but on the monthly chart, after a long series of years, these other angles should be carried along when the price begins to approach the levels where they would be broken, or where the price would rest on them and receive support.

45 Degree Angle From "O" to Top and Bottom: When a 45 degree angle moving up from O reaches the line or price of the bottom, it is very important. Then, again when it reaches the point of the extreme high price, it is very important for a change in trend.

You should carry 45 degree angles and other angles up from O from all important 1st, 2nd and 3rd higher bottoms, especially those where very much time has elapsed between these bottoms. You should also start the angle of 45 degrees up from O from the 1st, 2nd and 3rd lower tops, especially those which show much time period elapsed. These angles are the most important to be carried on the weekly and monthly charts.

Never overlook keeping up the angles from O because they will tell you when time is squaring out with price from tops and bottoms, and will locate support angles or moving trend lines at a point on the bear side, after the first 45 degree angle from a bottom is broken. You could not locate this support point in any other way except by the angles from O.

You should go back over past records and bring up these angles and square out different tops and bottoms so that you can prove to yourself the great value of using these angles.

ANGLES FROM TOPS DOWN TO "O" AND UP AGAIN

A 45 degree angle starting down from any important top on a monthly or weekly chart should be continued down until it reaches O, and then, started up again at the same rate. After a long number of years, between important tops and bottoms, this angle coming down and going up again is important. A 45 degree angle can also be continued down from any important bottom to O, and then started up again. This will show the squaring of price with time from either top or bottom. Also, some

ANGLES FROM TOPS DOWN TO "O" AND UP AGAIN (Contd.)

angles can be moved to base on lowest price, and then up again.

TWO 45° ANGLES FROM THE SAME BOTTOM

As we have previously explained, the 45 degree angle moves up at the rate of 1¢ per month and moves down at the rate of 1¢ per month. Refer to example on chart #8.

You will note that the low on this chart is shown as 52 and the price moves up to a high of 63. A 45 degree angle is drawn up from the bottom, and after the price reaches top and starts to work down, it breaks the 45 degree angle getting under it at a price of 59. You will note that I have drawn another 45 degree angle down from the bottom at 52. At the point where the price breaks under the 45 degree angle moving up from 52 to the 45 degree angle moving down from 52, the distance in points is 16. Therefore, the angles have widened until the price could decline 16¢, if it went straight down, before it reached the 45 degree angle moving down from the bottom.

Note that I have shown on the chart that the price continues down until it reaches 40, where it rests on the 45 degree angle from the bottom at 52. This would indicate the strongest support point and at least a temporary rally, especially as the price is down 23 points from the top. Later, you will find under "Resistance Levels," that 22-1/2¢ to 24¢ is a strong support point.

This shows that when an option gets into a very weak position by dropping under important angles moving down from bottoms, after having broken strong angles moving up from bottoms, it can decline to very low levels. These extreme fluctuations and declines have happened in the past and will happen again in the future. This proves the squaring out of time on the down side or the balancing up of Price and Time.

ANGLES OR MOVING TREND LINES FROM TOP TO THE NEXT TOP.
(Refer to example on Form #9.)

You will see that we have started the bottom at 60. The option advances 6 months to 74, to a point marked "T" and makes top, reacts for 3 months to 64 breaking the 45 degree angle but resting on the angle of 2 x 1 from the bottom, then starts advancing and finally crosses again the 45 degree angle from 60, getting into a stronger position, having regained this angle. In order to determine where it might meet resistance, as it is in new high territory, we draw a 45 degree angle from the top at 74. The price advances to 90 on the 22nd month from the bottom, striking the 45 degree angle from the first top at 74, on the 16th month from the 1st top. Being 16 points up above the 1st top, the time equals the advance in the price above the 1st top. The 45 degree angle shows that this is a strong resistance point and a place to go short with stop 1 to 3 points above the 45 degree angle. A decline starts and in the 3rd month the price again breaks under the 45 degree angle from the bottom (at 60) at a very high level. In other words, it is 24¢ up from the bottom and is now in a much weaker position because it is so far from the base of support, and indicates a decline again to the angle of 2 x 1 (marked in green).

Don't overlook this rule: After an option has advanced to a new high level, then declines to the old top at 74, this may be a support point unless it breaks 3¢ under it. If it does, and also breaks the angle of 2 x 1, it will be in a weaker position and the next point to watch for support and a rally would be the next bottom at 64.

ANGLES FROM BOTTOM OF FIRST SHARP DECLINE

When an option that has been advancing for sometime makes top and holds for several days, several weeks or several months, then turns the trend down andhas a sharp, severe decline, there is always a rally after this first decline. It usually makes a lower top on this secondary rally and then starts to work lower again. The bottom of the first decline is a very important point from which to draw angles especially the 45 degree angle moving down, as I have done on the chart marked "Form #10."

This chart shows the price rallying up to around 75, where the 45 degree angle coming up from the last bottom crosses the angle of 2 x 1 coming down from the top. Then the decline started and at 66 the price broke back under the angle of 45 degrees from the top, which put it in a very weak position. It declined to the angle of 45 degrees coming down from the bottom of the first sharp decline. This would be the squaring out of time from the bottom and would be a place to buy for a rally. An option will often decline and drop a little below this angle from the bottom. Then, if it holds for several days or weeks under this angle, or on it, it is a place to buy for a rally.

On a monthly chart always carry this angle down from the bottom of the first sharp decline, as it often becomes very important later on in a campaign.

After an option has been advancing for sometime and then has a sharp break lasting 2 to 3 days, 2 to 3 weeks or 2 to 3 months, then rallies and afterward breaks under the lows of this first sharp break, indicates that the main trend has turned down and that it is going lower.

Apply the same rule when any Grain has been declining for a long time and then makes a sharp, quick recovery for 2 to 3 days, 2 to 3 weeks or 2 to 3 months, then reacts and crosses this first rally point that it made, an indication of higher prices.

LAST SWING IN A BULL OR BEAR MARKET

It is important to draw angles from the price the market starts up, and makes its last run, in a bull market. Refer to Chart #11.

In this example note point marked "last bottom." In the last section of the bull market a fast advance follows to a price of 84. We have drawn the angle of 2 x 1 (a gain of 2¢ per day, week or month) and the 45 degree angle from this bottom. When the angle of 2 x 1 was broken, it indicated the trend had turned down. The market declined and rested on the 45 degree angle, then rallied and made a second lower top, then broke the 45 degree angle, declined sharply and rested on the 45 degree angle drawn from the top at 84, which indicated that time and price had squared out or were equal. This would be a buying level with a stop-loss order 2¢ to 3¢ under this angle for a rally back to the angle of 2 x 1 from the top, as shown on the chart.

In a very active fast-moving market the price may stay above the angle of 4 x 1 or the angle of 8 x 1 from the "last bottom," but on the daily or weekly chart, after this first acute angle is broken, it indicates that the trend has turned down.

Always remember that after a prolonged advance, when the main trend turns down, it is safer to wait for rallies and sell short than to buy against the trend.

All of these rules are reversed at the end of a bear market or sharp decline. It is important to note when the market starts down from the last top or rally, and makes its last run to bottom. Draw the angles from this last top and watch when the market reaches these important angles and crosses them.

After an option has been advancing for along time, in the last run when there is a lot of momentum, it may cross angles from previous tops or bottoms, then fall back under them which is an indication of weakness. When an option has a sharp decline and is making bottom, it will drop under important angles and then recover quickly getting above them, which shows that it is getting into a strong position and changing trend.

ANGLES FROM HIGHER BOTTOMS AND LOWER TOPS

What rule should be followed when Grain makes higher bottoms and lower tops?

As prices advance and make higher bottoms on the monthly, weekly or daily chart, you should always draw angles from higher bottoms. Then, in the last section of a bull market, if these important angles are broken from the last bottom, you know that the trend has turned down.

Apply this same rule as a market declines. Draw the angles from each lower top and watch the angles until the price again

ANGLES FROM HIGHER BOTTOMS AND LOWER TOPS (Contd.)

crosses the 45 degree angle from a 2nd, 3rd or 4th lower top. The 2nd lower top or 2nd higher bottom is always very important from which to draw angles and to measure time from as well.

SECTIONS OF MARKET CAMPAIGNS

All market campaigns, up or down, move in 3 to 4 sections. When an advance starts the market runs for several weeks or several months and then halts for several weeks or months, moving up and down over a range of 10¢ to 20¢ or more according to the price of the option, then the advance is resumed and the price crosses the high level of the 1st section, moves higher, halts again, and reacts for a period of time; then, crosses the top of the 2nd section and moves up again for another period of time and halts for the 3rd time, which is a very important point to watch as markets often culminate at the end of the 3rd section and a greater decline follows.

Most markets run out in 3 important sections or campaigns. However, after resting and reacting, if the price crosses the 3rd top, it will then move up to the top of the 4th section. This 4th advance may be a shorter period of time than the previous section, or, in some cases, may consume a greater period of time especially if the option is very active and high-priced. This 4th top is very important and generally marks a culmination and a reversal for a greater decline.

Reverse this rule in a bear market. Watch the action of the market when it makes the 3rd and 4th decline. But, remember, in a bear market, when rallies come, they may make only 1 section or 1 move, or, in extreme cases, only make the 2nd section, then reverse and follow the main trend down.

You will find it very helpful to study and watch these various section of a campaign and, by applying the angles from tops and bottoms, you can detect the first minor and major changes in trend.

STRENGTH OR WEAKNESS DENOTED BY POSITION ON ANGLES

The angles on the monthly and weekly charts are of greater importance than those on the daily chart because the daily trend can change quite often, while only the major changes are shown according to the angles on the monthly and weekly charts.

Always consider the distance an option is from its beginning price when it breaks any important angle or crosses any important angle. The further away from the beginning price, the more important the change in trend, whether this is crossing angles from the top or breaking under an angle from the bottom.

When an Option is in the Weakest Position

An option is in the weakest position when it has completed

distribution and broken under a 45 degree angle from an important bottom on the weekly or monthly chart. It is also in the weakest position when it has broken under the 1/2 point between any important top or bottom. The longer the time period has run and the higher the price, the weaker the position. Example: (Refer to 2-day and weekly chart on May Beans, 1947-48).

If an option has advanced to 150 and has only moved down 25¢ when the 45 degree angle from an extreme low on a weekly or monthly chart is broken, then it is in a very weak position because it is so far above the 1/2 point on its price movement, already having squared out the time period with price.

Weakness in price developes when it breaks the 3/4 point, the 2/3 point, the 1/2 point, etc., but the position on the timing angles from the bottom tells you still more about the weak position.

An option shows its first weakness when it breaks the first important angle coming up from the last bottom in the final run in a bull market.

When an Option is in the Strongest Position

An option is always in the strongest position coming up from a bottom when it is holding above the very acute angles on the daily, weekly or monthly charts especially on monthly and weekly charts.

As long as the option holds above the angle of 2 x 1 (a gain of 2¢ per day) on the daily chart, it is in a very strong position, as far as the bottom is concerned. In fact, it is always in a strong position on the daily as long as it holds above the 45 degree angle. The same applies to weekly and monthly charts which are the most important trend indicators.

I have found that the Grains which have the greatest advances are those that always hold above the angle of 2 x 1 on the monthly chart, or gain 2¢ per month for a long period of time. have seen prices rest 10 or 15 times on the angle of 2 x 1, and never break it until they have advanced 100¢ or more. In this way, the price stays ahead of time and stays within the square of time by being far above the angle of 45 degrees, and therefore is in a very strong position. But, the time must come when the cycle has run out and the main trend begins to change from a bull market to a bear market -- when the breaking of the angle from the last bottom shows a change in trend.

Another indication that an option is in a strong position is when it advances and moves up above the 1/2 point of the previous price movement, and then holds the 1/2 point, that is, advances above it and then reacts and fails to break under. This is just the same as resting on a 45 degree angle and indicates a very strong position.

Strongest Buying and Selling Points

The safest buying point is when the price rests on a 45 degree angle, placing a stop-loss order below it.

Another point to buy is on the 1/2 point of the price movement, placing a stop-loss order under the 1/2 point.

When the main trend is up, it is also safe to buy, when the option reacts to the angle of 2 x 1 (a gain of 2¢ per time period) on the weekly or monthly chart.

Regaining Angles or Crossing Lines

Remember, when any option breaks under the 45 degree angle from the extreme low price of a move on the daily, weekly or monthly chart, it is then in a very weak position and indicates a decline to the next angle. However, when an option can regain the 45 degree angle, it is in a stronger position.

The same rule applies to a 45 degree angle drawn up from any top. When the option crosses the angle on the daily, weekly or monthly, and stays above the 45 degree angle or any other angle to the left of the 45 degree angle, it is in a very strong position.

After the price once drops below or gets above any important angle, and then reverses its position by getting back above the angle or dropping back below it, it changes the trend again.

WHEN GRAIN IS IN A STRONG POSITION FROM BOTTOM AND IN A WEAK POSITION FROM TOP

An option is in a strong position from the bottom when it is keeping above the angle of 45 degrees, or the angle of 2 x 1, but at the same time it can be in a weak position when it rallies up and strikes against a 45 degree angle, or the angle of 2 x 1 coming down from the top, then it is a short sale until it can cross these angles or cross previous tops. When it breaks the angles from the bottom, it is in a weak position and indicates lower.

An option can be in a strong position from the top and in a weak position from the bottom, that is, it may cross some important angles from the top after a long period of time, but at the same time may break under the 2 x 1 angle or 45 degree angle from the bottom, which would indicate that it is in a weak position and getting ready to go lower.

When Angles from Extreme Top are Crossed

The 45 degree angle, drawn from the extreme high price of an option is most important and when it is crossed, a major move may be expected.

QUICK CALCULATION OF ANGLES

It is not necessary to draw these angles from a price a long way back. You can make the calculations and determine where they cross. Example: Suppose, in January, 1951, you wish to get the 45 degree angle from June, 1930, when Soy Beans were high at 216. This will make 247 months to January, 1951, and the 45 degree angle, moving up from zero, will be at the price of 247; therefore, you start the 45 degree angle at 247 and move it up 1¢ per month until the price declines below it.

1920, February 15, Soy Beans high, 405. This was the highest in history until 1947. To get the angle and time period to February 15, 1951, will be 31 years or 372 months and the 45 degree angle moving up from 0 will cross at 372. The 45 degree angle moving down from 405 will cross at 33. February, 1953, will be 396 months from 1920, and November 14, 1953, will be 405 months, which equals the highest price; and the 45 degree angle moving down from the top will reach 0. Time and price will have squared out on the monthly chart making November, 1953, a very important period for a change in trend.

LATITUDE AND LONGITUDE

On all charts -- daily, weekly or monthly -- the price must move up or down on the vertical angles. Therefore, the price movement is the same as latitude. You should begin with 0 on any chart -- daily, weekly or monthly -- and draw the important angles and resistance levels across which measures latitude.

Next, number the time points in days, weeks or months across and draw the horizontal angle at each important natural angle, such as, $11\frac{1}{4}$, $22\frac{1}{2}$, $33\frac{3}{4}$, 45, $56\frac{1}{4}$, $67\frac{1}{2}$, $78\frac{3}{4}$, 90, $101\frac{1}{4}$, $112\frac{1}{2}$, 120, etc. Then, you will know when price reaches these important angles and meets resistance.

Longitude measures the time running across the chart, as it moves over each day, week or month. Therefore, you must keep your chart numbered from each important top and bottom in order to get the time measurements, according to angles. These important angles, such as, $11\frac{1}{4}$, $22\frac{1}{2}$, $33\frac{3}{4}$, 45, $56\frac{1}{4}$, 60, $78\frac{3}{4}$, 90, etc., from each bottom and top will show you where the strongest resistance in price and time takes place. These angles prove the parallel or crossing point. Study past records and see what has happened when prices on monthly charts reached these important angles or time periods.

Example: 90 points up in price from 0, draw an angle horizontally across the chart. Then, 90 days, weeks or months, going to the right across the chart, draw a vertical angle up which will cross the horizontal angle at 90 and prove the square. By keeping all these angles up and understanding them on your charts, you will know when important time cycles are running out.

LATITUDE AND LONGITUDE (Contd.)

If the price of an option at 60 comes out on the 60th day, week or month, it will meet strong resistance because it has reached the square of price with time. It is at the same latitude or price, and the same longitude or time period. You can always put the square of 90 on a chart, either daily, weekly or monthly, and use the natural angles, but I advise only using this on the weekly and monthly. You can begin this square of 90 from any bottom or top, that is, going up 90 points or from the natural points which are 90, 135, and 180, but you must not fail to square the extreme low and high price, as well as the 2nd and 3rd lower tops and higher bottoms with time.

RULE FOR KEEPING TIME PERIODS ON CHARTS

It is very important that you keep the time periods on all of your charts, carrying them across from the bottom and top of each important move, in order to check up and know that you have your angles or moving trend lines at the correct point, and to see where major and minor cycles indicate changes in trend.

Time Periods from Bottoms

When an option makes bottom one month and then the following month makes a higher bottom and a higher top, or anyway, after it makes a higher bottom and rallies for one month or more, you can start numbering from that bottom. The month that it makes the low belongs to the old or downward movement and is the last move down. Count the first month up as 1, and then number across on the 1/2" squares running them across, adding 4 each time.

Example: If an option has made bottom and advanced 50¢, and you look down at the bottom of the chart and find that the price is on the 25th month, then the angle of 2 x 1, moving up 2¢ per month would cross at 50, while the 45 degree angle moving up 1¢ per month would be at 25; and if the price broke back under 50 the following month, it would be falling under the angle of 2 x 1 and indicate a further decline. If you had an error on the chart in the timing or numbering across from the bottom, the moving trend line or angle would not come out correctly.

Time Periods from Tops

After an option has advanced and made an extreme high and reacted for a few days, a few weeks or a few months, and you start putting on the angles from the top down, you must then begin to number the time periods across from the top. Apply the same rule for the top: The month, week or day that the option makes extreme high finishes the upward movement and is not to be counted. You can count the number of days, weeks or months moving across after that allowing the top month to be 0, the next month, week or day over to be 1, adding 4 across on the squares to get the correct position. If this time period is

Time Periods from Tops (Contd.)

carried across on all the charts correctly, then you can always check up and find out if you have made any mistake in bringing down the angles or moving trend lines.

This is a simple way to always know when the angles or moving trend lines are correct because you simply add the movement to the bottom and subtract it from the top. Suppose the price referred to above, when the price has declined 75¢ was 150, then subtracting 80 from the top at 150, the angle would cross at 70 and the price of the option down 75¢ would be at 75. Therefore, it would be above the angle of 2 x 1 from the top and in position for a rally if the time cycle indicated it.

Points from which to number Time Periods

The most important point on the monthly high and low chart to carry the time period is from the extreme low of the life of an option. From the extreme low price, the time period should always be carried across on the chart just the same as the important angles should be continued right along for years.

The next important point to number from is a 2nd or 3rd higher bottom, but you should not consider a bottom established until the market has held up or advanced 3 or 4 months, then commence numbering from that bottom, if it appears to be important.

Use this same rule at tops. After top iss reached and the trend turns down, carry the time numbers across from the top; but after any top is crossed or bottom is broken, that you are numbering from, do not count that top or bottom of importance to number from except to determine a time period on another cycle 3, 5, 7, 10 or 20 years ahead. Tops that stay for a long time without being crossed are always the most important from which to carry the time periods. The extreme high reached by an option is always most important until that high is crossed. Then, the next high price made on a secondary rally, which is always a lower top, is the next most important top from which to number.

Always note the number of months between extreme high and between extreme low points, and note what angle the tops and bottoms come out on.

Squaring the PriceRRange with Time

This is one of the most important and valuable discoveries I have ever made, and if you stick strictly to the rule, and always watch an option when Price is Squared by Time, or when Time and Price come together, you will be able to forecast the important changes in trend with greater accuracy.

The Squaring of Price with Time means an equal number of points up or down balancing an equal number of time periods, either days, weeks or months. Example: If an option has advanced 24¢ in 24 days, then moving the 45 degree angle or moving trend line up at the rate of 1¢ per day, the timing line or time period and the price of the option are at the same level, and the price is resting on a 45 degree angle. You should watch for an important change in trend at this point!

If an option is to continue up-trend and remain in a strong position, it must continue to advance and keep above the angle of 45 degrees. If it breaks back under this angle, then it is out of its square on the bear side of the 45 degree angle and in a weaker position. When you are squaring out time on a daily chart, look at the weekly high and low chart, and monthly high and low chart, and see if the option is in a strong position and has yet to run out the time periods because on a daily chart it has to react and then recover a position, squaring its price many times as long as the weekly and monthly charts point up. Market corrections or reactions are simply the squaring out of minor time periods and later the big declines or advances are the squaring out of major time periods.

Squaring the Range

Refer to Form #12, where a range of 12 points is shown from 48 low to 60 high. Now, suppose an option remains for several weeks or several months moving up or down in this range, never getting more than 12 points up from the bottom and not breaking the bottom, start the 45 degree angle from the bottom of 48 and move it up to the top of the range to 60, then, when we see the option is holding this range and not going higher, move the 45 degree angle back to the bottom; then, back to the top of the range again moving it up or down over this range until the price breaks out into new low levels or new high levels. You will find that every time the 45 degree angle reaches the top of this range, or the bottom, there is some important change in the trend of the option.

1949, Feb. 9, May Soy Beans low, 201½. To square this price with time on the weekly chart will require 201½ weeks, and the 45 degree angle moving up from 201½ will be at 403; but the 45 degree angle moving up from 0 will be at 201½ equalling the price.

The 1/8, 1/4, 1/3, 1/2 and other parts of 201½ must be watched in periods of time from 201½. 1/8 was 25¼ weeks or Aug. 6, 1949; 1/4 was Feb. 4, 1950; 1/2 was 101 weeks or Jan. 20, 1951. May and November Beans made high February 8, 1951, and the trend turned down.

1951, December 29, will be 150 weeks from February 9, 1949, and this is 3/4 of 201½, and is a very important date for a change in trend.

1952, January 15, will be 4 years from 1948, high 436-3/4, also important to watch for a change in trend.

Squaring the Range (Contd.)

1953, Dec.29, will be 202 weeks from Feb. 9, 1949, and this will square the price of 201½ with time. Watch this date for an important change in trend.

You can also use the angles of 2 x 1 to the right of the 45 degree angle and the 2 x 1 to the left, as they again divide the time period into 2 equal parts and are of some value.

If an option finally moves out of this range on the up side, then the angles would begin at the new and higher bottom and move up, but from the point where the price went into new high, or from any important bottom made while it was in the range especially the last bottom that it made, would be most important. You should then begin an angle at that bottom and continue on up again. Watch when this angle is broken or when time is squared out again with price which would be important for another change in trend, either major or minor.

Three Ways to Square Time and Price

We can square the range, that is, the number of cents from extreme low to extreme high with time; then square the extreme low price with time; and square the extreme high price with time. When the market passes out of these squares and breaks important angles, the trend changes up or down.

1. The range that any option makes between extreme high and extreme low can be squared, so long as it remains in the same price range. If the range is 25¢, it squares with 25 periods of time -- days, weeks or months. Continue to use this time period as long as it stays in the same range.

2. Squaring Time with Bottom or Extreme Low Price - The next important price to square with time is the lowest price or bottom of any important decline. Example: If the bottom of an option is 25, then at the end of 25 days, 25 weeks or 25 months time and price are equal Watch for a change in trend as based on its bottom or lowest selling price. As long as the option continues to hold one bottom and advances, you can always use this time period running across and continuing the time period, noting every time it passes out of the square. Watch especially when the price reaches the 3rd square, the 4th square, and again the 7th and 9th squares of its time period. These squares only occur frequently on the daily or weekly charts, as the monthly in most cases, would move out of a range, up or down, before it squared a bottom as many as 7 or 9 times. However, this does sometimes happen when an option is in a narrow range for many years.

   Example: May Beans, 1939, July 27 - low 67. This would require 67 months or 67 weeks to square the lowest price. Note monthly chart marked "Squares of 44 and 67."

3. Squaring Time with Top or Extreme High Price - The other important price with which to square time is the extreme high price of an option. The time period must be carried across from the high of the daily, weekly or monthly, and the square of the top price in time must be noted and watched for a change in trend. If the top of an option is 50 then, when it has moved over 50 days, 50 weeks or 50 months, it has reached its square in time and an important change is indicated. This can be determined by the position of the angles from top and bottom. Example: May Soy Beans, 1948, Jan. 15 - high 436-3/4. This requires 436-3/4 weeks to Square Price with Time.

Both major and minor tops and bottoms on all time periods must be watched as they square out right along. Most important of all is the extreme high price on the monthly high and low chart. This may be very high and work out a long time period before it squares the top, in which case you have to divide the price into 8 equal time periods and watch the most important points like 1/4, 1/3, 12, and 3/4, but most important of all is when Time equals Price.

When you are watching the position of an option, after it has squared out from a bottom or a top, always look up the time period and the angles from the opposite direction. If the market is nearing a low price, squaring out a top, see how its relation is to the bottom as it might be in the 2nd or 3rd square period from the bottom which would be a double indication for a change in trend.

Squaring Weekly Time Periods

The year contains 52 weeks and the square of this in time is 52 by 52. Therefore, you can make up a square of 52 wide and 52 high; put on all of the angles from 0; then, chart weekly high and low prices of an option in this square. Example: If the low price of an option is 50, then the top of this weekly square would be 52 added to 50, which makes 102 as top of the square. As long as the price stays above 50 and moves up, it will be working in the weekly square of 52. On the other hand, if the option makes top and works down, you would make up a weekly square 52¢ down from the top and 52 over to get the time period.

You can take the past movement of any option, put on a square of 52 x 52, and study the movement noting 13 weeks or 1/4, 26 weeks or 1/2, and 39 weeks or 3/4 points on time; and the changes in trend which take place when the price reaches these important resistance points in time and price. You would watch for a change in trend around these time periods.

Squaring Monthly Time Periods

At the time an option breaks a 45 degree angle, if it is selling at 135 on the 135th month, it is breaking a doubly strong resistance level -- a strong angle and a natural resistance level.

Squaring Monthly Time Periods. (Contd.)

This would be time and space for balancing at resistance levels or geometrical angles and would indicate a big decline to follow. Reverse this rule at the end of a bear campaign.

On a monthly chart, 12 months complete a year. Therefore, the square of 12 is very important for working out time periods on the monthly chart. The square of 12 is 144 and important changes often occur on even 12 months' periods from a bottom or top of an option. It will help, if you use the resistance levels on prices of the even 12's, noting 24, 36, 48, 60, 72, 84, 96, 108, etc. Watch how the option acts on angles when it reaches these important resistance points in price.

PRICE AHEAD OF TIME

Why do Grain options often cross the 45 degree angle on the daily, weekly or monthly chart, then have an advance for a short period of time, decline and rest on the same 45 degree angle?

Because, when the price crosses the 45 degree angle the first time, it has not run out or overcome the square of time with price. Therefore, on the secondary reaction, when it rests on the 45 degree angle, it is at a time when the price has reached the square of price in time. After that, a greater advance follows.

Reverse this rule at the top of a bull market. When an option breaks under the 45 degree angle, a long distance from the base or bottom, it is most important. Many times an option will rest on the 45 degree angle in the early stages of an advance, then later, on a reaction, rest on it again; then have a prolonged advance, react and rest on the 45 degree angle again, and then advance to a higher level; break the 45 degree angle the next time, which places it in an extremely weak position because it is so far away from the base and so much time has elapsed since the price made low. Don't forget: It is most important when angles are broken on the monthly and weekly charts.

This accounts for Grains that have a sharp, quick decline from the top and then advance and make a slightly higher top or a series of slightly lower tops, and work over until they overcome the square of the price range at a comparatively high level and break the 45 degree angle, then a fast decline follows.

STRONGEST ANGLES FOR MEASURING TIME AND PRICE

90° ANGLE - Why is the 90° angle the strongest angle of all? Because it is vertical or straight up and down.

180° ANGLE-What is the next strongest angle to the 90° angle? The 180° angle because it is square to the 90° angle being 90° from the 90° angle.

STRONGEST ANGLES FOR MEASURING TIME AND PRICE (Contd.)

270° ANGLE - What is the next strongest angle to the 180° angle? The 270° angle because it is in opposition to 90 or 180°, from the 90° angle which equals 1/2 of the circle, the strongest point. 270 months equals $22\frac{1}{2}$ years, which is 1/2 of 45.

360° ANGLE - What is the next strongest angle after 270°? It is 360° because it ends the circle and returns to the beginning degree, and is opposite 180° or the angle which equals 1/2 of the circle.

120° and 240° ANGLES - What angles are next strongest to 90°, 180°, 270° and 360°?

120° and 240° angles because they are 1/3 and 2/3 of the circle. 120° is 90° plus 30, which is 1/3 of 90°. 240° is 180° plus 1/3 or 60 which makes these strong angles especially strong for measurements of time.

45°, 135°, 225° & 315° ANGLES - What angles are next in strength?

45°	angle because	it is	1/2	of	90°
135°	"	"	" "	90 plus	45°
225°	"	"	" "	45 "	180°
315°	"	"	" "	45 from	270°

The angle of 225° is 180° from 45 and the angle of 315° is 180° from 135°.

CARDINAL FIXED CROSS - The angles of 90°, 180°, 270° and 360° form the first important cross, known as the Cardinal Cross. The angles of 45°, 135°, 225° and 315° form the next important cross, which is known as the Fixed Cross. These angles are very important for the measurements of time and space, or price and volume.

$22\frac{1}{2}$°, $67\frac{1}{2}$° and $78\frac{3}{4}$° - Why is the angle of $22\frac{1}{2}$° stronger than $11\frac{1}{4}$°? Because it is twice as much - the same reason that a 45° angle is stronger than a $22\frac{1}{2}$° angle. Again, the angle of $67\frac{1}{2}$° is $1\frac{1}{2}$ x 45, therefore, quite strong when anything is moving up toward 90°.

$78\frac{3}{4}$° is stronger than $67\frac{1}{2}$° because it is 7/8 of 90° and, therefore, one of the strongest points before 90 is reached -- important to watch on time, price and volume. Many Grains have important moves and make tops or bottoms around the 78th to 80th day, week or month, but don't overlook 84 months or 7 years -- a strong time cycle.

STRONGEST ANGLES FOR MEASURING TIME AND PRICE (Contd.)

Division of \$1 – 1/8 Points – Why are the angles of 1/8 of a circle most important for time and space measurements? Because we divide \$1 into 1/2, 1/4 and 1/8 parts. We use 25¢ or 1 quarter, 50¢ or half dollar, and many years ago we had 12½¢ pieces

While the most important figures of our basis of money are the 4 quarters, we do use the 1/8 part or 12½¢ in all calculations. Grain fluctuations are based on 1/8, 1/4, 3/8, 1/2, 5/8, 3/4, 7/8 and the whole figure. Therefore, any price measurement, as well as time, will work out closer to these figures when changed into angles of time rather than 1/2 or 2/3 points of price for the simple reason that the fluctuations moving in 1/8 proportions must come out closer to these figures. We use the denominations of 5¢ which equals 1/20 of a dollar, and 10¢ which equals 1/10 of a dollar.

Figuring \$100, or par, as a basis for Grain prices and changing these prices to degrees, 12½ equals 45°, 25 equals 90°, 37½ equals 135°, 50 equals 180°, 62½ equals 225°, 75 equals 270°, 82½ equals 315° and \$100 equals 360°.

Example: When an option sells at 50 on the 180th day, week or month, it is on the degree of its time angle.

Follow all the rules, study and experiment, and you will learn to do by doing, and make a success!

W. D. GANN

November 12, 1951

CHAPTER 7

RESISTANCE LEVELS

AUTHOR:
"Truth of the Stock Tape"
"Wall Street Stock Selector"
"New Stock Trend Detector"

W. D. GANN
Statistician and Economist
82 WALL STREET
NEW YORK, N. Y.

2101 N. W. 18th TERRACE
MIAMI, FLA.

MEMBER
New Orleans Cotton Exchange
Commodity Exchange, Inc. N.Y.
American Economic Ass'n
Royal Economy Society

RESISTANCE LEVELS

::::::::::::::

If we wish to avert failure in speculation we must deal with causes. Everything in existence is based on exact proportion and perfect relation. There is no chance in nature, because mathematical principles of the highest order lie at the foundation of all things. Faraday said: "There is nothing in the Universe but mathematical points of force."

Every stock makes a top or bottom on some exact mathematical point in proportion to some previous high or low level.

The movement of a stock between extreme high and extreme low, either in a major or a minor move, is very important and by a proper division of this range of fluctuation, we determine the points where resistance or support will be met on a reverse move, either up or down. By carefully watching these Resistance Levels in connection with your Trend Lines, you can make a greater success and trade with closer stop loss orders. You can tell by the Resistance Points why the averages or a stock should receive support or meet selling at old tops or bottoms.

RANGE OF FLUCTUATIONS

1/8 POINTS

Take the extreme low and extreme high of any important move; subtract the low from the high to get the range; then divide the range of fluctuation by 8 to get the 1/8 points, which are Resistance Levels or buying and selling points. When a stock stops around these levels and makes bottom or top on or near them and shows a turn on the Trend Line, this is the place to buy or sell. Sometimes the averages or a stock will hold for 3 to 7 days, making bottom or top around these important Resistance Levels, and at other times may hold for several weeks around them.

1/3 and 2/3 POINTS

After dividing a stock by 8 to get tho the 1/8 points, the next important thing to do is to divide the range of fluctuation by 3 to get the 1/3 and 2/3 points. These 1/3 and 2/3 points are very strong, especially if they fall near other Resistance Points of previous moves or when they are divisions of a very wide move.

HIGHEST SELLING PRICE

Next in importance is the division of the highest price at which a stock has ever sold and each lower top.

Divide the highest selling price by 8 to get the 1/8 points and also divide by 3 to get the 1/3 and 2/3 points.

This is very important as a stock, after breaking the half-way point of the fluctuating range, will often decline to the half-way point of the highest selling price, and will also work on the other Resistance Points in the same way.

When a stock is advancing, it will often cross the half-way point of the highest selling point and then advance to the half-way point of the fluctuation and meet resistance.

MOST IMPORTANT STOCK MOVEMENTS TO CONSIDER

The first and most important point: Consider the Resistance Levels between the extreme high and extreme low of the life of a stock.

Next important point to consider: Resistance Points or divisions of the highest price at which the stock has ever sold.

Then consider the fluctuation of each campaign which runs one year or more. Take the range between extreme high and extreme low and divide into 8 equal parts to get the Resistance Points.

Then take a third or fourth lower top and divide it by 8 to get the Resistance Points.

SECONDARY BOTTOMS AND TOPS

After the market has made final top in a Bear Campaign and the first rally takes place, then follows a secondary reaction, making a higher bottom, the half-way point between the high of the first rally and the low on secondary decline is very important to figure Resistance Levels from. The half-way point between the top of the first rally and the bottom of the secondary reaction is a strong support point.

Example: Dow-Jones Industrial averages - 1932 Bear Market
Jul. 8, 1932 final low 40-1/2;
Sep. 8, 1932 high of first rally 81-1/2;
Feb. 27, 1933 bottom of secondary reaction 49-1/2;
half-way point 61.

After final top in a Bull Campaign has been reached and the first sharp decline takes place and a secondary rally follows, making a lower top, this lower top is an important point to figure Resistance Levels from. The half-way point between the bottom of the first reaction and the secondary top is a strong Resistance Level.

Example: 1937, Mch. 8 high 195-1/2;
Jun. 17 low of first decline 163;
Aug. 14 high of secondary rally 190-1/2;
half-way point 179-1/4.

Also figure the half-way point between the secondary bottom of 49-1/2 made on February 27, 1933 and the secondary top of 190-1/2 reached on August 14, 1937.

This was 120, a very important Resistance Level. The low of April 11, 1939 was 120, where the trend turned up again. There were many other bottoms and tops formed around this level in the past.

ORDER OF RESISTANCE LEVELS

When a stock is advancing and crosses the 1/4 point, the next most important point to watch is the half-way point (1/2 point) or gravity center, or the average of the move or fluctuation.

Then the next point above the half-way point is the 5/8 point.

The next and strongest point after the half-way point is crossed is the 3/4 point.

Then, if the range is very wide, it is important to watch the 7/8 point of the move. This will often mark the top of an advance.

But in watching these Resistance Points, always watch your Trend Lines on the Weekly Chart and follow rules given on Formations. If the stock starts making tops or bottoms around these Resistance Points, it is safe to sell or buy.

THE AVERAGE OR HALF-WAY POINT

Always remember that the 50% reaction or half-way point of the range of fluctuation or of the extreme highest point of a stock or any particular move is the most important point for support on the down side or for meeting selling and resistance on the way up. This is the balancing point because it divides the range of fluctuation into two equal parts.

To get this point, add the extreme low of any move to the extreme high of that move and divide by 2.

When a stock advances or declines to this half-way point, you should sell or buy with a stop loss order 1, 2, or 3 points according to whether the stock is selling at very high or very low levels.

The wider the range and the longer the time period, the more important is this half-way point when it is reached.

You can make a fortune by following this one rule alone. A careful study and review of past movements in any stock or the averages will prove to you beyond doubt that this rule works and that you can make profits following it.

Buy or sell at the most important half-way point of the major move and place stop loss orders 1 to 3 points under the half-way point or 1 to 3 points above the half-way point. By major moves we mean the half-way point between the extreme low and extreme high when the range runs 25 to 100 points or more. A minor half-way point would be the 1/2 point between a minor top and a minor bottom. Reactions usually run back half of the last move or to the half-way point.

When the range between the 1/2 point and the 5/8 point is 5 to 10 points or more and the stock crosses the half-way point, it will go to the 5/8 point and meet resistance and then react or decline. The 5/8 point is a very important point to watch for top or reaction. A stock will often react from the 5/8 point back to the half-way point and be a buy again.

The same rule applies when a stock is declining. If the range is 5 to 10 points or more between the 1/2 point and the 3/8 point, then the stock breaks the half-way point, it will decline to the 3/8 point and make bottom and rally to the 1/2 point or higher.

When a stock is in a narrow trading range, it will often fluctuate between the 5/8 point on the upside and the 3/8 point below the half-way point, making bottoms and tops around the half-way point and at the 5/8 and 3/8 points, moving in 1/4 of the full range of fluctuation. See examples of 1/2, 3/8, 5/8 points on the Dow-Jones 20 Railroad averages 1896 to 1914 and the 30 Industrial averages 1903 to 1939.

When a stock advances to a half-way point and reacts several points from this level, then finally goes thru it, you can expect it to make the next resistance point indicated on your Resistance Level Card or the next old top.

The same applies when a stock declines and receives support several times on a half-way point, then breaks thru it. It will then indicate the next resistance point on your Resistance Level Card or the next important bottom.

The greatest indication of strength is when a stock holds one or more points above the half-way point, which shows that buying or support orders were placed above this important Resistance Level.

A sign of weakness is when a stock advances and fails to reach the half-way point by one or more points; then declines and breaks the Trend Line or other Resistance Points.

NEXT RESISTANCE LEVELS AFTER THE MAIN HALF-WAY POINT HAS BEEN BROKEN

The next Resistance Level to watch after the main half-way point has been broken is the next half-way point of some previous move. By main half-way point I mean, the half-way point of the extreme fluctuating range of the life of a stock.

Another very important Resistance Level after the main half-way point is crossed is the half-way point or 1/2 of the highest selling price. This is a stronger support level than the half-way point of minor fluctuating moves because it cuts the highest selling price in half, and is a strong buying or selling point until it is crossed by 1, 2, or 3 points, according to the price of a stock, whether it is very high-priced, medium or low-priced.

RESISTANCE POINTS NEAR SAME LEVELS

When two half-way points or any other two Resistance Points, either in the range of fluctuation or the division of the highest selling price, occur near the same level, you should add these two points together and divide by 2, as the half-way point between these two points will often be a support point on a decline or a selling point on a rally.

HOW TO LOOK UP RESISTANCE LEVELS

When you find an important Resistance Level or the strongest one - the half-way point - at a certain level, look to see if any other Resistance Level, whether it be 1/8, 1/4, 3/8, 5/8 or 2/3 point, falls around this same price. You may find 3 or 4 Resistance Levels around the same price. The more you find, the stronger resistance the stock will meet when it reaches this level. Then take the highest Resistance Level around this same price and the lowest, and add them together to get the average point of resistance.

Watch the activity of the stock when it reaches these Resistance Levels. If it is advancing very fast or declining very fast on large volume, do not consider that it is going to stop around these Resistance Levels unless it stops or holds one or two days around these levels; then sell or buy with stop loss orders. Also consider whether the market is in 3rd or 4th section from bottom or in 3rd or 4th section from top down.

AVERAGE AND EXTREME FLUCTUATIONS

In normal markets the rallies and reactions on the Dow-Jones 30 Industrial averages run 10 to 12 points and when they exceed this number of points they run 20 to 24 points and then 30 to 40 points. When there are great extremes between main tops and main bottoms, like August 8, 1896, low 28-1/2 to September 3, 1929, high 386, and from 386 high to a low of 40-1/2on July 8, 1932, you can divide by 16 and 32 to get closer mathematical points instead of dividing by 8 to get the 1/8 points. These points will correspond to minor tops and bottoms of other movements.

Use all the rules and figure that the important tops and bottoms will come out on the strongest points, like the 1/3, 2/3, 1/4, 3/8, 1/2, 5/8 and 3/4 points.

Do not overlook the fact that it requires time for a market to get ready at the bottom before it advances and requires time to distribute at the top. The longer a market has been running, the more time it will require to complete accumulation or distribution.

WHEN STOCKS DECLINE UNDER OLD TOPS

When stocks drop back under old tops of previous campigns, the Resistance Levels between old bottoms and these old tops will be important points for support and resistance.

Example: After the 1929 high the averages dropped back below 119-5/8, the top of 1919, and declined to 85-1/2 in October, 1931, which was also the low of October 27, 1923. On November 9, 1931, they rallied to 119-5/8, the old top of 1919. After that, as long as the averages stayed below 120, you would watch the old Resistance Levels from 28-1/2 low, 38-1/2 low, 42 low, 52 low to 119-5/8 high. Then, when the averages advanced above 120, you would watch Resistance Levels to higher tops. The important ones were at 195-1/2 to 197.

SMALL GAINS IN LAST STAGE OF BULL OR BEAR MARKET

When a bull or advancing market is nearing the end of a campaign, the gains or runs will often get smaller, which is a sign that the averages or stocks are meeting with greater selling pressure.

Example: Suppose a stock is moving up and crosses a previous top and advances 20 points, then reacts 10 points; then crosses the last top and advances 15 points and reacts 5 to 7-1/2 points; again advances above the last top but only goes 10 points above it and reacts 5 points or more, this would be a sign of weakness or that the top was near because each move was making a smaller gain. In very active fast markets, when volumes of sales are large, the last run may be a greater number of points. Reverse this rule in a declining market.

If a stock has made several moves down of 10, 15 or 20 points and each one gets shorter or when the stock breaks bottom and the declines get smaller, it is a sign that the selling pressure is decreasing and that a change in trend is near, but in fast panicky markets the last decline may be a large number of points with very small rallies. This is a final wave of liquidation.

In the last stages of Bull or Bear Campaigns use only the half-way point of short or minor moves. It is most important to watch the Resistance Levels of the final move, which may run several weeks or months, particularly the half-way point. When it is exceeded by 3 full points, the trend usually reverses.

LOST MOTION

As there is lost motion in every kind of machinery, so there is lost motion in the stock market due to momentum, which drives a stock slightly above or below a Resistance Level. The average lost motion is 1-7/8 points.

When a stock is very active and advances or declines fast on heavy volume, it will often go from 1-7/8 points above a half-way point or other strong Resistance Level and not go 3 points. The same rule applies on a decline. It will often pass an important Resistance Point by 1-7/8 points but not go 3 full points beyond it.

This is the same rule that applies to a gravity center in anything. If we could bore a hole thru the earth and then drop a ball, momentum would carry it beyond the gravity center, but when it slowed down, it would finally settle on the exact center. This is the way stocks act around these important centers.

A study of the Resistance Levels between bottoms and tops of individual stocks or the averages will prove how accurate the market works out to these important points.

July 6, 1939

RESISTANCE LEVELS

DOW JONES 30 INDUSTRIAL AVERAGES

COMPARATIVE BOTTOMS AND TOPS

Resistance points are figured to show you why bottoms and tops were made around these levels. You can use your resistance cards and levels in the same way to determine future bottoms and tops.

1896 Aug. 8 — Low 28½ — was 3/8 of 78 3/4 the Last High
1896 Nov. 12 — High 45 — was 1/2 of 78 3/4 to 28½
1898 Mar. 19 — Low 42 — was 1/4 of 94½ to 28½
1898 Aug. 7 — High 61 — was 1/2 of 94½ to 28½
1898 Oct. 22 — Low 51 5/8 — was 1/2 of 78 3/4 to 28½
1900 Sept. 29 — Low 53 — was 1/2 of 77 5/8 to 28½

From 42 Low to 78 5/8 the 1/2 point was 60 1/4
From 53 Low to 78 1/4 the 1/2 point was 65 6/8
From 53 Low to 78 1/4 the 5/8 point was 68 3/8

1902 Apr. & Sept.)
1904 Feb.) — Tops 68 1/2 to 67 3/4 was 5/8 of 53 to 78 1/4

1904 — Broke 65 6/8 was 1/2 of 53 to 78 1/4
1903 Nov. 9 — Low 42 1/8 an old bottom of March 1898 and was 1/4 of 28½ to 78 3/4
Later crossed 53 5/8 was 1/2 of 28½ to 78 3/4
and a big Bull Market followed.

1906 Jan. 19 — High 103 A sharp decline followed.
1906 May 5 — Low 86½ — was 3/4 of 38½ to 103
1906 July 14 — Low 85½ — was 3/4 of 28½ to 103
1906 Aug. 13 — High 96
1907 Jan. 12 — High 96 3/4 — was 7/8 of 53 to 103
and 3/4 of 76½ to 103
Later broke 85
declined to 78 was 1/2 of 53 to 103
A Bear Market followed.

1907 Nov. 23 — Low 53 (same as 1900) was 1/3 of 28½ to 103
and 1/4 of 38½ to 103
(Note: 1/2 of 103 is 51½. Holding above this 1/2 point was a strong support and buying point at 53, the old bottom.)

1908 Jan. 18 — High 66 3/4 — was 5/8 of 103 to 53
1908 Sept. 22 — Low 77 1/4 — was 1/2 of 103 to 53
1909 Oct. 2 — High 100½ — was
(Note: 3 bottom at 96 was 7/8 of 53 to 103
and 94½ was 7/8 of 53 to 100½
Then broke 96 and 96½ and declined fast.)

RESISTANCE LEVELS, Cont'd

DOW JONES 30 INDUSTRIAL AVERAGES

COMPARATIVE BOTTOMS AND TOPS

1910 July 26	Low 73 5/8	was 1/2 of 42	to 103
1911 June 24	High 87	was 1/2 of 73 5/8	to 100½
1911 Sept. 25	Low 73	was 1/2 of 42	to 103
	and same low as July 26, 1910. A double bottom and place to buy.		
1912 Oct. 10	High 94	was 3/4 of 73 5/8	to 100½
Made several bottoms around	88	was 3/4 of 53	to 100½
Later Broke	87	was 1/2 of 73 5/8	to 100½
1913 June 14	Low 72 1/8	was 3/8 of 53	to 103
		and 1/2 of 42	to 103
	A third time at this level - a buying point.		
1913 Sept. &) 1914 March)	High 83 3/8	was 1/2 of 72 1/8	to 94 1/8
		and 3/8 of 73	to 100½
1914 July declined to	71 1/4	under three old bottoms	
	and under	1/2 of 42	to 103
	and	3/8 of 53	to 103
	A sure sign of lower prices.		
1914 Dec. 24	Low 53 1/8 This was third time at this level.		
	1900-- Low 53		
	1907-- Low 53		
	1914-- Low 53 1/8		
	Holding above 51½	the 1/2 of 103	
		and 1/3 of 28½	to 103
		and 1/4 of 38½	to 103
	Made this a good support and buying point in a panic.		
	The War Bull Market Followed.		
1915 May	High 71 3/4 just under the 3/8 of 53		to 103
	and under three old bottoms.		
1915 June	Low 60½ a secondary reaction		
	60½	was 1/3 of 38½	to 103
	and 62 3/8	was 1/2 of 53 1/8	to 71 3/4
1919 Jan.	High 99		
1916 Apr.	Low 85	was 5/8 of 53	to 103
1916 Nov. 21	High 110 1/8	a sharp reaction followed.	
1917 Feb. 2	Low 87	was 5/8 of 53 1/8	to 110 1/8
1917 June 9	High 99	was 7/8 of 28½	to 110 1/8
		and 1/2 of 85	to 110
	Later broke all important 1/2 points		
	including 81½	was 1/2 of 53	to 110 1/8

RESISTANCE LEVELS, Cont'd

DOW JONES 30 INDUSTRIAL AVERAGES

COMPARATIVE BOTTOMS AND TOPS

1917	Dec. 19	Low 66	was 1/3 of 42	to 110 1/8
			and 3/8 of 38½	to 110 1/8
1918	Oct. 19	High 89	was 3/4 of 28½	to 110 1/8
			and 5/8 of 53	to 110 1/8
1919	Feb. 8	Low 79 1/8	was 1/2 of 53	to 110 1/8
			and 5/8 of 28½	to 110 1/8
		A Big Bull Market followed.		
1919	Nov. 3	A New High 119 5/8	A sharp decline followed.	
1920	Feb. 25	Low 90	was 3/4 of 28½	to 110 1/8
			and 5/8 of 42	to 119 5/8
			and 2/3 of 28½	to 119 5/8
1920	Apr. 8	High 105	was 5/8 of 79 1/8	to 119 5/8
			and 3/4 of 66	to 119 5/8
			and 1/2 of 90	to 119 5/8
		Later declined, to 99	was 1/2 of 79 1/8	to 119 5/8
1921	Aug. 24	Low 64 Just 2 points under 1917 Lows.		
		" 64	was 1/3 of 38½	to 119 5/8
		62 5/8	was 3/8 of 28½	to 119 5/8
		This was a final low and the greatest Bull Market in history followed.		
		(Note: When averages crossed 80 they were above	1/2 of 42	to 119 5/8
		and	1/2 of 38½	to 119 5/8

Note: 91 7/8 was 1/2 of 119 5/8 to 64 and after averages crossed 92 did not reach 91 before they advanced to 105 5/8

1923	Mar. 20	High 105 5/8	was 3/4 of 64	to 119 5/8
1923	Oct. 27	Low 85 3/4	was 3/8 of 64	to 119 5/8
			5/8 of 28½	to 119 5/8
			1/2 of 53	to 119 5/8
		A Strong Support Point.		
1924	May 20	Last Low 88 3/8	was 2/3 of 28½	to 119 5/8
1924	Dec.	Crossed old top of 1919 at 119 5/8		

A Big Bull Market followed.

In view of the fact that the averages made - High 103 in 1906 and in 1916 made a new High of 110 1/8 and in 1919 another record High 119 5/8 and in 1921 decline to 64, holding more than 4 points above 1/2 of 119 5/8, was a strong indication of much higher prices because of such a long period of time between these top levels. From January 1906 to December 1924, when averages went above 119 5/8, was nearly 19 years. You could figure they would first double the highest selling price or made 240. After that figure was crossed, you figure three times 119 5/8 of about 360.

RESISTANCE LEVELS, Cont'd

DOW JONES 30 INDUSTRIAL AVERAGES

COMPARATIVE BOTTOMS AND TOPS

1929 Sept. 2	High 386 If you take the range from extreme Low 28½ to 119 5/8 the range was 91 1/8. Multiply this range by 4 and we get 364½ as a probable top. The proper procedure after the averages were in new high, was to follow the trend and use all rules until there was a change in the main trond.
1926 July	High 162¼
1926 Apr.	Low 135 1/8 was just under 1/2 of 115 to 162¼ 150 5/8 was 1/2 of 162¼ to 135 1/8 When the averages crossed this level the second time they went right up to new highs.
1927 Oct.	High 199 7/8
1927 Oct.	Low 179 was 1/2 of 165 3/4 the last low to 199 7/8 189 3/8 was 1/2 of 119 7/8 to 179 When crossed this level never sold below 190½ again.
1928 Dec.	High 299
1928 Dec. 12	Low 254½ was near 250 the 1/2 of 200 7/8 to 299 Holding above the 1/2 of last move indicated higher.
1929 Jan.	High 324½
1928 Mar. 30	Low 281½ 279 was 1/2 of 234 to 374½ the last low, and holding above 1/2 point was strong.
1929 May	High 331 Last reaction before top
End of "	Low 290 3/4 of 281½ to 331 was 287½ holding above this indicated support.
Then when crossed	306 the 1/2 of 281½ to 331
and crossed	310½ the 1/2 of 331 to 290 indicated higher.
1929 Sept. 3	High 386 Final Top.

After the trend turned down, we calculated the Resistance Points from bottoms from 1896 to date, to get points to watch on the way down. The first 1/2 point of the last move from 281½ to 386, making 333 3/4, - this was broken on the first decline to 321, which was 1/2 of 255 to 386.

1929 Oct. Last Rally	358 the 1/2 of 386 to 321 was 253½, did not go 5 points above it -- then broke wide open.
1929 Oct. 29	Low 213 was 1/2 of 38½ to 386
1929 Oct. 31	High 273½ was 2/3 of 42 to 386 and 2/3 of 53 to 386 and just under 2/3 of 64 to 386

RESISTANCE LEVELS, Cont'd

DOW JONES 30 INDUSTRIAL AVERAGES

COMPARATIVE BOTTOMS AND TOPS

1929 Nov. 13 — Low 195½
This was a very important panic bottom and there was a strong mathematical point which indicated they should stop around this level.

When			
225	was 1/2 of	64	to 386 was broken
219½	was 1/2 of	53	to 386
214	was 1/2 of	42	to 386
207¼	was 1/2 of	28½	to 386

The extreme high according to our rules is the next important point, or 1/2 of 386 the highest selling point - which is 193 - and the averages held 2½ points above this strong point, indicating bottoms for a big rally.

1930 Apr. 17 — High 296 3/8 was 3/4 of 28½ to 386
and just 5 points above
291 the 1/2 of 386 to 195 3/8
when the averages dropped back under 290
they never rallied to 291 again
245 3/4 was 1/2 of 195 3/8 to 296 3/8, they never broke this 1/2 point, never sold at 250 again.

1930 June to Aug. Bottoms at — 208 to 214 which was 1/2 of 28½ to 386
and 42 to 386

1930 Sept. 10 — Last High 247 was 1/2 of 195 3/8 to 296 3/8
Then followed a big decline breaking all main 1/2 points and when the average broke 193 the 1/2 of 386 in Oct. 1930 they never sold above 198½ again.

1930 Dec. 17 — Low 155½ was 1/3 of 38½ to 386
1/3 of 42 to 386

1931 Jan. — High 175½ was 3/8 of 53 to 386
1/3 of 64 to 386

1931 Jan. 24 — Low 160 was 1/4 of 85 3/4 to 386
165½ was 1/2 of 155½ to 175½
When it crossed this level it never sold at 163 until it made next Top.

1931 Feb. 24 — High 197¼ was just above
193 the 1/2 of 386 and under low of Nov. 1929 and last Top of Nov. 1930 - making this a safe point to Sell Short.

The next important point to watch... 176 7/8 was 1/2 of 155½ to 197¼

1931 Mar. 14 — Low 175 3/4 was 1/2 of 155½ to 197¼

1931 Mar. 20 — High 189 was 5/8 of 297
1/3 of 85 3/4 to 386
3/8 of 64 to 386

Latter part of Mar. broke 176 the 1/2 of 155½ to 197¼
and a panic decline followed.
Later broke 161 which was 1/4 of 85 3/4 to 386
Then broke Low 155½ and declined fast.

RESISTANCE LEVELS, Cont'd

DOW JONES 30 INDUSTRIAL AVERAGES

COMPARATIVE BOTTOMS AND TOPS

1931	June	2	Low	120	was 1/4 of 85 3/4	to 386
					and 3/4 of 157½	
			and back to 1919 Top. A strong support for a rally.			
1931	June	27	High	157½	was 1/3 of 42	to 386
			and just under		1/2 of 197¼	to 120
			and at Lows of Dec. 1930 made this a Sure Selling Level.			
1931	Oct.	5	Low	85½	Same Low as Oct. 27, 1923	
				85	was 1/8 of 386	to 42
1931	Nov.	9	High	119 5/8	was under 1/2 of 157¼	to 85½
					and 1/4 of 28½	to 386
					and 1/8 of 85 3/4	to 386
			A sharp decline followed.			
1932	Jan.	7	Low	70	was 1/8 of 28½	to 386
1932	Mar.	8	High	89½	was 3/8 of 119 5/8	to 70
				79 3/4	was 1/2 of 70	to 89½
			When it broke under 79 it declined fast.			
1932	July	8	Low	40½		
			Final Low - End of Great Bear Market Down to Lows of 1898.			
1932	Sept.	8	High	81½	was 1/2 of 119 5/8	to 40½
					under 3/8 of 386	to 40½
					1/3 of 157½	to 40½
				61	was 1/2 of 40½	to 81½
1933	Feb.	27	Low	49½	was 3/4 of 40½	to 81½
1933	Mar.	18	High	64½	was 1/2 of 49½	to 81½
1933	Apr.	1	Last Low 54 3/4 not 3 points under		1/2 of 49½	to 64½
			A rapid advance followed,			
			crossed		1/2 of 49½	to 81½
			and		1/2 of 40½	to 81½
1933	July	17	High	110½	was 3/8 of 296 3/4	
			just under		5/8 of 146½	to 40½

Why did prices of the Dow Jones 30 Industrial Averages make High at 110½ and 111½ in 1933 and 1934?

The highest selling point in 1929 was 386. 1/3 of this is 128 5/8. 1/4 of 386 is 96½. The half-way point between 1/3 and 1/4 points is 112½. This is one of the reasons that so many tops were made around this level for such a long period of time before they were crossed.

RESISTANCE LEVELS, Cont'd

DOW JONES 30 INDUSTRIAL AVERAGES

COMPARATIVE BOTTOMS AND TOPS

Why 82½ Low, October, 1933?

In September 1932, the old Top 81. From the low of 49½ to 111½, the half-way point is 80½. From the breakaway point 55½ to 111½ the half-way point is 83½. The fact that the averages held above the extreme half-way point was a sign of strength and good support. From 111½ to 82½, the half-way point was 97.

In March, 1935, the averages started up from 95½, not 3 points under this half-way point and on March 31, 1939, the averages declined to 97½ which was also the half-way point of the highest selling point 195½ in 1937.

1933	Oct.	21	Low 82½ was above 1/2 of 49½ to 110½ and 1/8 of 386 to 40½ and 1/2 of 54 3/4 to 110½ Holding above these important 1/2 points, indicated strong support.
1934	Feb.	5	High 111½ Low 82½ to 111½ made 97 the 1/2 point.
1934	Mar.	31	Low 97 rallied to 107
1934	July	26	Low 84½ was 3/8 of 157½ to 40½ From 111½ To 84½ the 1/2 point was 98
1935	Feb.	18	High 108½
1935	Mar.	18	Low 95½ just under 1/2 of 87½ to 111½ and 1/2 of 195½ and 1/4 of 386 From 108 To 95½ the 1/2 was 101 3/4 Crossed this minor 1/2 point and crossed Old Tops 110½ to 111½ and Big Bull Market followed.
1936	Apr.	6	High 163½ was 3/8 of 28½ to 386 was 3/8 of 386 to 49½
1936	Apr.	30	Low 141½ was 7/8 of 40½ to 157½ Just 3 points under 1/2 of 176½ to 163½
1937	Mar.	10	High 195½ Same as Low Nov. 13, 1929 and Last High Oct. 1930. Just under High of Feb. 1931. This was not 3 points above 193, the 1/2 of 386 and a sure place to go Short.
1937	June	17	Low 163 was 3/8 of 28½ to 386 was 1/2 of 141½ to 195½

RESISTANCE LEVELS, Cont'd

DOW JONES 30 INDUSTRIAL AVERAGES

COMPARATIVE BOTTOMS AND TOPS

1937 Aug. 14	High 190½	just 2½ points under 1/2 of 386 and a lower Top- a sign of weakness.	
	The 1/2 point from 163 to 195 was 179¼ and 163 to 190½ was 176 3/4. When these levels were broken a panicky decline followed.		
1929 Oct. 19	Low 115½	was 1/2 of 195½	to 40½
1929 Oct. 29	High 141½	was 2/3 of 195½	to 40½
	and under	3/8 of 386	
1937 Nov. 23	Low 112½	was 3/8 of 196 3/4	
1938 Jan. 15	High 134¼	was 3/8 of 40½	to 296 3/4
		and 3/8 of 95½	to 195½
1938 Mar. 31	Low 97½		
Final Bottom of Panic	97½	was 1/2 of 195½	
		and 3/8 of 40½	to 195½
		and 1/3 of 296 3/4	
		and 1/4 of 386	
	This was a safe buying point.		
1938 Apr. 18	High 121¼	just above 1/2 of 40½	to 195½
		and 2/3 of 157½	to 140½
		and 5/8 of 195½	
1938 May 27	Low 106½	just above 1/4 of 40½	to 296 3/4
		and 1/8 of 195½	to 97½
	109¼	was 1/2 from 97½	to 121½
	When it crossed 110 showed strong up and advanced fast.		
1938 July 25	High 146¼	was 1/2 of 195½	to 97½
1938 Sept. 26	Low 128	was 1/3 of 386	
		and 1/3 of 195½	to 97½
		and 1/2 of 106½	to 146¼
	A Strong Support Level and Buying Point.		
1938 Nov. 10	High 158 3/4		
	When the averages crossed 146½	1/2 of 97½	to 195½
	indicated the 5/8 point at 158 3/4.		
	158 3/4	was 5/8 of 97½	to 195½
		and 1/3 of 40½	to 386
		and 3/4 of 195½	to 40½
	Making this a sure point to Sell Shirt.		

RESISTANCE LEVELS, Cont'd

DOW JONES 30 INDUSTRIAL AVERAGES

COMPARATIVE BOTTOMS AND TOPS

1939 Nov. 28	Low	145	was 1/2 of 195½	to 97½
			and 3/4 of 195½	
			1/2 of 128	to 158 3/4
			3/8 of 97½	to 158 3/4
			and 5/8 of 40½	to 195½
1939 Mar. 10	High	152½	was 7/8 of 97½	to 158 3/4
	Last Low 136 1/8			
	to 158 3/4 the 1/2 was 148½			
			and 1/3 of 136 1/8	to 152½
			was 144½	
	When broke this 1/2 point declined fast.			
1939 Apr. 11	Low	120	was 3/8 of 97½	to 158 3/4
			and 3/4 of 158 3/4	
	Note	118	was 1/2 of 40½	to 195½
	This was the strongest 1/2 point and the averages held 2 points above, also 118½ was			
			1/4 of 28½	to 386
1939 May 10	High	134 5/8	was 3/8 of 158 3/4	to 120
			also 3/8 of 195½	to 97½
1939 May 17	Low	128 3/8	was 1/2 of 97½	to 158 3/4
1939 June 9	High	140 3/4	was 1/2 of 120	to 158 3/4
1939 June 30	Low	129	was 1/2 of 97½	to 158 3/4
			and 1/3 of 386	

A strong support point and buying level.
The Market rallied and crossed 139 3/8
the 1/2 of 120 to 158 3/4
and on July 25th advanced to 145 3/4 just
under 1/2 of 97½ to 195½
and 2/3 of 120 to 158 3/4

RESISTANCE LEVELS. Cont'd

DOW JONES 20 RAILROAD AVERAGES

Aug. 8, 1896	....	Low	42 WHY?	
			46	was 1/2 of 92, the last high
			49½	was 1/2 of 99, the extreme high
Apr. 1897	Low of reaction		48¼	was 1/2 of 54¼ to 42
Sept. 1897	....	High	67½	was 1/2 of 42 to 92
Nov. 1897	....	Low	57½	was 1/2 of 48¼ to 67¼
Apr. 1898	....	Low	58 3/4	was 1/2 of 42 to 67¼
Aug. 1898	....	High	70¼	was 1/2 of 42 to 99
Oct. 1898	....	Low	65 3/4	was 1/2 of 42 to 92 close

After averages crossed 70½, the 1/2 of 42 to 99 never sold lower and advanced to 138 3/ Jan. 19, 1906.

Apr. 1899	....	High	87	was 7/8 of 99
				and 2/3 of 42 to 99
June 1899	....	Low	77¼	was 1/2 of 66 to 87
Dec. 1899	....	Low	72½	
			just above	1/2 42 to 99
				and 1/2 of 56 to 87

(Note triple bottom near this level)

June	....	Low	73	
Oct.	....	Low	73 3/4	
(Note)	....		79 3/4	was 1/2 87 to 72½
		and	80½	was 1/2 of 62 to 99 and in

Nov. 1899 the breakaway came when averages crossed 80½ after making triple bottoms above the 1/2 of 42 to 99, - later crossed 99, the old top advancing quickly to 117 3/4 May, 1901 and on Sept. 30, 1902 made high at 129¼.

May 9, 1901	....	Low	103¼	was 1/8 of 42 to 117 3/4
				and 1/4 of 56 to 117 3/4
				and 1/3 of 72½ to 117 3/4
(Note)	....		106¼	was 1/4 of 72½ to 117 3/4

and on secondary reaction after double top, the market made 3 bottoms: 105, 105¼, 106¼, starting up from 106¼ and advancing to new highs.

Sept. 10, 1902	....	High	129¼	
Dec. 1902	....	Low	113¼	
			just above	3/4 of 56 to 129¼
Jan. 1903	....	High	121¼	at 1/2 of 110¼ to 129¼

(Note) 101¼ was 1/2 of 72½ to 129½, broke this level and rallied 2 points above, then broke under and declined further.

Oct. 1903	....	Low	89 3/8	at 1/2 of 48¼ to 129¼
Jan. 1904	....	High	99 3/4	at 1/4 of 129¼ to 89 3/8
			and under	1/2 of 72½ to 129¼

Aug. 1904 crossed old top and crossed 1/4 of 129¼ to 89 3/8, then came the breakaway and rapid advance to new highs.

Later crossed 1/2 point 129¼ to 89 3/8

RESISTANCE LEVELS, Cont'd

DOW JONES 20 RAILROAD AVERAGES

Mar.&Apr. 1905 made double tops at 127
July 1905 .... Low 114½ at 3/4 of 89 3/8 to 129¼, later crossed
121 above 1/2 of 114½ to 127 advanced to
138 3/8 Jan.19, 1906.
May 1906 .... Low 120¼ (This was first sharp reaction).
....at 3/4 of 89 3/8 to 129¼
Last Low 114½ .... to 138 3/8, the 1/2
point............................. 126½ and 1/2 of 138 3/8 to 120¼ was 129.
The first rally was to............ 131
Then secondary reaction........... 121 3/4
Then crossed...................... 129
And advanced to................... 137 3/4, making triple tops.

Showed down when they broke the .... 1/2 of 120¼ to 138 3/8 and was
still weaker when they broke .... 1/2 of 98 3/8 to 138 3/8.

Mar. 14, 1907.............. Low 98 3/8 at 3/8 of 138 3/8 to 72¼
and 1/2 of 56 to 138 3/8
May 1907.............High 110 3/8 at 1/4 of 98 3/8 to 138 3/8
and 2/3 of 56 to 138 3/8

(Note.. 1/2 of 98 3/8 to 110 3/8 was 104.
When they broke this level, they declined to new lows.

Nov. 23, 1907 ....Low 81 3/8 at 3/8 of 48¼ to 138 3/8
Jan. 1908 ....High 95 3/4 at 1/2 of 81 3/8 to 110 3/8 and later
a secondary reaction to....... 86¼
Just under 1/2 of 81 3/8 to 95 3/4. Later
crossed top at............... 95 3/4 and 1/4 of 138 3/8 to 81 3/8.

Sept. 1908 ....High 110¼ at 1/2 of 138 3/8 to 81 3/8
Sept. 22, 1908 reacted to 103 3/8 the 1/2 of 98 to 110 3/8
Jan. 1909 ....High 120 3/4 at 2/3 of 138 3/8 to 81 3/8
Mar. 1909 ....Low 113 3/4 above 1/2 of 103 3/8 to 120 3/4
Aug. 14, 1909 ....High 134¼
(Note)........................... 131 was 1/8 of 138 3/8 to 81 3/8
Last move up 113 3/4 to 134¼
the 1/2 at 124.
When the averages broke this level they never sold above.......... 125 3/4
Until declined to 105 5/8
On July 26, 1910. This Low was just under 1/8 of 81 3/8 to 134¼

Oct. 1910 ....High 118 3/8 the 1/2 of 105 5/8 to 118 3/8 was 112
Dec. 1910 ....Low 111½
good support @ 1/2 point
July 1911 ....High 124 at 2/3 of 105 5/8 to 134¼
.... 3/4 of 81 3/8 to 134 3/8 at 121
and.................................. 1/2 of 105 5/8 to 134¼ at 120
When this level was broken, sharp decline followed.

RESISTANCE LEVELS, Cont'd

DOW JONES 20 RAILROAD AVERAGES

Sept. 25, 1911 ....Low 109 3/4 at 3/8 of 105 5/8 to 124
(Note)......................... 117 was 1/2 of 124 to 109 3/4.
Averages advanced to............ 119
Reacted to...................... 115
Then crossed the 1/2 at 117 and went higher.

Oct. 1912.............High 124 5/8 at 2/3 of 105 5/8 to 134¼
(Note) .... 117 was 1/2 of 109 3/4 to 124 5/8
When averages broke this level never rallied above.,.....118
June 1913 ....Low 100½ at 3/8 of 81 3/8 to 134¼
Sept. 1913
and
Jan. 1914 ....High 100¼ at 3/8 of 105 5/8 to 124 5/8
.........................and under .... 1/2 of 124 5/8 to 100½
Later broke under............. 105 the 1/2 of 100½ to 109¼
and declined with very small rallies.

July 30, 1914 ....Low 89½

(Note) From 1896 ....Low 42
to
Jan. 19, 1906 ....High 138 3/8 the 1/2 was 90 1/8
and on July 30, 1914 the averages closed under the 1/2 point from exteeme low to the extreme high, closing, in a panic under this strongest point indicated lower prices later.

When Exchange opened in December 1914, the 20 RAILROAD AVERAGES declined to 87¼.

NAME Inc.

YEARS		19..... to 19.....	19..... to 19.....	19..... to 19.....	19..... to 19.....	19..... to 19.....	19..... to 19.....	19..... to 19.....	19..... to 19.....	19..... to 19.....	19..... to 19.....	19..... to 19.....	19..... to 19.....	19..... to 19.....	19..... to 19.....	19..... to 19.....	19..... to 19.....	19..... to 19.....	19..... to 19.....	19..... to 19.....	19..... to 19.....	19..... to 19.....	19..... to 19.....	19..... to 19.....	19..... to 19.....
PRICE	HIGH LOW																								
	⅛																								
	¼																								
	⅓																								
	⅜																								
	½																								
	⅝																								
	⅔																								
	¾																								
	⅞																								
	0																								

CHAPTER 8

TIME AND PRICE RESISTANCE LEVELS

TIME AND PRICE RESISTANCE LEVELS
by
W.D. GANN

WEEKLY HIGH AND LOW CHART

The Weekly Chart is one of the most reliable trend indicators that we use. The Weekly Tables for Price and Time Resistance are very valuable and enable you to determine ahead of time the prices at which highs and lows will be made and the time or date when these extreme high or low prices will be reached.

These Weekly Tables cover periods of 7 days or 1 calendar week. Howeve you do not start to number time periods from January 1 or the 1st day of any month. You begin to count the time periods from the exact dates of any extreme high or low price. You also use the dates of the minor high and low prices both to begin to count time periods from and to get price resistance and determine a change in trend.

NATURAL SEASONAL TIME PERIODS

These periods do not start with the calendar year but start with the Spring Season March 20. The year is divided up into 8 equal parts and also divided into 1/3's which give two more time periods. These Time Periods are as follows:

Mar. 20 to May 5 is 1/8 of a year or 46 days
June 21 is 1/4 of a year or 91 days
July 23 is 1/3 of a year or 121 days
Aug. 5 is 3/8 of a year or 136 days
Sept 22 is 1/2 of a year or 182 days
Nov. 8 is 5/8 of a year or 227 days
Nov. 22 is 2/3 of a year or 242 days
Dec. 21 is 3/4 of a year or 273 days
Feb. 4 is 7/8 of a year or 319 days
Mar. 20 is 1 year or 365 calendar days

All of these periods are important to watch for changes in trend. The most important are 1/2 and the end of the season; next important 1/4 and 3/4, and 1/3 and 2/3.

MID-SEASON POINTS

These are May 5, August 5, November 8 and February 4. By checking over past records of prices, you will see how often highs and lows have occurred during these periods.

TABLES FOR TIME PERIODS AND PRICE RESISTANCE

The Tables for Time Periods and Price Resistance are made up to cover 40 years in the future. You can also use them for 40 years in the past

These Tables measure Price and Time Resistance from 6½ to 2080. Each period of one year or 52 weeks is shown at the bottom of the Table and the division of the yearly time periods are shown both for the Seasonal and Natural Time Periods and for the proportionate parts of a year starting from the date of any high or low price.

Below we give the Tables showing the Price and Time Periods.

1/8	of	year	46 days	6½ weeks	Price	6½
1/4	"	"	91 days	13 "	"	13
1/3	"	"	121 days	17 "	"	17
3/8	"	"	136 days	19½ "	"	19½
1/2	"	"	182 days	26 "	"	26
5/8	"	"	227 days	32½ "	"	32½
2/3	"	"	242 days	35 "	"	35
3/4	"	"	273 days	39 "	"	39
7/8	"	"	319 days	45½ "	"	45½
1		"	365 days	52 "	"	52

From the above you can see that the year is divided into 10 divisions of Time and starting with 6½ to 52, the price is also divided into 10 divisions. These Tables continue the same for 40 years or more, making equal divisions of Time and Price.

PRICE RESISTANCE

The Price Resistance is calculated in the same way at Time Periods from highs and lows. Always calculate how much the price is up from the low levels or how much it is down from high levels. In this way you are able to determine all of the important Price Resistance Levels. Example

Suppose the low price is 50 and the current price is 102. This is up 52 from the low and equals 52 weeks or 1 year in time, making this price important to watch for change in trend because it is a Time and Price Balance.

Suppose the high price has been 182 and at the time you look it up, the stock or grain is selling at 130. This is at 1/2 or 2½ years in time and the price is down 52 from the high which equals 1 year in time. This is also a Price and Time Balance and is important to watch for change in trend.

Suppose the price makes high or low on 1/4 and the next high or low is on 1/4 of 1/2. This would be important for change in trend.

From the low, suppose the time is on 1/4 and 3/4 and from the high the time is on 1/3 or 2/3, this is important for change in trend, especialy if the price is at 1/2 or 3/4 resistance. (for more proof see example of actual market moves in the past.)

INDICATIONS FOR CHANGE IN TREND

1. TIME AND PRICE BALANCE -- Suppose you wish to look up the time period for 5 years, you look at the bottom of column 5 where you find 260, which is 260 weeks. Suppose the price is at 260. This is a Time and Price Balance and is very important for a change in trend.

   Suppose at the end of 262 weeks the price is at 234, which is 1/2 and equals 4½ years in Time. This is next in importance for change in trend.

2. ANNIVERSARY DATES -- Always consider the anniversary date from extre highs and lows as important for a change in trend.

3. DIVISIONS OF TIME -- Next consider 1/4, 1/3, 1/2, 2/3, and 3/4 of th time periods important for a change in trend.

4. PRICE RESISTANCE LEVELS -- These same Resistance Levels in Price are also important to watch for change in trend, especially when the Time Period comes out at one of these important divisions of price.

5. WEEKLY BOTTOMS AND TOPS -- When you are studying the Weekly Chart, always look to see if a weekly bottom has been broken or a weekly high level has been crossed, which would be important for a change in trend. The greater the time period from any high or low level, the more important it is when prices cross these levels.

6. DOUBLE AND TRIPLE TOPS AND BOTTOMS -- When these occur on important Time Periods and at important Price Resistance Levels, they are very important to watch for change in trend and to expect a move to start that will last for a considerable length of time.

7. SWING BOTTOMS AND TOPS -- The breaking of a swing bottom or the crossing of a swing top is very important for a change in trend.

   SWING CHART -- You can make up a Swing Chart by moving the price up to the top of each week; then the first time the low of the previous week is broken, you move the swing line down to the low of that week When that week's bottom has been broken, continue to move the line down as long as the price makes lower tops and lower bottoms. The first week that the price makes a higher bottom and a higher top, you move the line on the Swing Chart up to the top of that week and continue to move it up each week until there is a reversal.

WHEN MOST IMPORTANT CHANGES IN TREND OCCUR

These are:

1. Anniversary dates of previous highs and lows
2. Next is 1/2 of each yearly period or 182 days from any high or low
3. Next in importance is 1/4 and 3/4 or 13 weeks and 39 weeks

4. Next is 1/3 and 2/3 or 17 weeks and 35 weeks.
5. Next is 3/8 and 7/8 of a year or 19½ and 35½ weeks.

You can prove to yourself how well these rules work by going back and checking the Time Periods from highs and lows for several years and checking the price at which the stock or commodity was selling and see how it compares on the Tables for Price and Time Resistance. This will give you the value of these Time Tables and Price Resistance Levels.

W.D. GANN

January 26, 1955

CHAPTER 9

ENHANCED MASTER CHARTS

W. D. GANN
78 WALL STREET
NEW YORK

SCIENTIFIC ADVICE
AND ANALYTICAL REPORTS
ON STOCKS AND COMMODITIES
AUTHOR OF "TRUTH OF THE STOCK TAPE"
"THE TUNNEL THRU THE AIR"

MEMBER
AMERICAN ECONOMIC ASS'N
ROYAL ECONOMIC SOCIETY
CABLE ADDRESS
"GANWADE NEWYORK"

MASTER CHARTS

::::::::::::::::

The Master Charts are permanent and represent natural angles and permanent resistance points for either price, time or volume. These points do not change and you should study them carefully on each different Master Chart and learn how to apply them.

MASTER "12" CHART

The MASTER CHART is the Square of "12" or 12 x 12, making the first square end at 144. The Second Square of "12" ends at 288, the Third Square of "12" at 432, and the Fourth Square at 576, which will cover most anything that you want, but you can make up as many more squares as you need.

This chart may be used and applied to anything--TIME, SPACE, PRICE OR VOLUME, the number of points up or down; days, weeks, months and years.

On Square No. 1, which runs from 1 to 144, I have drawn the finer angles to show the grand-center or strongest resistance point in each minor square. The minor centers, which are the strongest for minor tops and bottoms are 14, 17, 20, 23, 50, 53, 56, 59, 86, 89, 92, 95, 122, 125, 128, 131.

The major center is where the strongest resistance is met. These numbers are 66, 67, 78 and 79. Stocks going up or coming down to these prices will meet with stubborn resistance. The next strong angle is the 45°, and the numbers of greatest resistance on it are 14, 27, 40, 53, 66, 79, 92, 105, 118, 131 and 144. The other diagonal 45° angle from 12 is equally strong. The numbers are 12, 23, 34, 45, 56, 67, 78, 89, 100, 111, 122 and 133.

The numbers which are cut by the 45° angles thru the center of each of the 1/4 squares are next in strength. These numbers are 7, 20, 33, 46, 59, 72, 61, 50, 39, 28, 17 and 6, and on the other side of the square, after you pass the half-way point, these numbers are 73, 86, 99, 112, 125, 138, 139, 128, 117, 106, 95 and 84.

The numbers at the tops and bottoms of the squares are important prices for important tops and bottoms to be made because they are opposition numbers and are equal to the half-way point. These numbers for Square No. 1 are 1, 13, 25, 37, 49, 61, 73, 85, 97, 109, 121, 133. The top numbers are 12, 24, 36, 48, 60, 72, 84, 96, 108, 120, 132, and 144. These are very important to measure time in days, weeks, months and years.

The opposition angle, which runs thru the center of the Square, from east to west, equally dividing it, is one of the very strong angles because it equals one-half. Any stock moving up or down and reaching these prices will meet with any resistance and make tops or bottoms. These numbers are 6, 7, 18, 19, 30, 31, 42, 43, 54, 55, 66, 67, 78, 79, 90, 91, 102, 103, 114, 115, 126, 127, 138, 139.

Remember, when anything has moved three sections over from the beginning, it reaches the square of its own place, which is the first strong resistance. When it has moved six sections over, it reaches the opposition, or what equals the half-way point of its own place and meets still stronger resistance. Moving over nine places or sections from its own place, it reaches the 3/4 point, another square. The 8th and 9th sections are the strongest and hardest points to pass because this is the "death" zone. The next and still stronger is the 12th section or column which ends at 144. Anything getting into this section meets the strongest resistance but once it moves out of this square and gets as much as 3 points into Square #2, that is, making 147, will indicate much higher. But after reaching this, it should not drop back to 141 or 3 points into Square #1.

When a stock gets into the Second Square of "12", it has faster moves, and when the time or number of months from any bottom or top moves into the Second Square, it is an indication of faster moves, both up and down.

Apply the same rule to the 3rd, 4th, 5th and 6th Squares. In the 3rd and 4th squares of the Master "12", you will find that most of the big bull and bear campaigns culminate, when measured by months, which determines the division, according to time. All of the other rules given you to apply to Space movements, angles and time, can be used with the Master "12" tables.

SQUARE OF NINE

You have already had the MASTER SQUARE OF TWELVE explained, which represents days, weeks, months and years, and the measurements of TIME in the Square of Twelve or the square of the Circle; also used to measure price movements and resistance levels.

The SQUARE OF NINE is very important because nine digits are used in measuring everything. We cannot go beyond 9 without starting to repeat and using the 0. If we divide 360° by 9, we get 40, which measures 40°, 40 months, 40 days, 40 weeks or 40 months, and shows why bottoms and tops often come out on these angles measured by one-ninth of the circle. This is why the children of Israel were 40 years in the wilderness.

If we divide our 20-year period, or 240 months, by 9, we get 26-2/3 months, making an important angle of 26-2/3°, months, days or weeks. Nine times 9 equals 81, which completes the First Square of Nine. Note the angles and how they run from the main center. The Second Square of Nine is completed at 162. Note how this is in opposition to the main center. The Third square of Nine is completed at 243, which would equal 243 months or 3 months over our 20-year period and accounts for the time which often elapses before the change in the Cycle, sometimes running over 3 months or more. The Fourth Square of Nine ends at 324. Note the angles of 45° cross at 325, indicating a change in cycles here. To complete the 360° requires Four Squares of Nine and 36 over. Note that 361 equals a Square of 19 times 19, thus proving the great value of the Square of Nine in working out the important angles and proving up discrepancies.

Beginning with "1" at the center, note how 7, 21, 43, 73, 111, 157, 211, 273 and 343 all fall on a 45° angle. Going the other way, note that 3, 13, 31, 57, 91, 133, 183, 241, and 307 fall on an angle of 45°. Remember there are always four ways you can travel from a center following an angle of 45°, or an angle of 180° or an angle of 90°, which all equal about the same when measured on a flat surface. Note that 8, 23, 46, 77, 116, 163, 218, 281 and 352 are all on an angle from the main center; also note that 4, 15, 34, 61, 96, 139, 190, 249, and 316 are on an angle from the main center, all of these being great resistance points and measuring out important time factors and angles.

Study the SQUARE OF NINE very carefully in connection with the MASTER TWELVE and 360° CIRCLE CHART.

SIX SQUARES OF NINE

You will receive six Permanent Charts, each containing 81 numbers. The First Square of Nine runs from 1 to 81. Everything must have a bottom, top, and four sides to be a square or cube. The first square running up to 81 is the bottom, base, floor or beginning point. Squares #2, 3, 4, and 5 are the four sides, which are equal and contain 81 numbers. The Sixth Square of Nine is the top and means that it is times times as referred to in the Bible, or a thing reproducting itself by being multipled by itself. Nine times nine equals 81 and six times 81 equals 486. We can also use 9 times 81, which would equal 729.

The number 5 is the most important number of the digits because it is the balance or main center. There are four numbers on each side of it. Note how it is shown as the balancing or center number in the Square of Nine.

We square the Circle by beginning at 1 in the center and going around until we reach 360. Note that the Square of Nine comes out at 361. The reason for this is: It is 19 times 19, and the 1 to begin with and 1 over 360 represent the beginning and ending points. 361 is a transition point and begins the next circle. Should we leave the first space blank or make it "0", then we would come out at 360. Everything in mathematics must prove. You can begin at the center and work out, or begin at the outer rim and work in to the center. Begin at the left and work right to the center or to the outer rim or square.

Note the Square of Nine or the Square of the Circle, where we begin with 1 and run up the side of the column to 19, then continue to go across until we have made 19 columns, again the square of 19 by 19. Note how this proves up the circle. One-half of the circle is 180°. Note that in the grand-center, where all angles from the four corners and from the East, West, North and South reach gravity center, number 181 appears, showing that at this point we are crossing the Equator or Gravity center and are starting on the other half of the circle.

We have astronimical and mathematical proof of the whys and wherefores and the cause of the workings of geometrical angles. When you have made progress, proved yourself worthy, I will give you the Master Number and also the Master Word.

THE HEXAGON CHART

Since everything moves in a circle and nothing moves in straight lines, this chart is to show you how the angles influence stocks at very low levels and very high levels and why stocks move faster the higher they get, because they have moved out to where the distance between the angles of 45° are so far apart that there is nothing to stop them and their moves are naturally rapid up and down.

We begin with a circle of "1" in the center and while this only contains 1, yet the circle is 360° just the same. We then place a circle of circles around this circle and six circles complete the second circle, making a gain of 6 over the first one, ending the second circle at 7, making 7 on this angle a very important month, year, and week as well as day, the seventh day being sacred and a day of rest. The third circle is completed at 19. The fourth circle around is completed at 37, a gain of 18 over the previous circle. The fifth circle is completed at 61, a gain of 24 over the previous circle. The sixth circle is completed at 91, a gain of 30 over the previous circle, and the seventh circle at 127, a gain of 36 over the last circle. Note that from the first the gain is 6 each time we go around. In other words, when we have traveled six times around we have gained 36. Note that this completes the first Hexagon and as this equals 127 months, shows why some campaigns will run 10 years and seven months, or until they reach a square of the Hexagon, or the important last angle of 45°.

The eighth circle around is completed at 169, a gain of 42 over the first. This is a very important angle and an important time factor for more reasons than one. It is 14 years and one month, or double our Cycle of 7 years. Important tops and bottoms culminate at this angle as you will see by going over your charts.

The ninth circle is completed at 217, a gain of 48 over the previous circle. The tenth circle is completed at 271, a gain of 54. Note that 271 is the 9th circle from the first, or is the third 90° angle or 270°, three-fourths of a circle, a very strong point. All this is confirmed by the Master Twelve Chart, by the four seasons and by the Square of Nine Chart, and also confirmed by the Hexagon Chart, showing that mathematical proof is always exact no matter how many ways or from what directions you figure it.

The eleventh circle is completed at 331, a gain of 60 over the last circle. The twelfth circle is completed at 397, which completes the Hexagon, making a gain in 11 circles of 66 from the beginning. 66 months, or 5 years and six months, marks the culmination of major campaigns in stocks. Note how often they culminate on the 60th month, then have a reaction, and make a second top or bottom in the 66th month. Note the number 66 on the Master Twelve Chart. Note it on the Square of Nine and see that 66 occurs on an angle of 180° on the Hexagon Chart, all of which confirms the strong angle at this point.

We have an angle of 66°, one of 67½, and one of 68, confirming this point to be doubly strong for tops and bottoms or space movements up or down.

Note the number 360 on the Hexagon Chart. It completes a circle of 360°. From our beginning point this occurs at an angle of 150° on the Hexagon Chart going around, but measuring from the center, it would equal an angle of 90° or 180°, making this a strong point, hard and difficult to pass, and the ending of one campaign and the beginning of another.

Again with the center of the Hexagon Chart at "1" notice that 7, 9, 37, 61, 91, 127, 169, 217, 271, 331, and 397 are all on this direct angle and are important points in time measurement. Beginning with "1" and following the other angle, note that 2, 9, 22, 41, 66, 97, 134, 177, 226, 281, and 342 are all on the same angle of 90°, or an angle of 60° and 240° as measured by the Hexagon Chart.

Go over this Chart and the important angles each way and you will see why resistance is met either on days, weeks, months, or years, and why stocks stop and make tops and bottoms at these strong important points according to time and price.

When any stock has passed out above 120° or especially above 127° or 127 points and gone out of the square of the first Hexagon, its fluctuations will be more rapid and it will move faster up and down. Notice near the center that in traveling from 6 to 7 it strikes the angle of 180° or 90°, but when the stock gets out to 162, it can travel up to 169 before striking another strong angle. That is why fast moves occur up and down as stocks get higher and as they move from a center in time.

Remember that everything seeks the center of gravity and important tops and bottoms are formed according to centers and measurements of time from a center, base or beginning point, either top or bottom. The angles formed going straight up and across, may form just the same going across as the stock travels over for days, weeks, months or years. Thus, a stock going up to 22½ would strike an angle of 22½°. If it moves over 22½ days, 22½ weeks, or 22½ months, it would also strike an angle of 22½°, and the higher it is when these angles are struck and the angle it hits going up, the greater the resistance to be met. Reverse the rule going down.

Market movements are made just the same as any other thing which is constructed. It is just the same as constructing a building. First the foundation has to be laid and then the four sides have to be completed and last, but not least of all, the top has to be put on. The cube or hexagon proves exactly the law which works because of time and space in the market. When a building is put up it is built according to a square or hexagon. It has four walls or four sides, a bottom and a top; therefore, it is a cube.

In working out the 20-year Cycle in the stock market, the first 60°, or 5 years, from the beginning forms the bottom of the cube. The second 60°, running to 120, completes the first angle or the first side and runs out the 10-year Cycle. The third 60°, or the second side, ends 15 years or 180°. It is very important because we have the building half completed and must meet the strongest resistance at this point. The fourth 60°, or the end of 20 years or 240 months, completes the third side. We are now two-thirds around the building, a very strong point which culminates and completes our 20-year Cycle. The fifth 60°, or 300° point, days, weeks, or months, completes 25 years, a repetition of the first 5 years, but it completes the fourth side of our building and is a very important angle. The 6th 60° or 360°, completing the circle and ending 30 years as measured by our Time Factor, which runs 1° per month on an angle of 45°, completes the top. This is a complete cube and we begin over again.

Study this in connection with the Hexagon Chart. It will help you.

W. D. GANN

91 WALL STREET
NEW YORK

Scientific Advice
and Analytical Reports
Stocks and Commodities
Author of "Truth of the Stock Tape"
and "The Tunnel Thru the Air"

Member
American Economic Ass'n
Royal Economic Society
Cable Address
"Ganwade New York"

MASTER CHARTS (continued)

THE MASTER CHART OF 360°.

This chart begins at "0" and runs around the circle to "360". We first divide by two and get 180°; then divide 180 by 2 and we get 90°; then divide 90 by 2 and we get 45°; then divide 45 by 2 and we get 22½°; then 22½ by 2 and we get 11¼°; then divide 11¼ by 2 and we get 5-5/8°, - all of which form the important angles around the circle.

I have only shown all the important angles from 3-3/4 to 360°. All the angles drawn in red because they are the important square angles.

After dividing the circle by 2, the next important number to divide by is 3. Dividing by 3, we get 120°, 240° and 360°, making the important triangle points. We then divide 120 by 2 and get the angles of 60°, 150°, 210°, 300° and 330°. We divide 60 by 2 and get the angles of 30° and their proportionate parts around. Then divide 30 by 2 and get the angles of 15° and their proportionate angles around the circle. Then divide 15 by 2 and we get the angles at 7½° around the circle.

24 hours in a day divided into the circle equals 15° for each hour. There are 48 divisions of the circle of 7½°, which are important in measuring day, weekly and monthly time periods.

Study the Major Chart of 360° carefully and you will see why cycles repeat. When anything has traveled up 180°, it starts to go down to the opposite point and each angle up to 180° is the opposite on the other side of the circle. That is why tops and bottoms come out at each one of these degrees. For instance, top coming out at 90° or 90 months at one time will occur 90° or 90 months apart and there will be similar tops causing rapid fluctuations and fast moves up and down because this angle is so acute that stocks can not remain long before starting in the opposite direction.

Note the culminations that occur every 14 and 15 years, 180 months, or when an 180° angle or an angle straight up and down is reached. How rapid the moves are when they near this angle and how fast they move up and down and how quickly reverse. It is the same with the 45°, the 135°, the 225° and the 315° angle. Note how this proves the important campaigns when tops and bottoms work out in regularity an equal number of months apart. Note the 22½° and then follow the next important angle, the 30° angle, then the 45°, then note the 60 and 67½° are close together but both very strong angles. Note also 112½° and 120°, both strong angles and close together, indicating important tops and bottoms. Also note 150° and 157½°, strong angles close together, indicating important tops and bottoms, and so on all the way around.

When the circle is divided by 2 and 3 and redivided, we get the following important angles and measurements of time, space and volume around the circle of 360°:-

5-5/8, 7-1/2, 11-1/4, 15, 16-7/8, 22-1/2, 27-7/8, 30, 33-3/4, 37-1/2, 39-3/8, 45, 50-5/8, 56-1/4, 60, 61-7/8, 67-1/2, 73-1/8, 75, 78-3/4, 82-1/2, 84-3/8, 90, 95-5/8, 101-1/4, 105, 106-7/8, 112-1/2, 118-1/8, 120, 123-3/4, 129-3/8, 135, 140-5/8, 146-1/4, 150, 152-7/8, 157-1/2, 163-1/8, 168-3/4, 174-3/8, 180, 185-5/8, 191-1/4, 196-7/8, 202-1/2, 208-1/8, 210, 213-3/4, 219-3/8, 225, 230-5/8, 236-1/4, 240, 241-7/8, 247-1/2, 253-1/8, 258-3/4, 264-3/8, 270, 275-5/8, 281-1/4, 286-7/8, 292-1/2, 298-1/8, 300, 303-3/4, 309-3/8, 315, 320-5/8, 326-1/4, 330, 331-7/8, 337-1/2, 343-1/8, 348-3/4, 354-3/8, 360, which completes the circle.

These points are all made by a division of angles and are measurements of one-half, one-third, one-fourth, one-eight, one-sixteenth, one-thirty-second and one-sixty-fourth.

Compare these points with your Master Twelve Chart, your Square of Nine Chart, your Hexagon Chart and your Major Chart of 360°. You will see how they all confirm the important angles and time factors.

The number "7" being so important in determining the culmination in weeks, days, months and years, we must divide the circle by 7 to get the important points, or the one-seventh points in the circle, which are vital and important angles.

The first one-seventh of 360 equals 51-3/7, the second equals 102-6/7, the third equals 154-2/7, the fourth equals 205-5/7, the fifth equals 257-1/7, the sixth equals 308-4/7 and the seventh completes the circle, equalling 360 degrees, days, weeks, months or years. If you divide each of these points by 2, you will also get other important and valuable angles which will confirm and correspond to the other angles in the other charts.

One-seventh of a year or one-seventh of a circle shows why so many fast market movements culminate in the 49th day or the 52nd day and why the 7th week is so very important in culminations and also the 7th month as well as the 7th year.

1½ times 51-3/7 equals 77-1/8 and shows why the angles are so very strong around that point and why the 77th day, 77th week and 77th month are so important for culminations.

MASTER 360° CIRCLE CHART SQUARED

The Master 360 Circle Chart when squared is 90 x 90, and contains 8,100 cells, zones or spaces. Therefore, the square of 360 will contain 32,400 spaces. This shows you why a stock fluctuates up and down so many times over the same territory, because it is working out the number of cells or vibrations of each space in a square. For example:-

1/8 of 90 equals 1,012-1/2
1/4 of 90 equals 2,025
1/2 of 90 equals 4,050
3/4 of 90 equals 6,075
1/3 of 90 equals 2,700
2/3 of 90 equals 5,400

The square of 360, or 360 times 360, equals 32,400.

1/4 of 360 equals 8,100
1/3 of 360 equals 10,860
1/2 of 360 equals 16,200
2/3 of 360 equals 21,600
3/4 of 360 equals 24,300
7/8 of 360 equals 28,350

These points are very important to use for volume of sales as well as time and price measurements.

Suppose you want to know the number of days required to fill or work out the square of 90. There are 365 days in a year. 20 years will give you 7,300 days, and in counting the leap years will run a little over this. Therefore, about 22 years, 2 months and 10 days are required to work out each vibration in the square of 90.

THE SPIRAL CHART

The Spiral Chart represents the correct position, time and space of anything that begins at zero and begins to move round and round. It shows just exactly how the numbers increase as the spiral moves round and round, and why stocks move faster as they grow older, or swing so much more rapidly as the price reaches higher levels. At center, beginning point or zero, it requires 45° to represent one point. When the stock traveled seven times around from the center, it then required seven points to strike a 45° angle. When it has traveled around the spiral twelve times, it will then require a space of ten points before striking a 45° angle. It would also mean that the stock could move in one direction ten months without striking anything to cause any very great reaction. On this chart, we have only shown the 45, 60, 90, 120, 135, 180, 225, 240, 270, 300, 315 and 360 degree angles. This shows the division of the circle by 2, 4 and 8, and also shows the one-third point and the two-thirds point; being the vital and most important angles, we place them so you can see how space or time makes rapid fluctuations.

NEW YORK STOCK EXCHANGE PERMANENT CHART.

This Chart is a square of 20, or 20 up and 20 over, making a total of 400, which can be used to measure days, weeks, months or years, and to determine when tops and bottoms will be made against strong angles, as indicated on this Permanent Chart.

For example:- The New York Stock Exchange was incorporated May 17th, 1792. Therefore, we begin at "0" on May 17, 1792. 1793 ends on 1, when the Stock Exchange was 1 year old. 1812 will come out on 20;

1832 on 40	1892 on 100
1852 on 60	1912 on 120
1872 on 80	1932 on 140

Note that 139, or 1931, strikes the 45° angle, running from 20 down, and that this is in the 7th zone, or the 7th space over, which indicates that 1931 is the ending of a bear campaign, and the starting of a bull market. But we must watch out for a break around May and June, 1931, when this angle is hit at the end of the 139th year.

You will notice that the numbers which divide the square into equal parts, run across 10, 30, 50, 70, 90, 110, etc., and that the year 1802 comes out on 10, the year 1822 on 30, the year 1842 on 50, the year 1862 on 70. Note that the year 1861, when the Civil War broke out, was on the number 69, which is a 45° angle. Then note that 1882 ended in May on the 90° angle, and at the 1/2 point, 180° angle, running horizontally across.

Again in 1902, it was at 110, the 1/2 point, and in 1903 and 1904, hit the 45° angle.

Note that the years 1920 and 1921 hit the 45° angle on No. 129 and 1922, the first year of the bull market, was at 130 at the 1/2 point.

Note that 1929 was on the 137th number, or 137th month, and hit an angle of 45°, and that the year 1930 was at the 1/2 point on the 4th square, a strong Resistance Point, which indicated a sharp, severe decline.

Again, 138 is at the 1/2 point on the Master 12 Chart.

1933 will be on 141, in the 8th Zone, and at the center or 1/2 point of the 2nd quarter of the Square of 20.

The years 1934 and 1935, ending in May, will be on 142 and 143, and 1935 will come out on the 45° angle at the grand center in the 8th Zone and at the 1/2 point of the 2nd square, going to 1/2 of the total square, which will indicate a decline and bottom for an advance to run up in 1936, with 1937 striking at 145, which is 1/4th of the column on the way up in the square.

If you will study the weeks, months, as well as the years, and apply them to these important points and angles, you will see how they have determined the important tops and bottoms in the past campaigns.

UNITED STATES STEEL NAME CHART

The name, United States Steel, contains 17 letters. Therefore, to make up a Permanent Square for United States Steel according to its name, will require 17 x 17, or a square of 289. Therefore, 17, which is really 2½ times the lowest price at which Steel ever sold is an important point.

The prices 34, 51, 68, 85, 102, 119, 136, 153, 170, 187, 204, 221, 238, 255, 272 are all important because they strike important vibrations on the name and angles of U. S. Steel.

The basic number or low point, for example 9, the lowest digit on U. S. Steel, and its vibrations according to its name, all cause slight variations at times from other stocks, because each stock works according to its own base, beginning point, numbers and name.

U. S. Steel works good to the natural angles and Master Chart, because its digit is 9 and comes out on exact 9 vibrations all the way through, finishing at 261, which was 28 nines from its beginning point, or lowest level.

A study of all these various tables will help you to understand Resistance Levels.

UNITED STATES PERMANENT MASTER CHART

We use the square of 7 for the United States because the name of America contains 7 letters, and this square is 49, a very important and fatal number.

We begin the United States Chart on October 12th, 1492. Make up these Squares of 7 and put on the years. You will note how this indicates the panic years in the United States and the years of prosperity.

You can also make up a square of 21 x 21, which is the number of letters in the name of United States of America. These angles and important points will all come out about the same as when we use America, because three times 7 is 21. However, you will get some stronger angles and more important points if you make up the square of 21 x 21, which will run out to 441, with the 1/2 point at 220-1/2.

The more you study these Permanent Charts, the more you will appreciate their great value, and will see that numbers do determine everything in the future, and that geometrical angles and mathematical points measure every Resistance Level, time, price, space or volume.

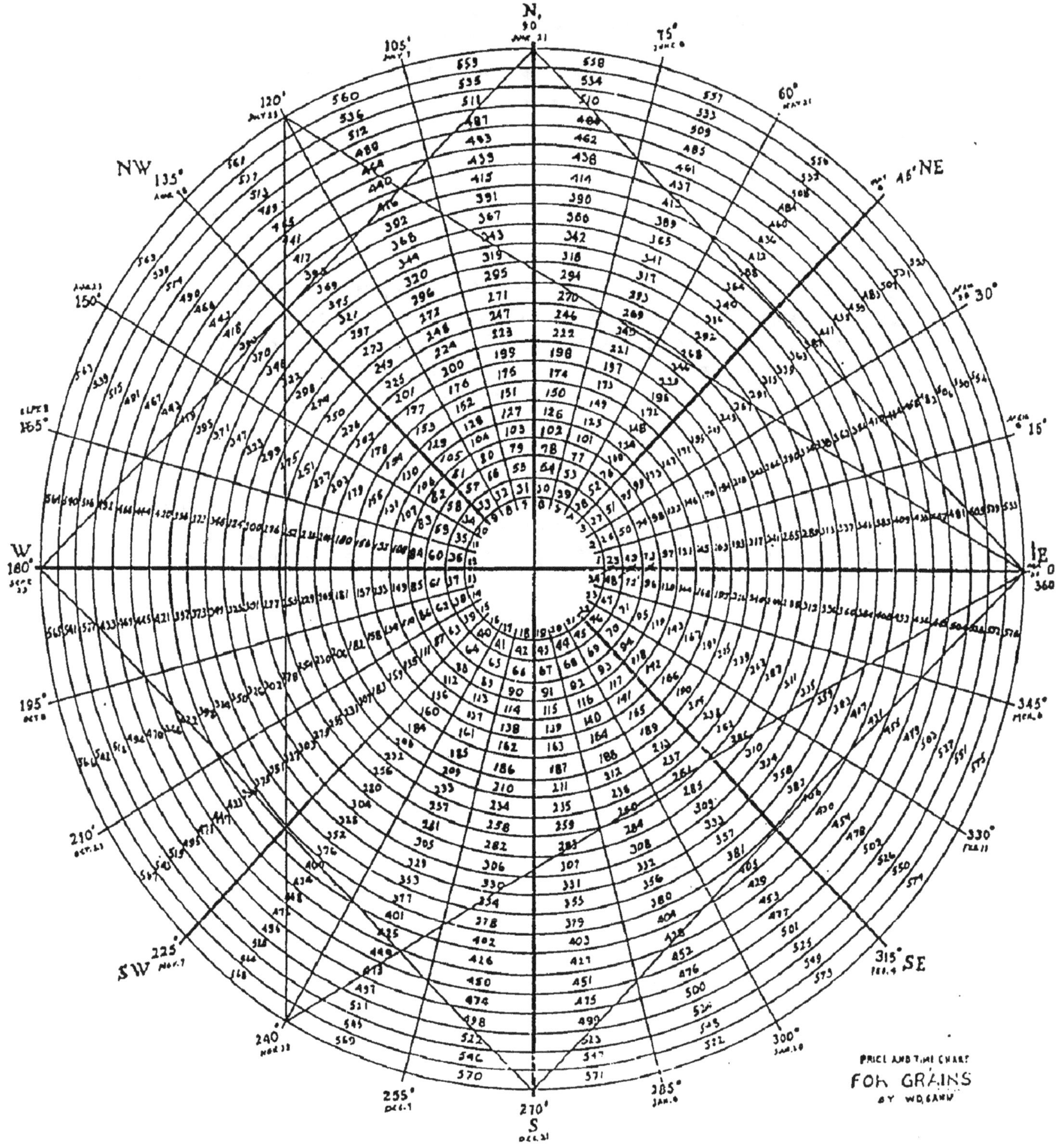

PRICE AND TIME CHART
FOR GRAINS
BY W.D. GANN

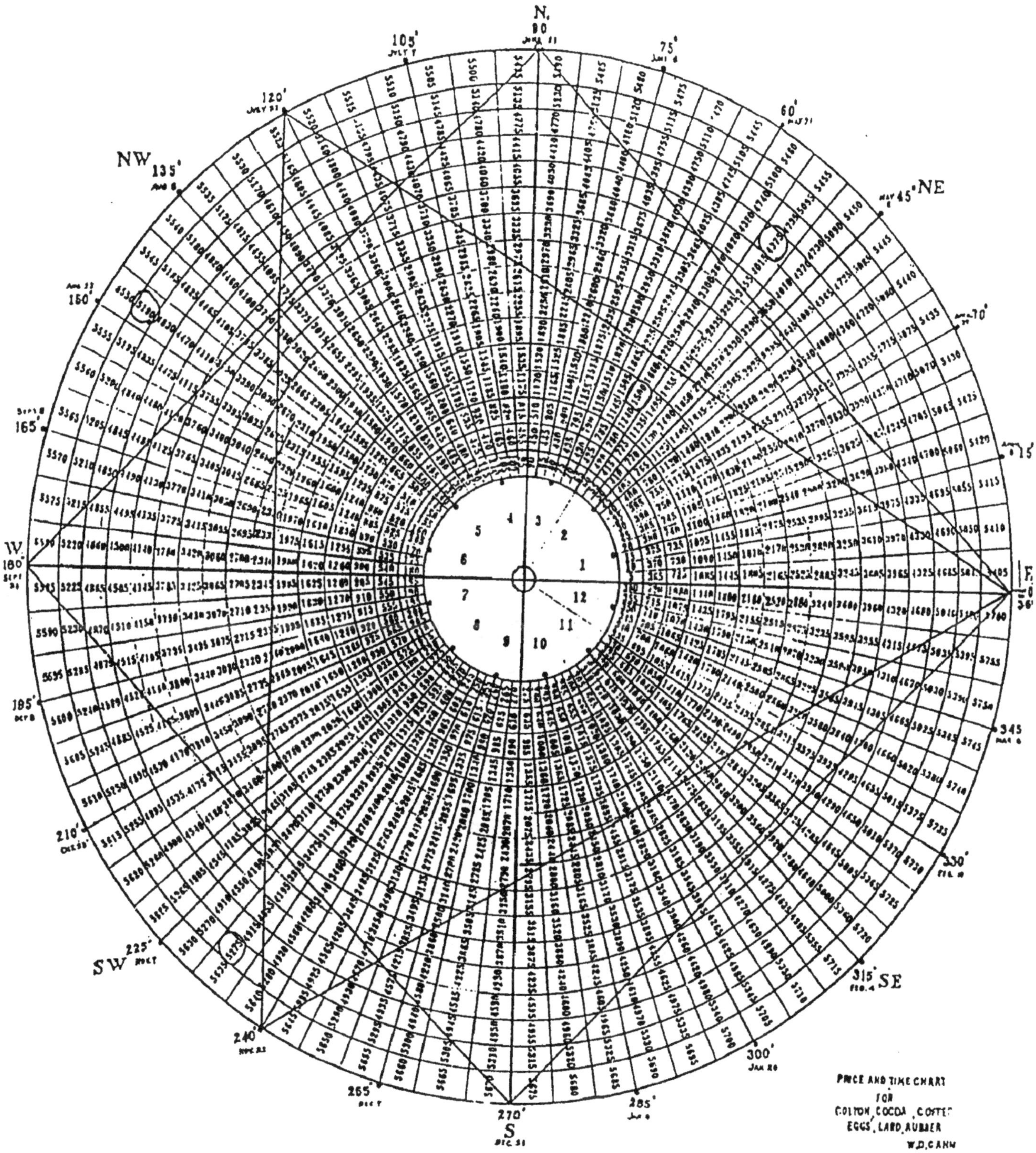

PRICE AND TIME CHART
FOR
COTTON, COCOA, COFFEE
EGGS, LARD, RUBBER
W.D. GANN

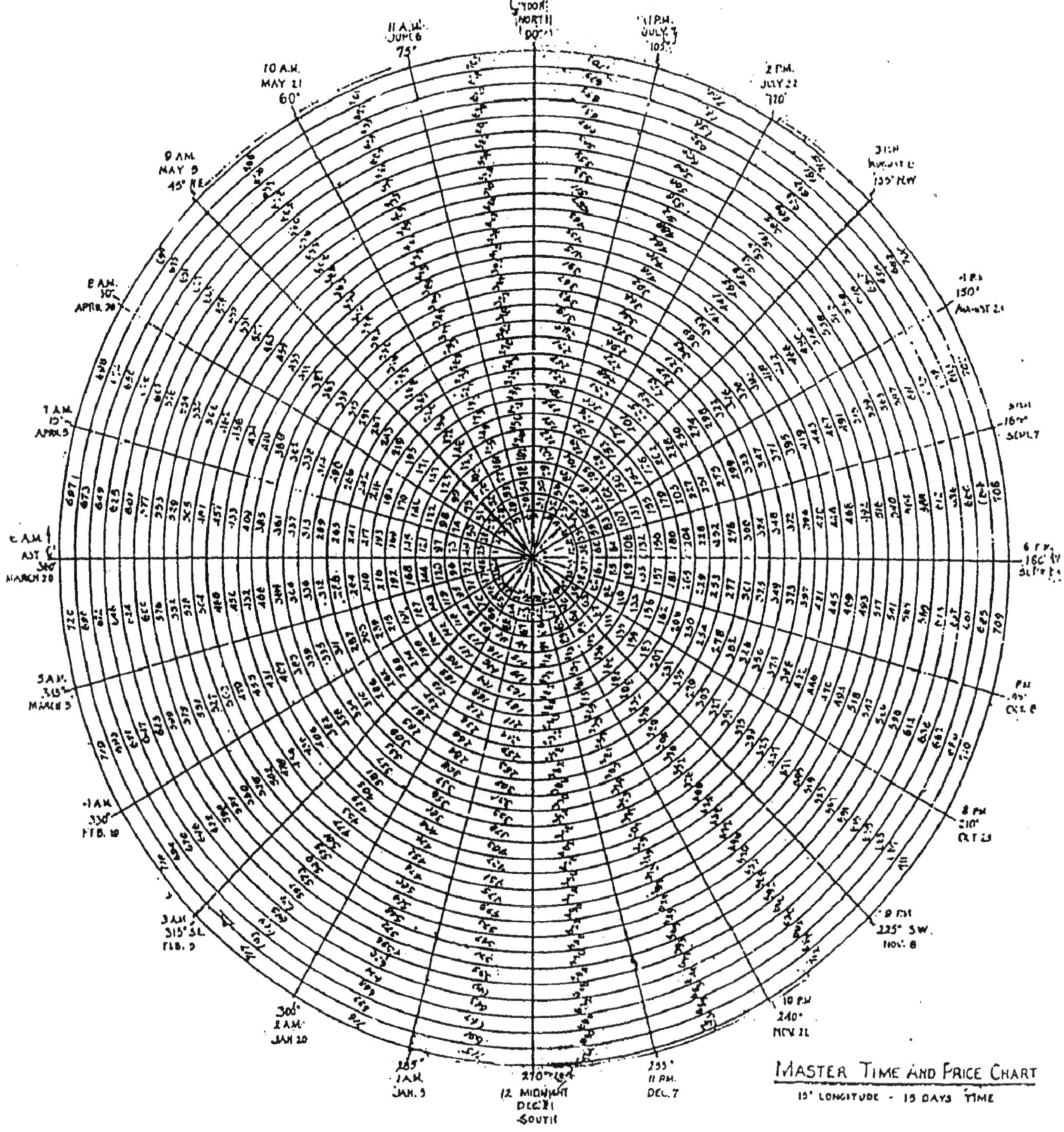

MASTER TIME AND PRICE CHART

15° LONGITUDE - 15 DAYS TIME

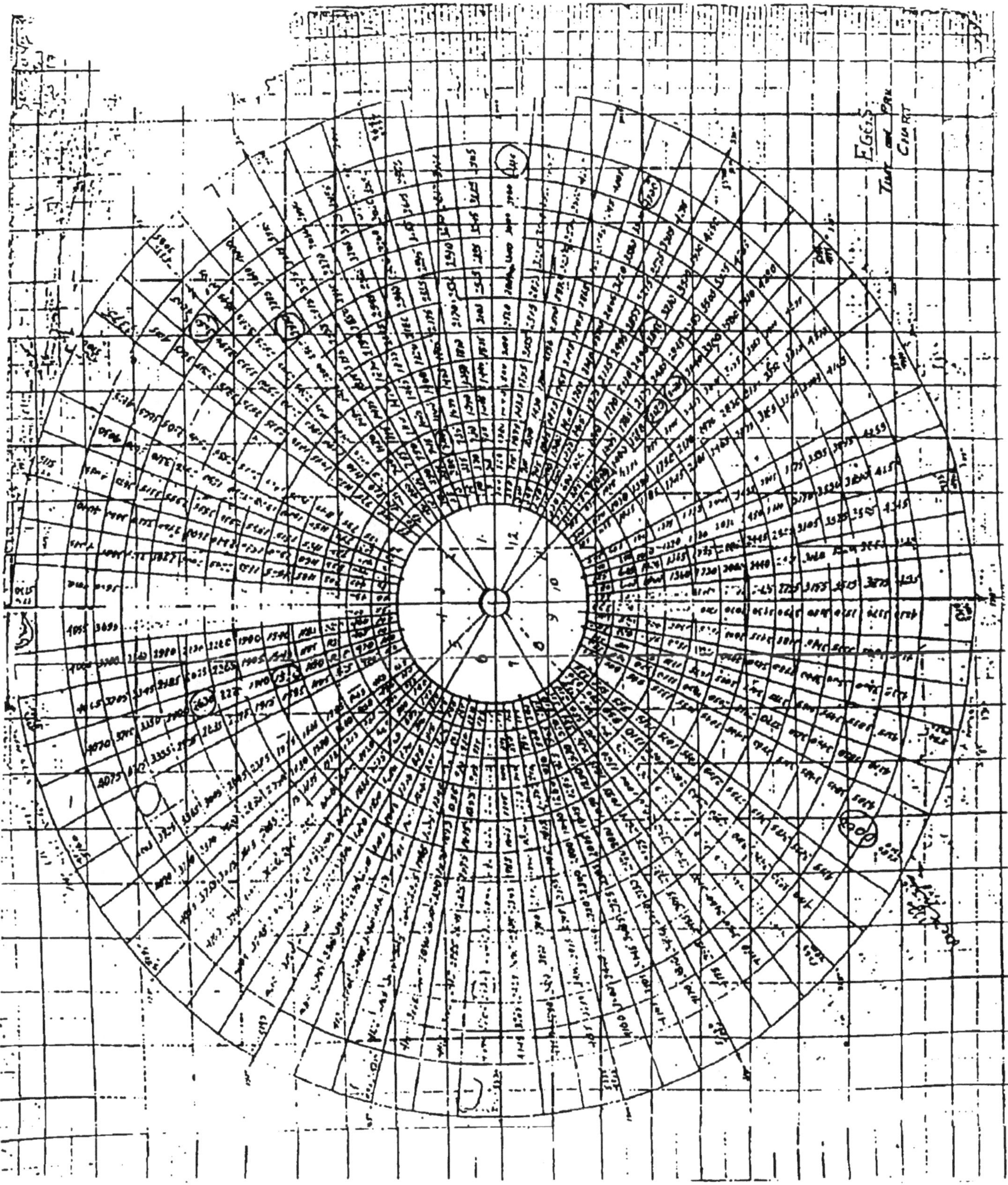

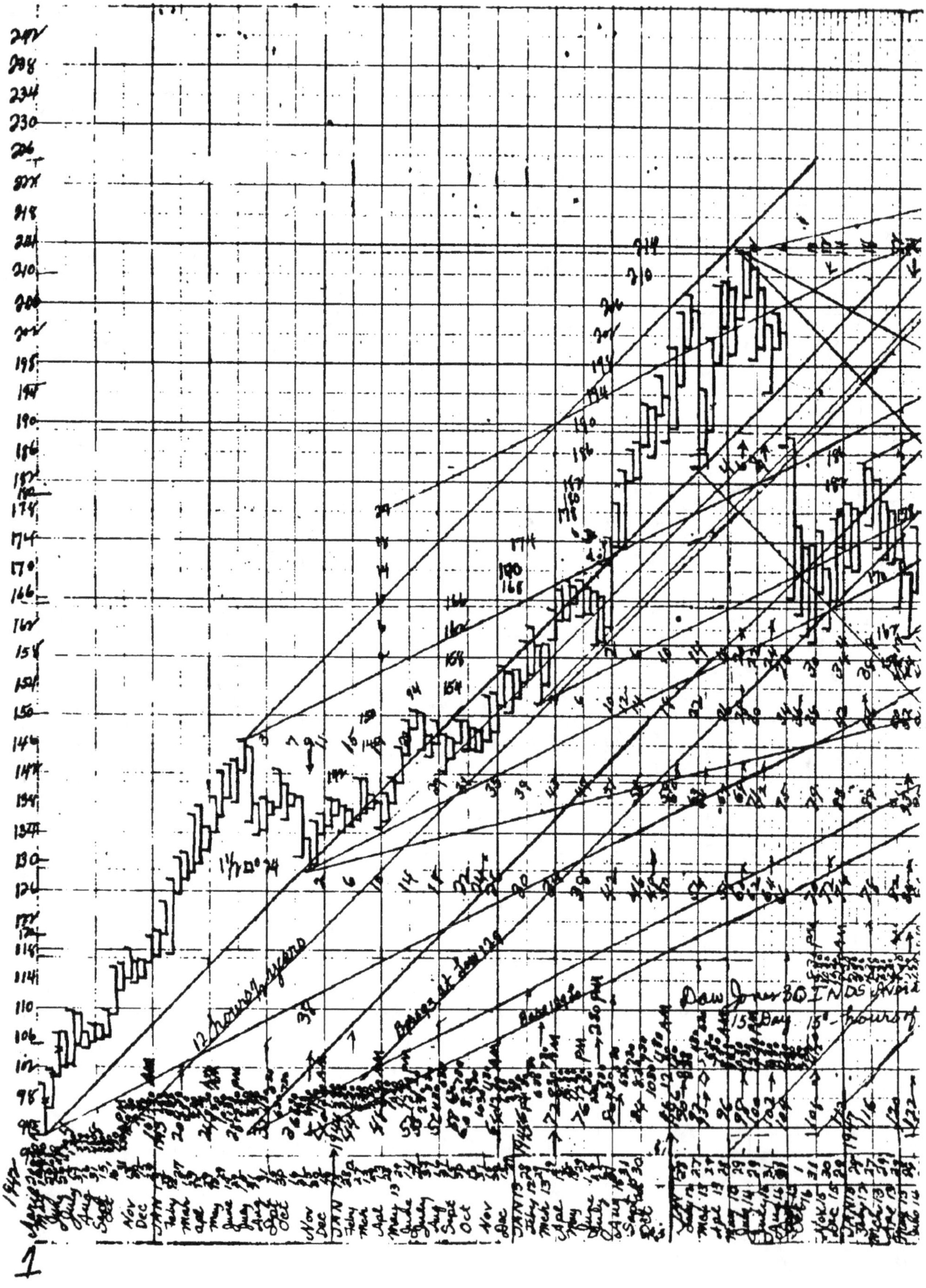

1

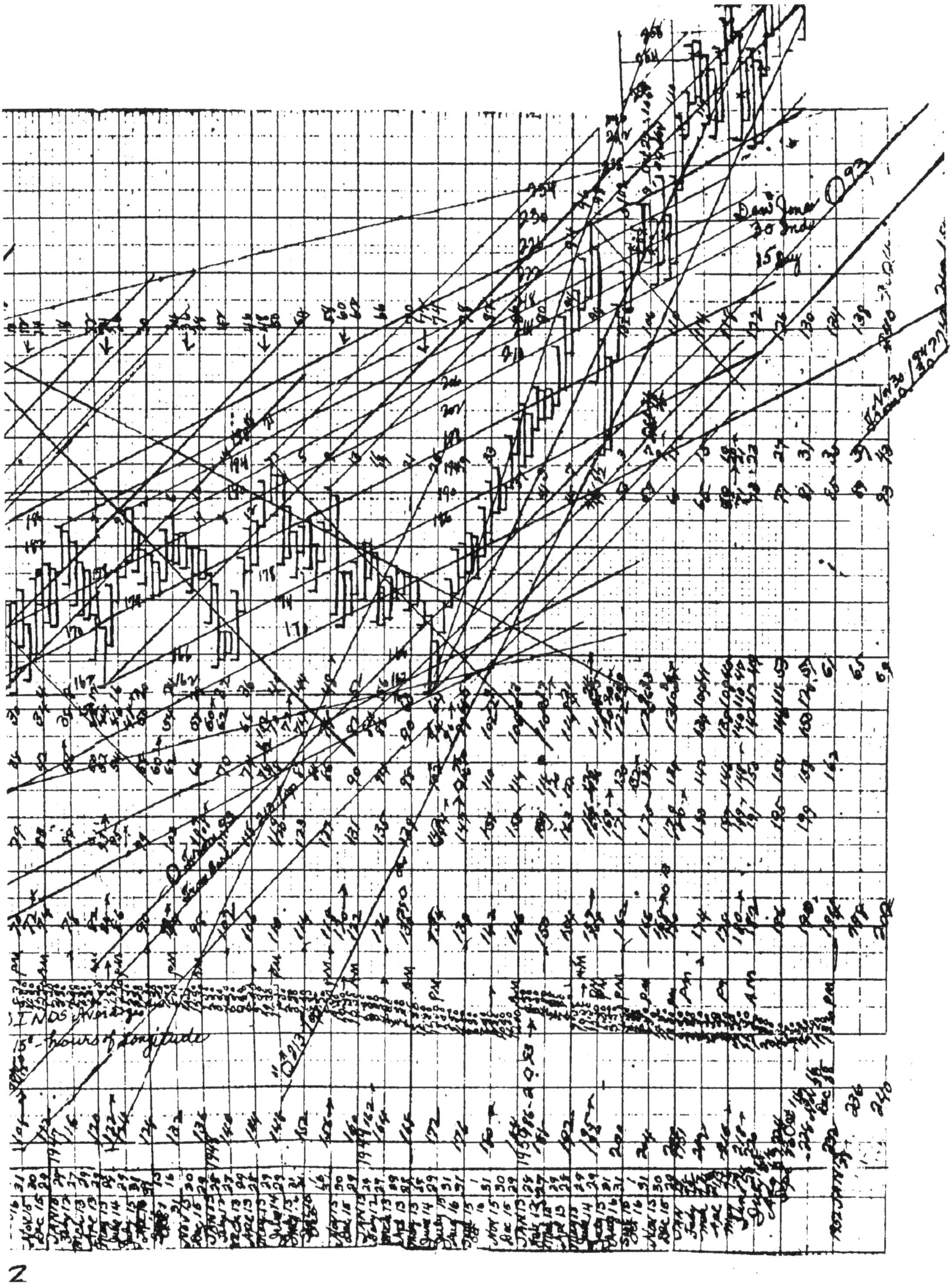
Dow Jones
30 Indu
15 day
INDS Averages
15° hours of longitude

MASTER 360° CHART

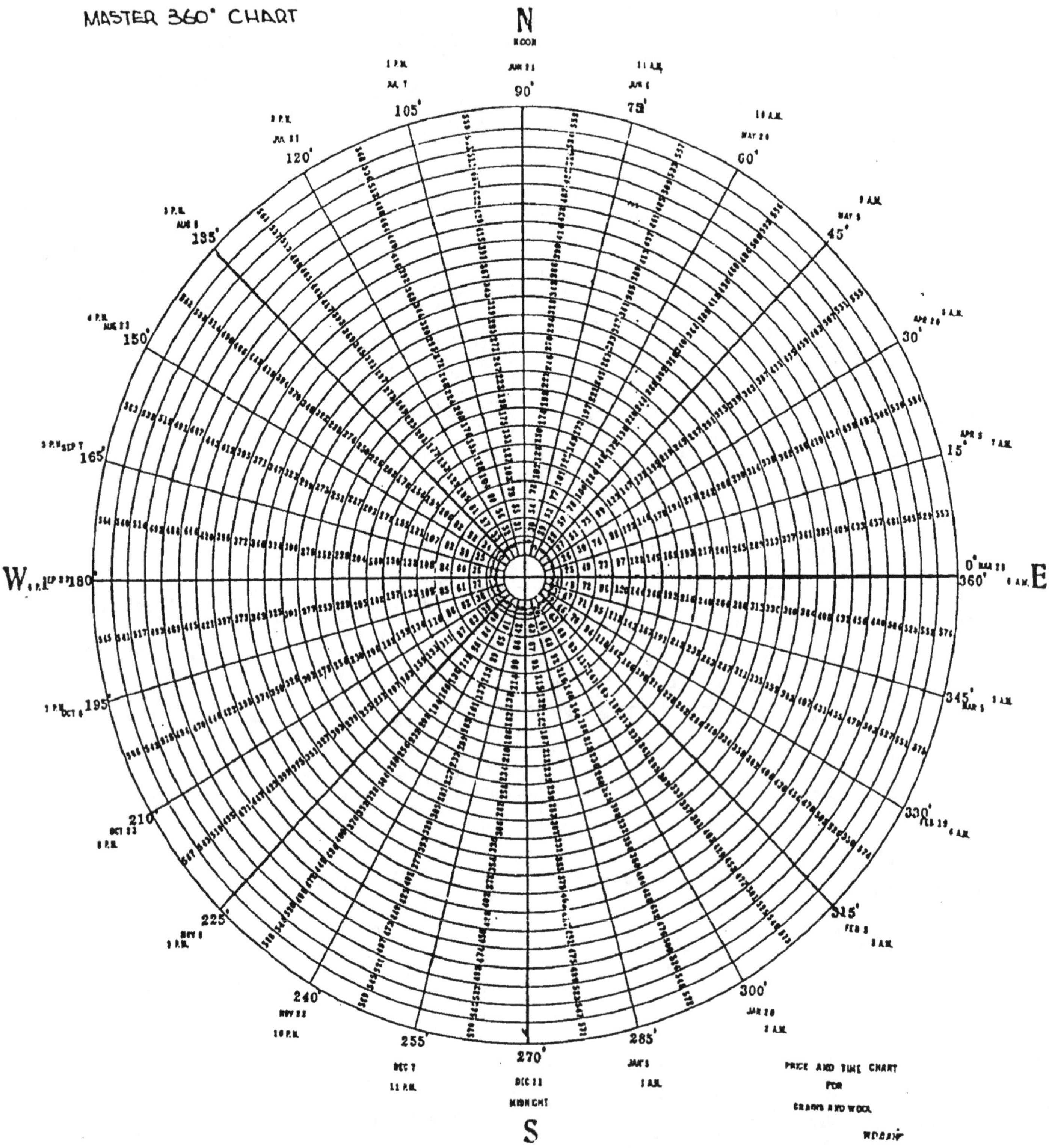

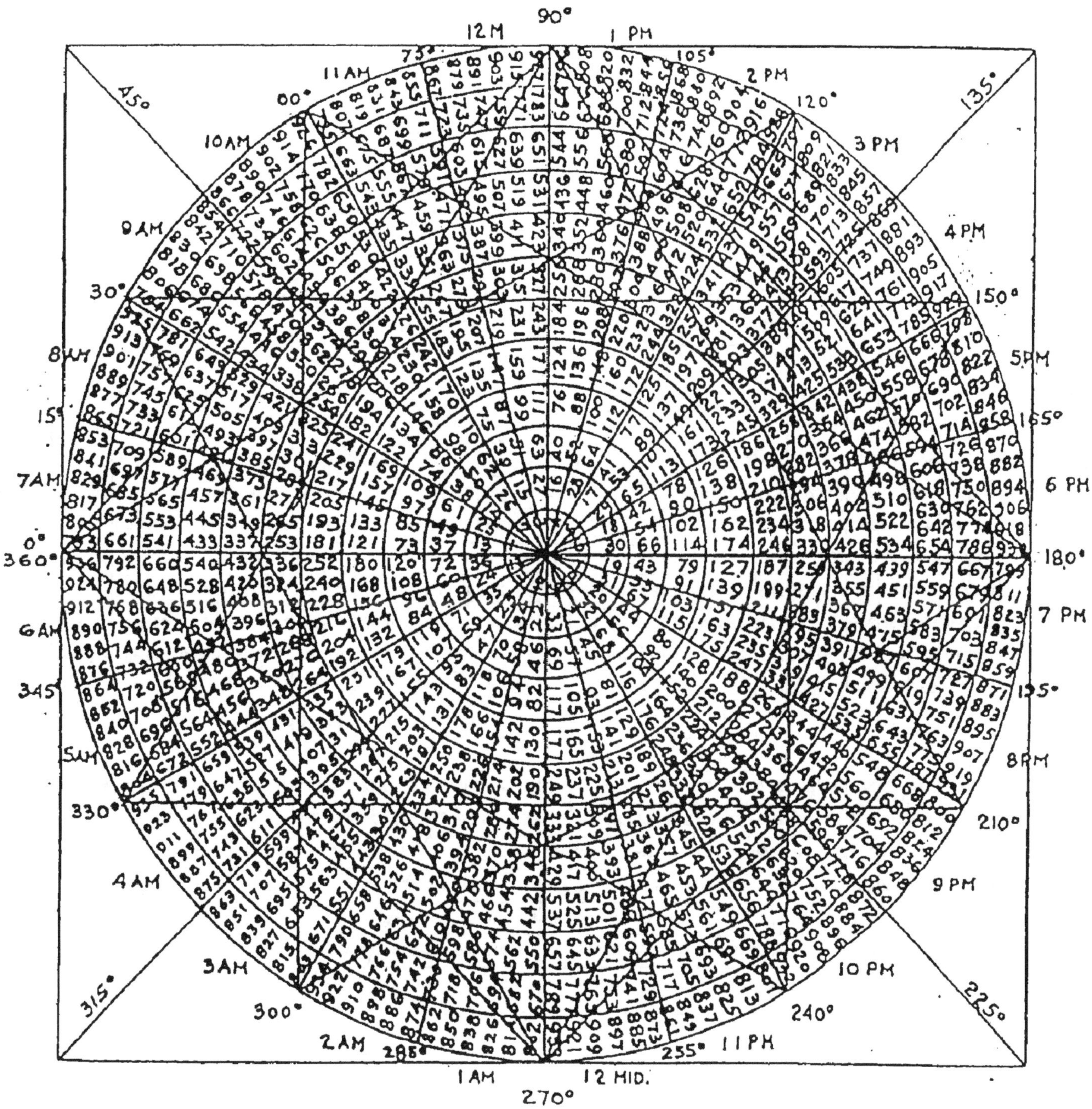

90°
12 M
1 PM
105°
2 PM
120°
135°
3 PM
4 PM
150°
5 PM
165°
6 PM
180°
7 PM
195°
8 PM
210°
9 PM
10 PM
225°
240°
255°
11 PM
12 MID.
270°
1 AM
2 AM
285°
300°
315°
3 AM
4 AM
330°
5 AM
345°
6 AM
360°
0°
7 AM
15°
8 AM
30°
9 AM
10 AM
45°
60°
11 AM
75°

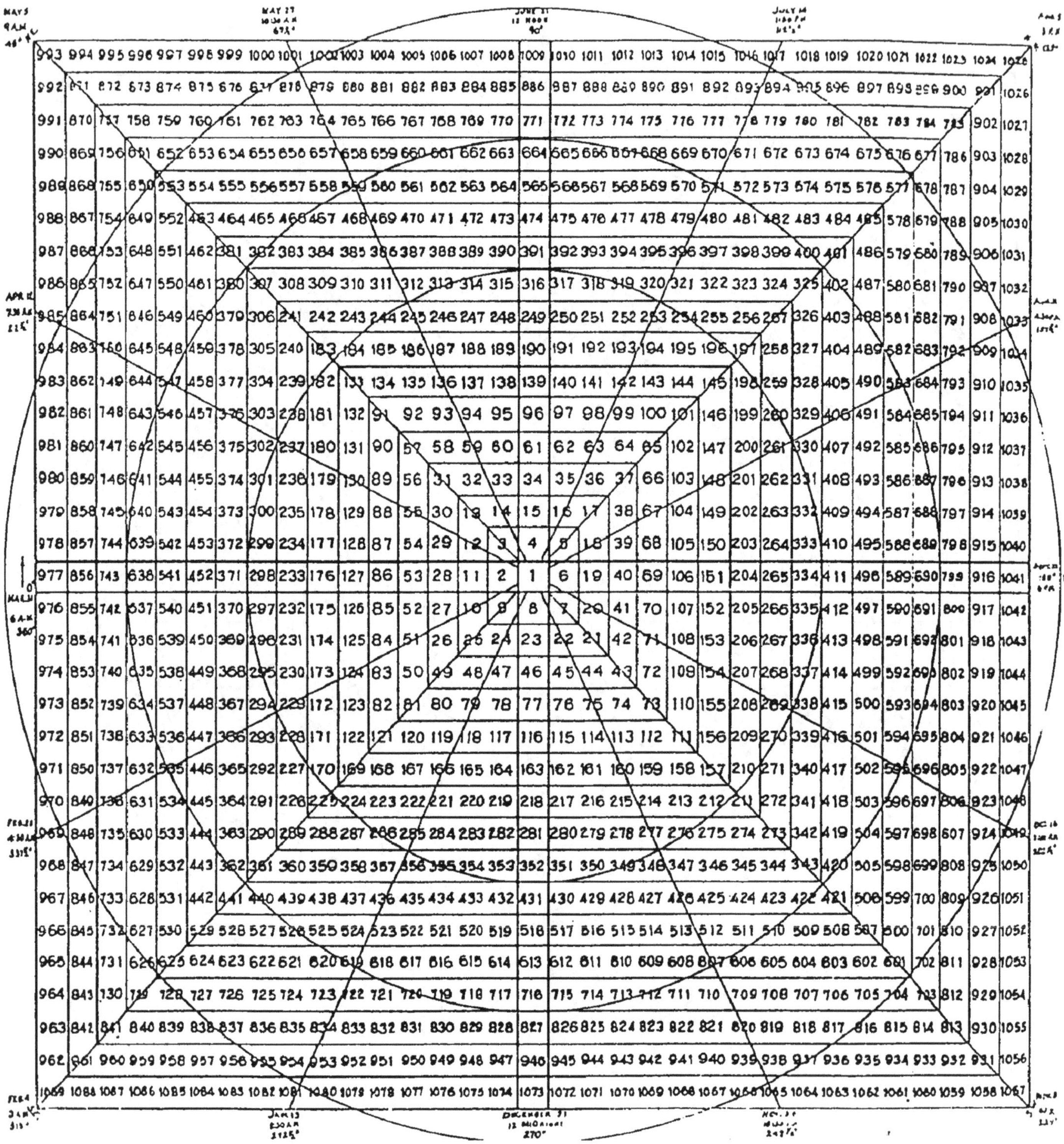
90°
DECEMBER 21
270°

MASTER TIME & PRICE CHART

[illegible] OF OPPOSITE POINTS

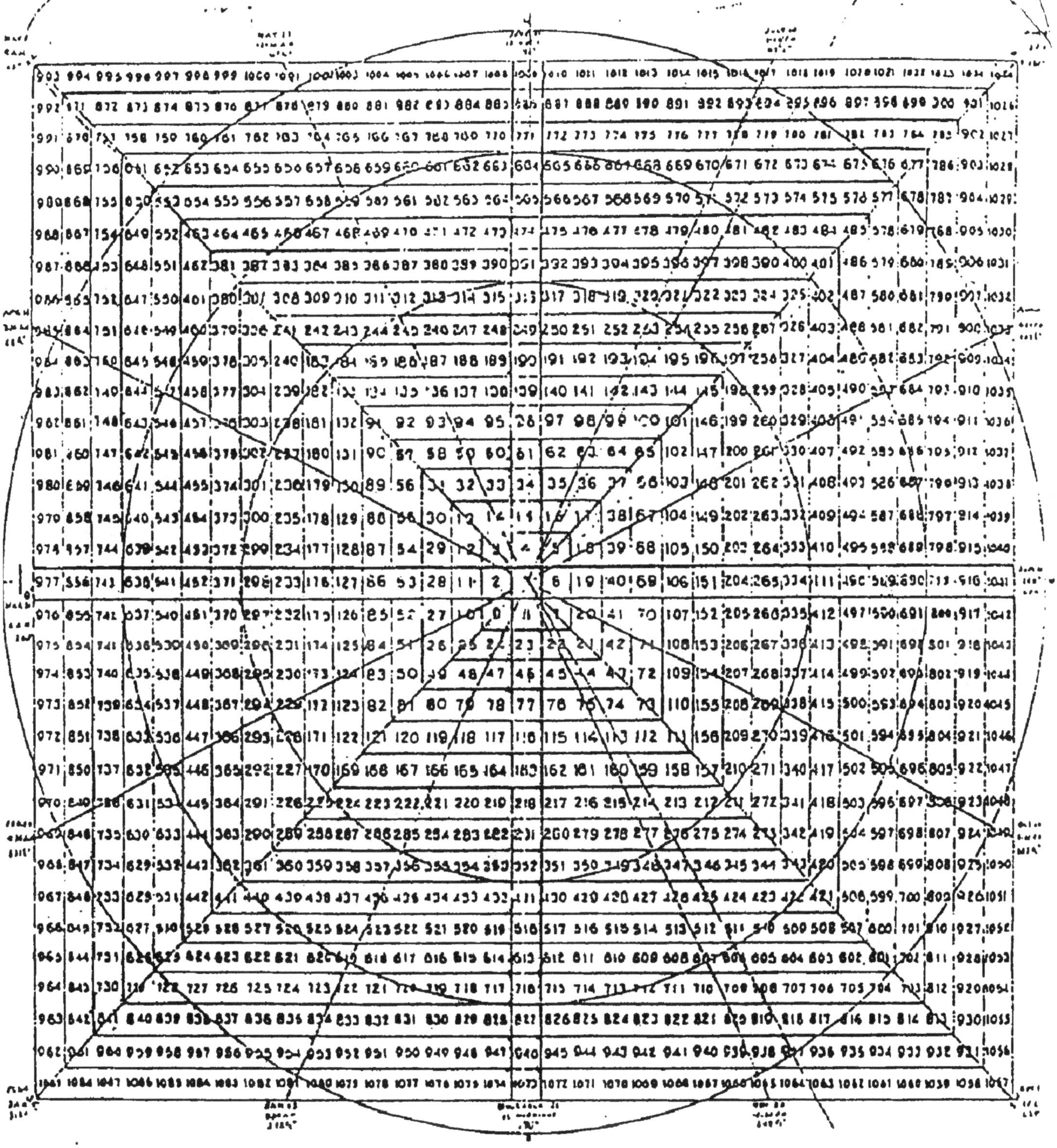

PRICES OR TIME ON ORANGE LINES [illegible] ARE

OR [illegible] PRICES OPP. [illegible]

TIME ON [illegible] ARE TURNING POINTS-

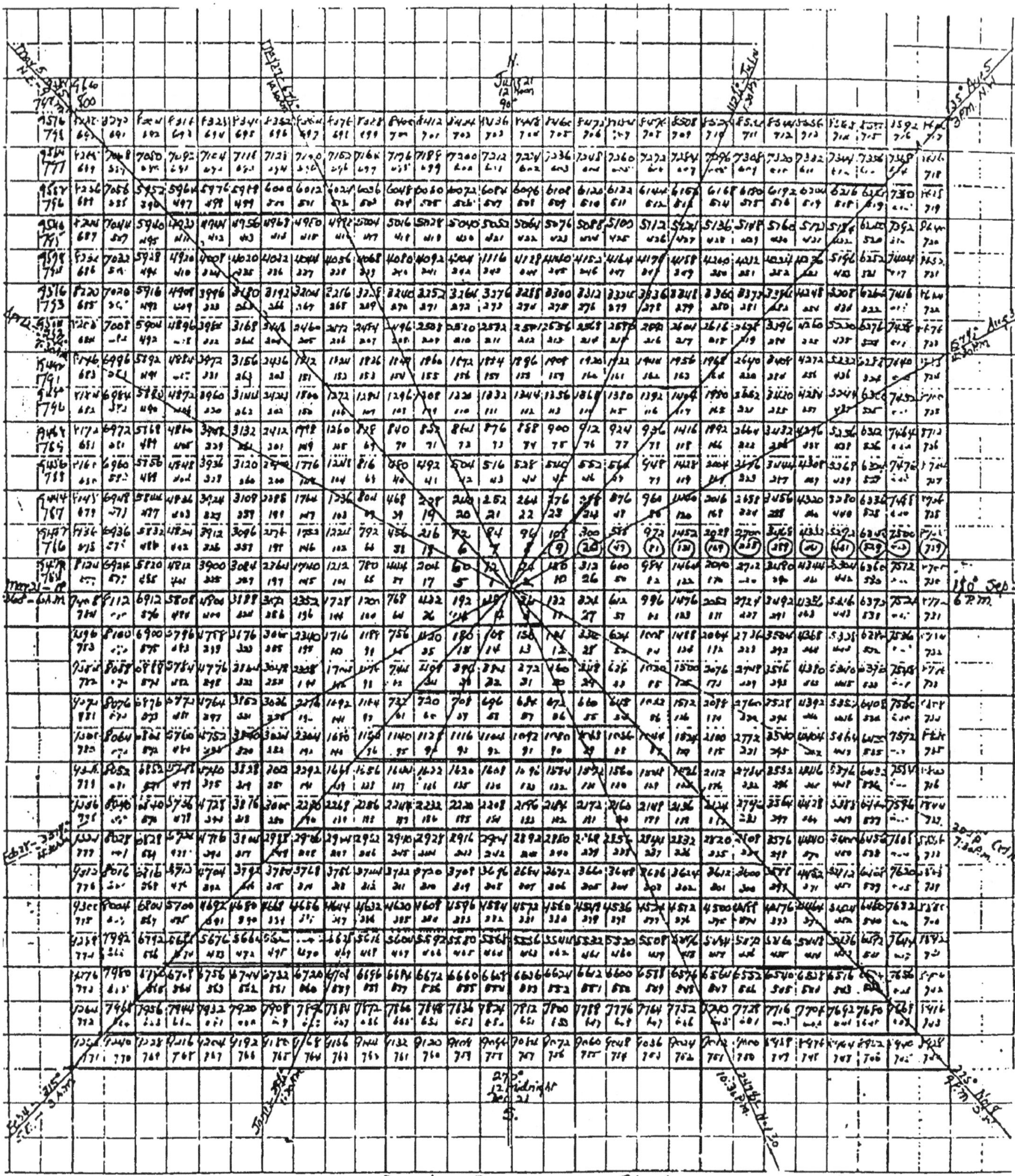

Master Price & Time Chart
for
Cotton, Coffee, Cocoa, Hogs,
and Grain

MASTER CHART

MAY SOY BEANS

PRICE & TIME

4	443	442	441	440	439	438	437	436	435	434	433	432	431	430	429	428	427	426	425	424
	368	367	366	365	364	363	362	361	360	359	358	357	356	355	354	353	352	351	350	423
	369	300	299	298	297	296	295	294	293	292	291	290	289	288	287	286	285	284	349	422
	370	301	240	239	238	237	236	235	234	233	232	231	230	229	228	227	226	283	348	421
	371	302	241	188	187	186	185	184	183	182	181	180	179	178	177	176	225	282	347	420
	372	303	242	189	144	143	142	141	140	139	138	137	136	135	134	175	224	281	346	419
	373	304	243	190	145	108	107	106	105	104	103	102	101	100	133	174	223	280	345	418
	374	305	244	191	146	109	80	79	78	77	76	75	74	99	132	173	222	279	344	417
	375	306	245	192	147	110	81	60	59	58	57	56	73	98	131	172	221	278	343	416
	376	307	246	193	148	111	82	61	48	47	46	55	72	97	130	171	220	277	342	415
	377	308	247	194	149	112	83	62	49	44	45	54	71	96	129	170	219	276	341	414
	378	309	248	195	150	113	84	63	50	51	52	53	70	95	128	169	218	275	340	413
	379	310	249	196	151	114	85	64	65	66	67	68	69	94	127	168	217	274	339	412
	380	311	250	197	152	115	86	87	88	89	90	91	92	93	126	167	216	273	338	411
	381	310	251	198	153	116	117	118	119	120	121	122	123	124	125	166	215	272	337	410
	382	313	252	199	154	155	156	157	158	159	160	161	162	163	164	165	214	271	336	409
	383	314	253	200	201	202	203	204	205	206	207	208	209	210	211	212	213	270	335	408
	384	315	254	255	256	257	258	259	260	261	262	263	264	265	266	267	268	269	334	407
	385	316	317	318	319	320	321	322	323	324	325	326	327	328	329	330	331	332	333	406
	386	387	388	389	390	391	392	393	394	395	396	397	398	399	400	401	402	403	404	405

NYSE

PERMANENT CHART

1	2	3	4	5	6	7	8	9	10	11	12	13	14	15	16	17	18	19	20
20	40	60	80	100	120	140	160	180	200	220	240	260	280	300	320	340	360	380	400
19	39	59	79	99	119	139	159	179	199	219	239	259	279	299	319	339	359	379	399
18	38	58	78	98	118	138	158	178	198	218	238	258	278	298	318	338	358	378	398
17	37	57	77	97	117	137	157	177	197	217	237	257	277	297	317	337	357	377	397
16	36	56	76	96	116	136	156	176	196	216	236	256	276	296	316	336	356	376	396
15	35	55	75	95	115	135	155	175	195	215	235	255	275	295	315	335	355	375	395
14	34	54	74	94	114	134	154	174	194	214	234	254	274	294	314	334	354	374	394
13	33	53	73	93	113	133	153	173	193	213	233	253	273	293	313	333	353	373	393
12	32	52	72	92	112	132	152	172	192	212	232	252	272	292	312	332	352	372	392
11	31	51	71	91	111	131	151	171	191	211	231	251	271	291	311	331	351	371	391
10	30	50	70	90	110	130	150	170	190	210	230	250	270	290	310	330	350	370	390
9	29	49	69	89	109	129	149	169	189	209	229	249	269	289	309	329	349	369	389
8	28	48	68	88	108	128	148	168	188	208	228	248	268	288	308	328	348	368	388
7	27	47	67	87	107	127	147	167	187	207	227	247	267	287	307	327	347	367	387
6	26	46	66	86	106	126	146	166	186	206	226	246	266	286	306	326	346	366	386
5	25	45	65	85	105	125	145	165	185	205	225	245	265	285	305	325	345	365	385
4	24	44	64	84	104	124	144	164	184	204	224	244	264	284	304	324	344	364	384
3	23	43	63	83	103	123	143	163	183	203	223	243	263	283	303	323	343	363	383
2	22	42	62	82	102	122	142	162	182	202	222	242	262	282	302	322	342	362	382
1	21	41	61	81	101	121	141	161	181	201	221	241	261	281	301	321	341	361	381

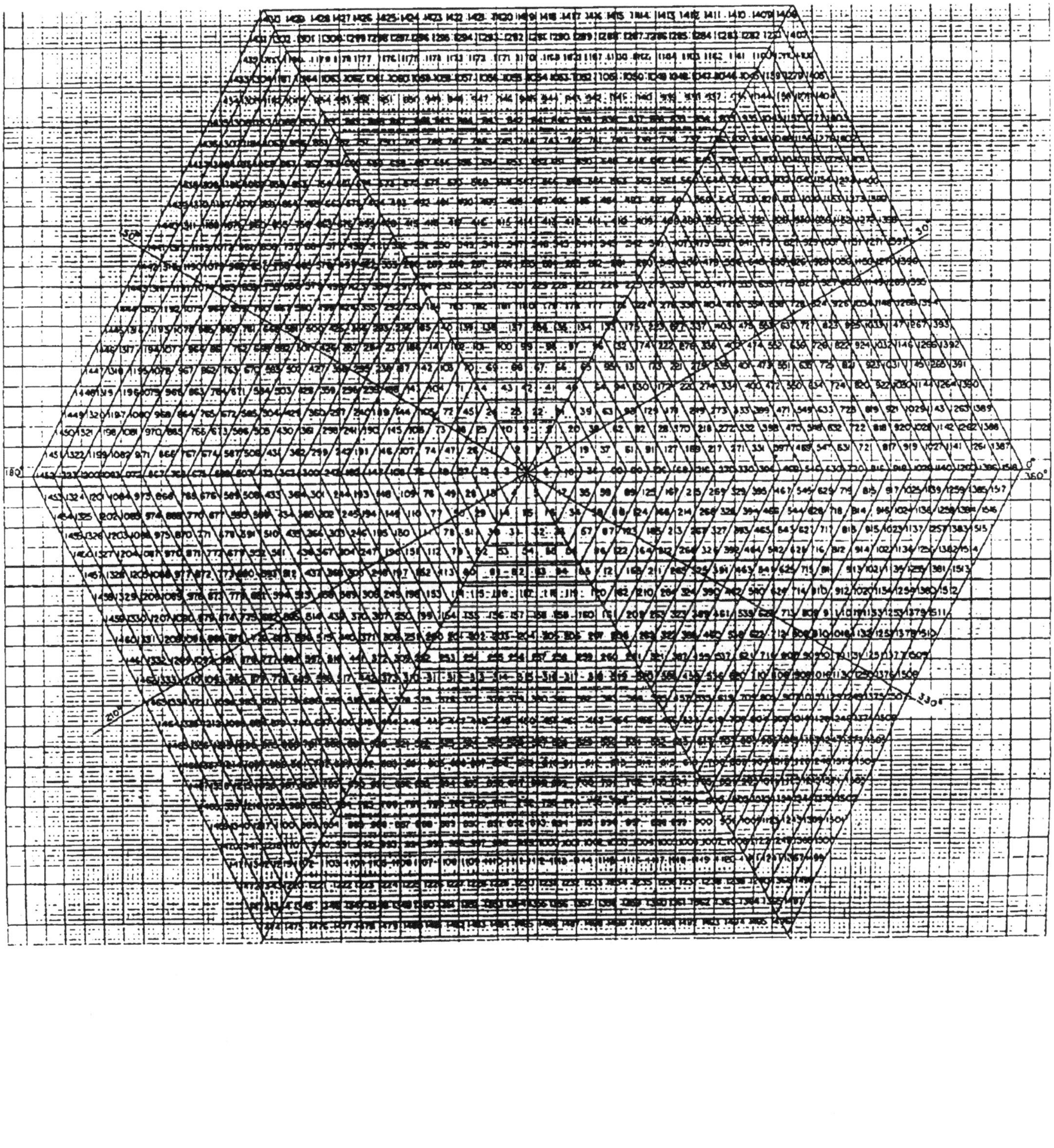
180°
0°
360°
30°
150°
210°
330°

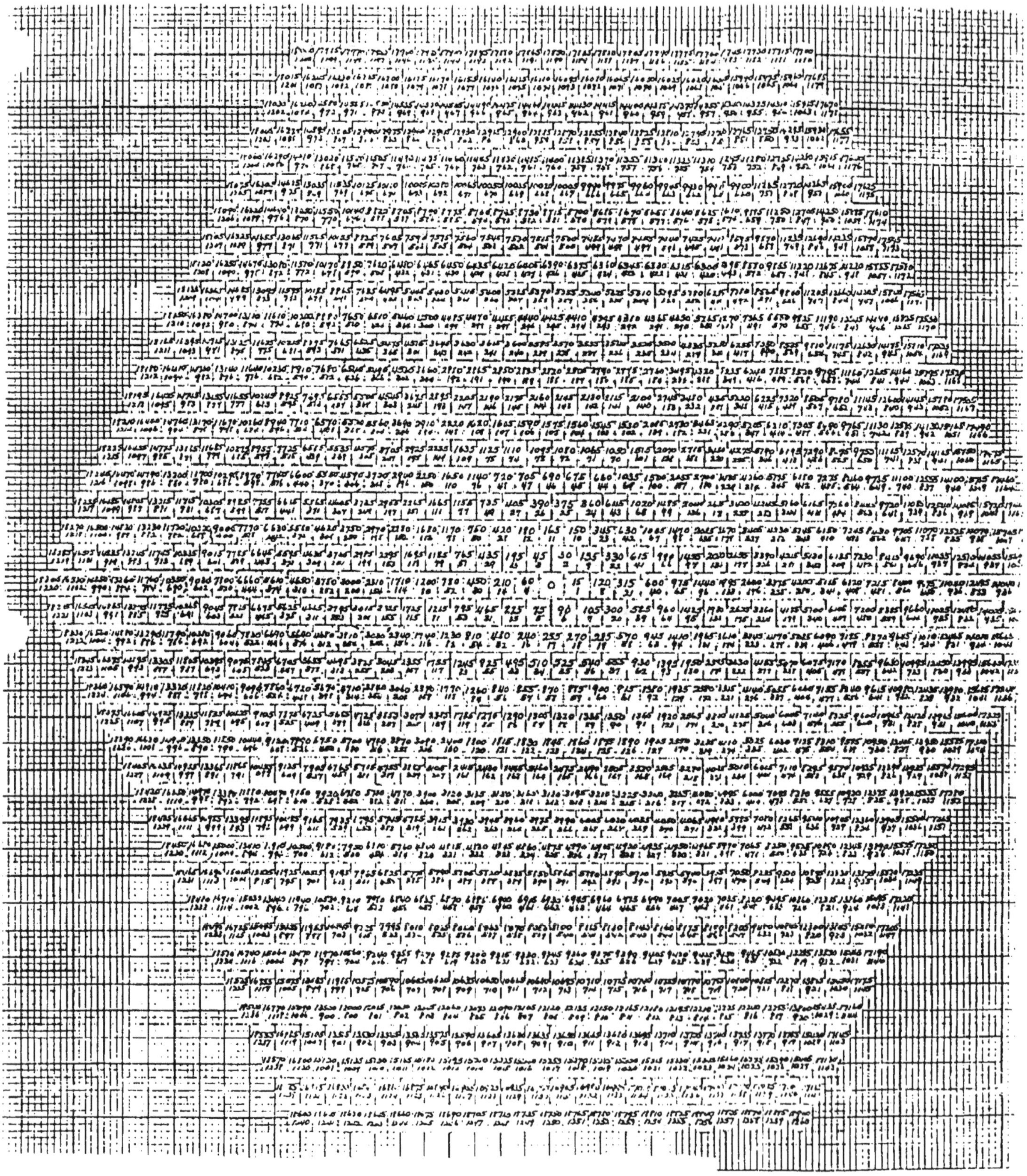

Coffee Rio Jan 300 Oct 2 1936

20 9300 9330 9360 9390 9420 9450 9480 9510 9540 9570 9600 9630

7½ 8640 [illegible] 8850 8880 [illegible] 8970 9000 9030 9060 [illegible] 9120 9150 9180 9210 9240 9270

[illegible] 7920 7950 [illegible] 8010 8040 8070 8100 8130 [illegible] 8190 8220 8250 8280 8310 8340 8370 8400 8430 8460 8490 8520 8550 [illegible]

7260 7290 7320 7350 7380 7410 7440 7470 7500 7530 7560 [illegible] 7620 7650 7680 7710 [illegible] 7770 7800 7830 7860 7890 [illegible]

6600 6630 6660 6690 6720 6750 6780 6810 6840 6870 6900 6930 6960 6990 7020 7050 7080 7110 7140 7170 7200 7230

6000 6030 6060 6090 6120 6150 6180 6210 6240 6270 6300 6330 6360 6390 6420 6450 6480 6510 6540 6570 6600

5460 5490 5520 5550 5580 5610 5640 5670 5700 5730 5760 5790 5820 5850 5880 5910 5940 5970 6000

4920 4950 4980 5010 5040 5070 5100 5130 5160 5190 5220 5250 5280 5310 5340 5370 5400 5430

4410 4440 4470 4500 4530 4560 4590 4620 4650 4680 4710 4740 4770 4800 4830 4860 4890

3930 3960 3990 4020 4050 4080 4110 4140 4170 4200 4230 4260 4290 4320 4350 4380

3480 3510 3540 3570 3600 3630 3660 3690 3720 3750 3780 3810 3840 3870 3900

3060 3090 3120 3150 3180 3210 3240 3270 3300 3330 3360 3390 3420 3450

2670 2700 2730 2760 2790 2820 2850 2880 2910 2940 2970 3000 3030 [illegible]

2310 2340 2370 2400 2430 2460 2490 2520 2550 2580 2610 [illegible]

1980 2010 2040 2070 2100 2130 2160 2190 2220 2250 2280 [illegible]

1680 1710 1740 1770 1800 1830 1860 1890 1920 1950

1410 1440 1470 1500 1530 1560 1590 1620 1650 [illegible]

1170 1200 1230 1260 1290 1320 1350 1380

960 990 1020 1050 1080 1110 1140

750 780 840 870 900 930

560 660 690 720 750

510 540 570 600

390 420 440

360 390

330

Jan 300

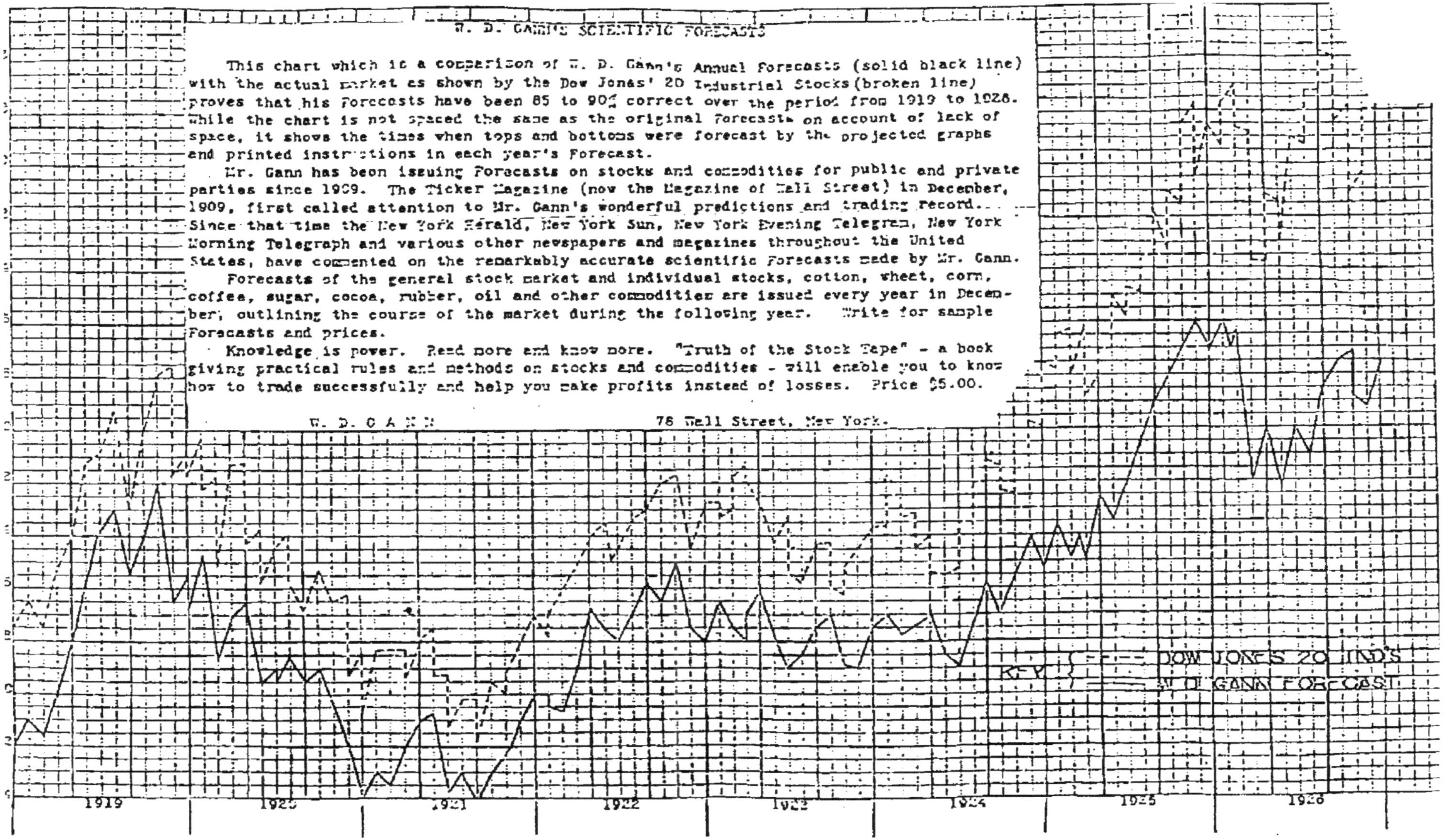

W. D. GANN'S SCIENTIFIC FORECASTS

This chart which is a comparison of W. D. Gann's Annual Forecasts (solid black line) with the actual market as shown by the Dow Jones' 20 Industrial Stocks (broken line) proves that his Forecasts have been 85 to 90% correct over the period from 1919 to 1928. While the chart is not spaced the same as the original Forecasts on account of lack of space, it shows the times when tops and bottoms were forecast by the projected graphs and printed instructions in each year's Forecast.

Mr. Gann has been issuing Forecasts on stocks and commodities for public and private parties since 1909. The Ticker Magazine (now the Magazine of Wall Street) in December, 1909, first called attention to Mr. Gann's wonderful predictions and trading record. Since that time the New York Herald, New York Sun, New York Evening Telegram, New York Morning Telegraph and various other newspapers and magazines throughout the United States, have commented on the remarkably accurate scientific Forecasts made by Mr. Gann.

Forecasts of the general stock market and individual stocks, cotton, wheat, corn, coffee, sugar, cocoa, rubber, oil and other commodities are issued every year in December, outlining the course of the market during the following year. Write for sample Forecasts and prices.

Knowledge is power. Read more and know more. "Truth of the Stock Tape" - a book giving practical rules and methods on stocks and commodities - will enable you to know how to trade successfully and help you make profits instead of losses. Price $5.00.

W. D. GANN 78 Wall Street, New York.

Master 360° Circle Chart

		1	2	3	4	5	6	7	8	9	10	11	12	1	2	3	4	5
12	24	360	720	1080	1440	1800	2160	2520	2880	3240	3600	3960	4320	4680	5040	5400	5760	6120
	23	345	705	1065	1425	1785	2145	2505	2865	3225	3585	3945	4305	4665	5025	5385	5745	6105
11	22	330	690	1050	1410	1770	2130	2490	2850	3210	3570	3930	4290	4650	5010	5370	5730	6090
7/8	21	315	675	1035	1395	1755	2115	2475	2835	3195	3555	3915	4275	4635	4995	5365	5715	6075
10	20	300	660	1020	1380	1740	2100	2460	2820	3180	3540	3900	4260	4620	4980	5340	5700	6060
	19	285	645	1005	1365	1725	2085	2445	2805	3165	3525	3885	4245	4605	4965	5325	5685	6045
9 3/4	18	270	630	990	1350	1710	2070	2430	2790	3150	3510	3870	4230	4590	4950	5310	5670	6030
	17	255	615	975	1335	1695	2055	2415	2775	3135	3495	3855	4215	4575	4935	5295	5655	6015
8 2/3	16	240	600	960	1320	1680	2040	2400	2760	3120	3480	3840	4200	4560	4920	5280	5640	6000
5/8	15	225	585	945	1305	1665	2025	2385	2745	3105	3465	3825	4185	4545	4905	5265	5625	5985
7	14	210	570	930	1290	1650	2010	2370	2730	3090	3450	3810	4170	4530	4890	5250	5610	5970
1/2	13	195	555	915	1275	1635	1995	2355	2715	3075	3435	3795	4155	4515	4875	5235	5595	5955
6	12	180	540	900	1260	1620	1980	2340	2700	3060	3420	3780	4140	4500	4860	5220	5580	5940
	11	165	525	885	1245	1605	1965	2325	2685	3045	3405	3765	4125	4485	4845	5205	5565	5925
5	10	150	510	870	1230	1590	1950	2310	2670	3030	3390	3750	4110	4470	4850	5190	5550	5910
	9	135	495	855	1215	1575	1935	2295	2655	3015	3375	3735	4095	4455	4815	5175	5535	5895
4 1/3	8	120	480	840	1200	1560	1920	2280	2640	3000	3360	3720	4080	4440	4800	5160	5520	5880
	7	105	465	825	1185	1545	1905	2265	2625	2985	3345	3705	4065	4425	4785	5145	5505	5865
3 1/4	6	90	450	810	1170	1530	1890	2250	2610	2970	3330	3690	4050	4410	4770	5130	5490	5850
	5	75	435	795	1155	1515	1875	2235	2595	2955	3315	3675	4035	4395	4755	5115	5475	5835
2 1/6	4	60	420	780	1140	1500	1860	2220	2580	2940	3300	3660	4020	4380	4740	5100	5460	5820
1/8	3	45	405	765	1125	1485	1845	2205	2565	2925	3285	3645	4005	4365	4725	5085	5445	5805
1	2	30	390	750	1110	1470	1830	2190	2550	2910	3270	3630	3990	4350	4710	5070	5430	5790
	1	15	375	735	1095	1455	1815	2175	2535	2895	3255	3615	3975	4335	4695	5055	5415	5775
		30° 1/12	60° 1/6	90° 1/4	120° 1/3	150° 5/12	180° 1/2	210° 7/12	240° 2/3	270° 3/4	300° 5/6	330° 11/12	360° 0	30° 1/12	60° 1/6	90° 1/4	120° 1/3	150° 5/12

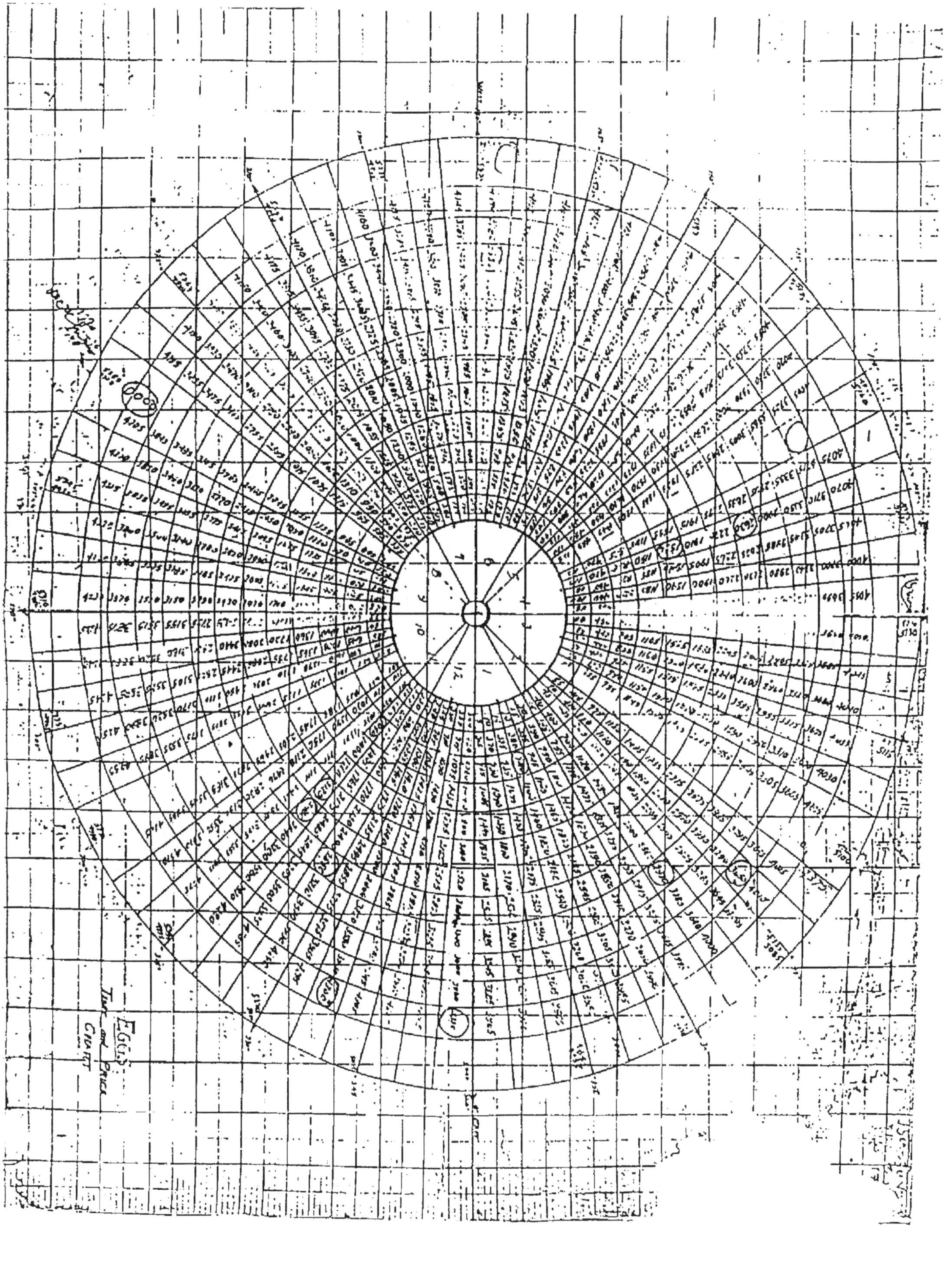

May 28, 1932

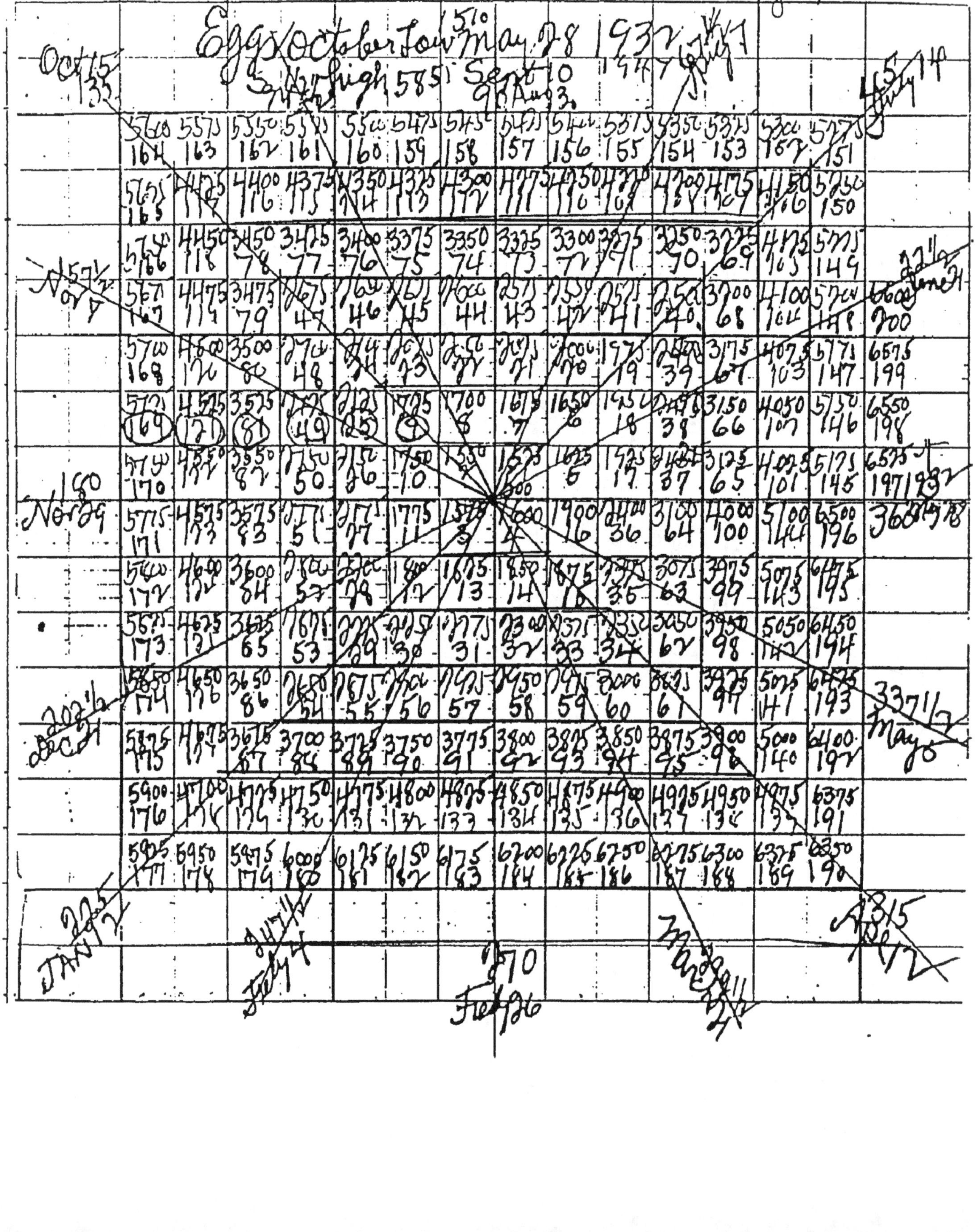
Eggs October Low May 28 1932
Oct 15
Nov 29
Dec 21
Jan 21
Feb 26
May 6
270
225
315
337½
202½

EVEN SQUARES for COTTON & EGGS

Time and Price

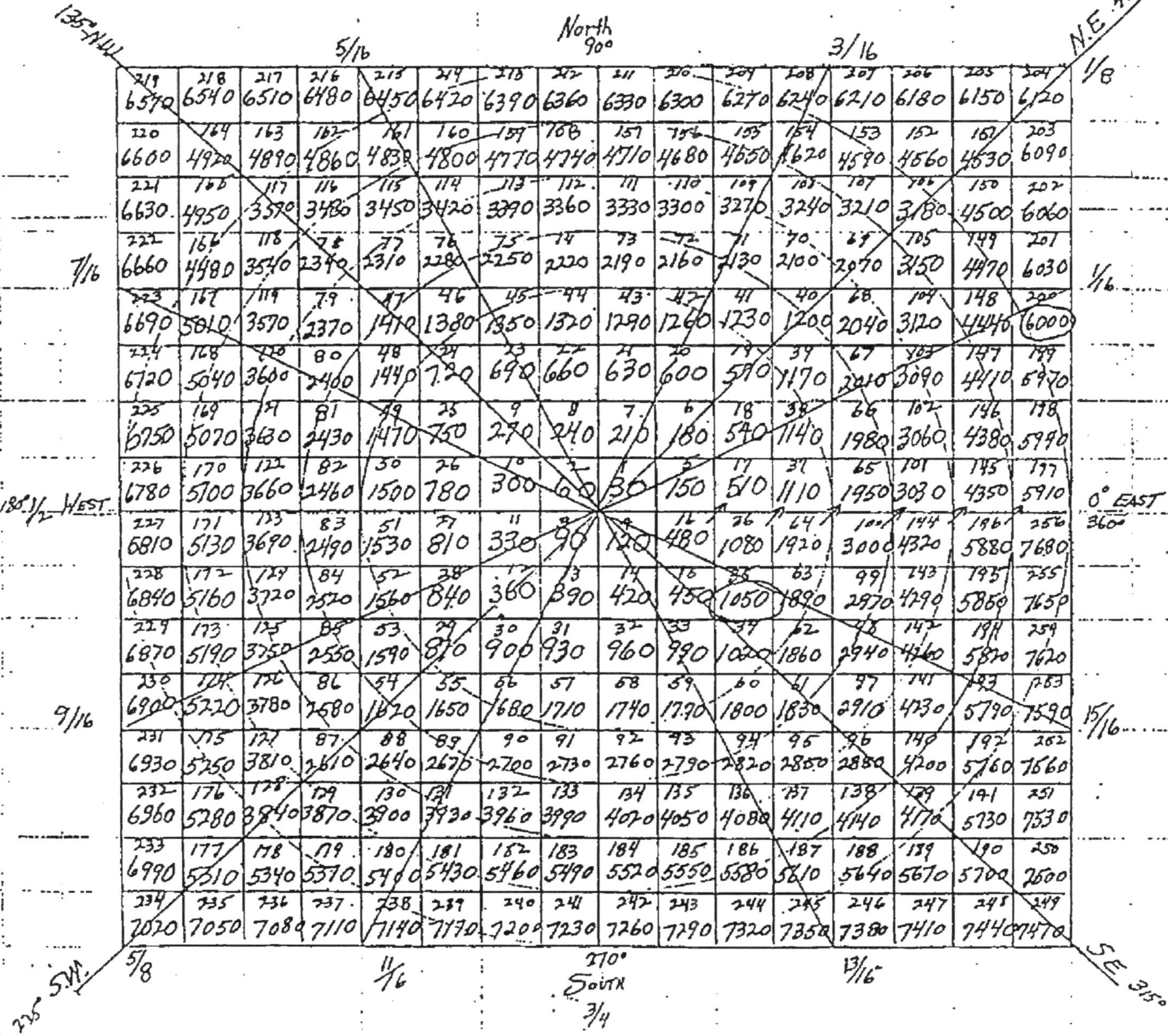

DEC-28-1920
DEC-28 1948 = 336 Months
April/28-1949 = 4 "
340 "
JULY 28-1949 = 343 "
7 X 49 = 343 "

DEC. 28.-1920 - High 60¢
MAY 2. 1949 = 1481 weeks

Square of 38 = 1444
" " 39 = 1521
" " 40 = 1600

From □ 38 to 39
1/4 = 19 1/4 Weeks
1/2 = 38 1/2 "
1481 + 38 1/2 = 1482 1/2
MAY 13-1949 = 1482 1/2

1440 = 4 X 360

MAY 30, 1949 = 45 Weeks
In New 360 cycle.

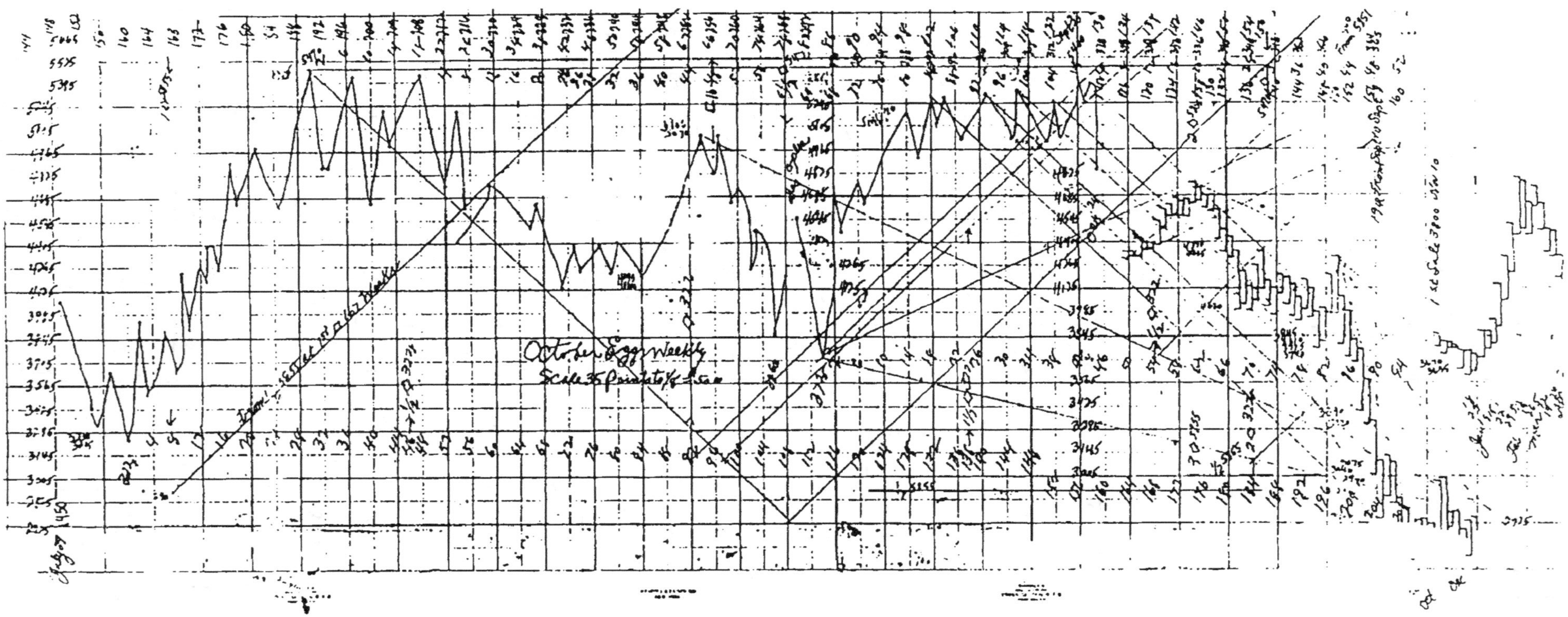
October Eggs Weekly
Scale 35 Points to 1/8 inch

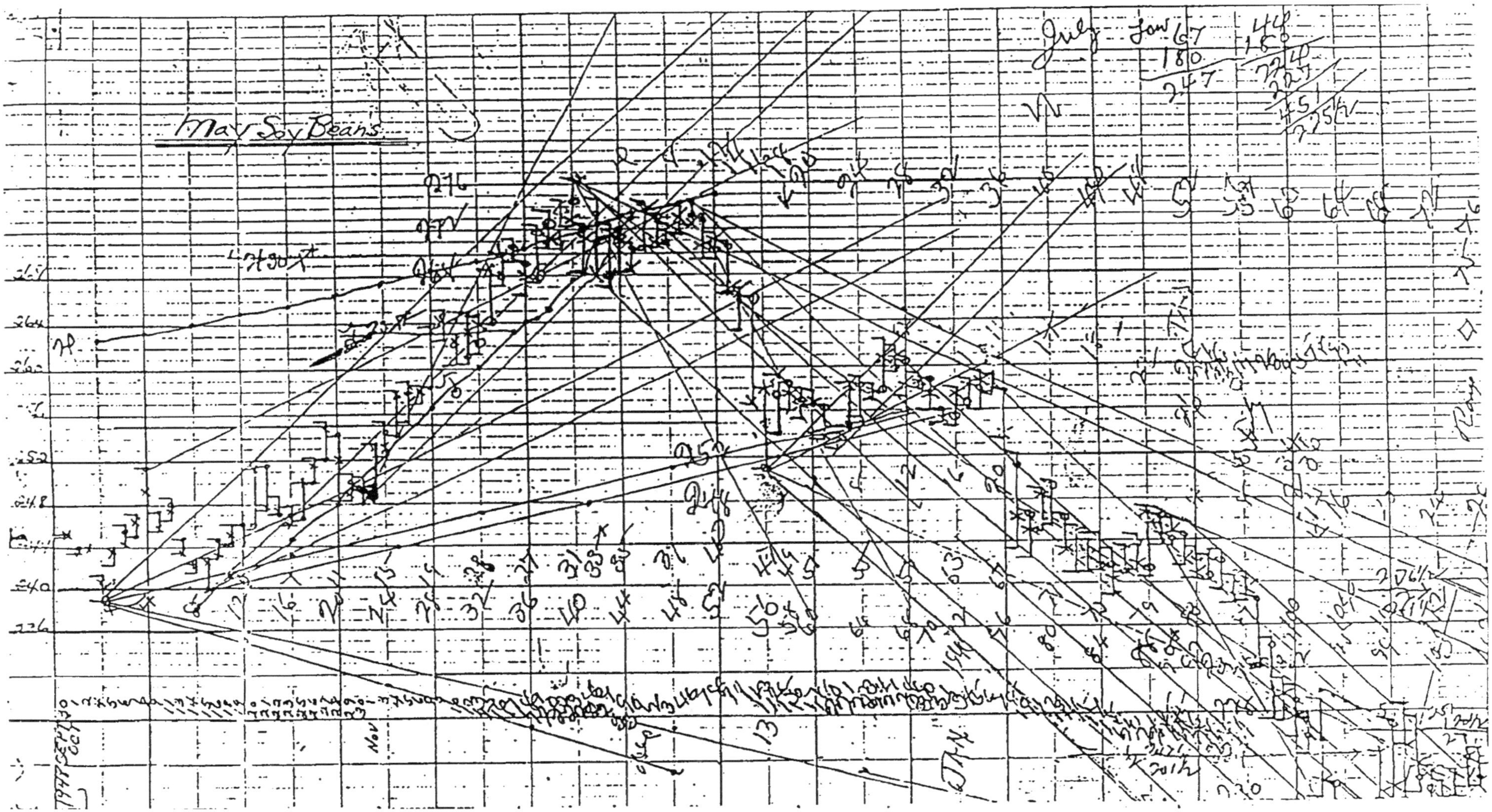
May Soy Beans

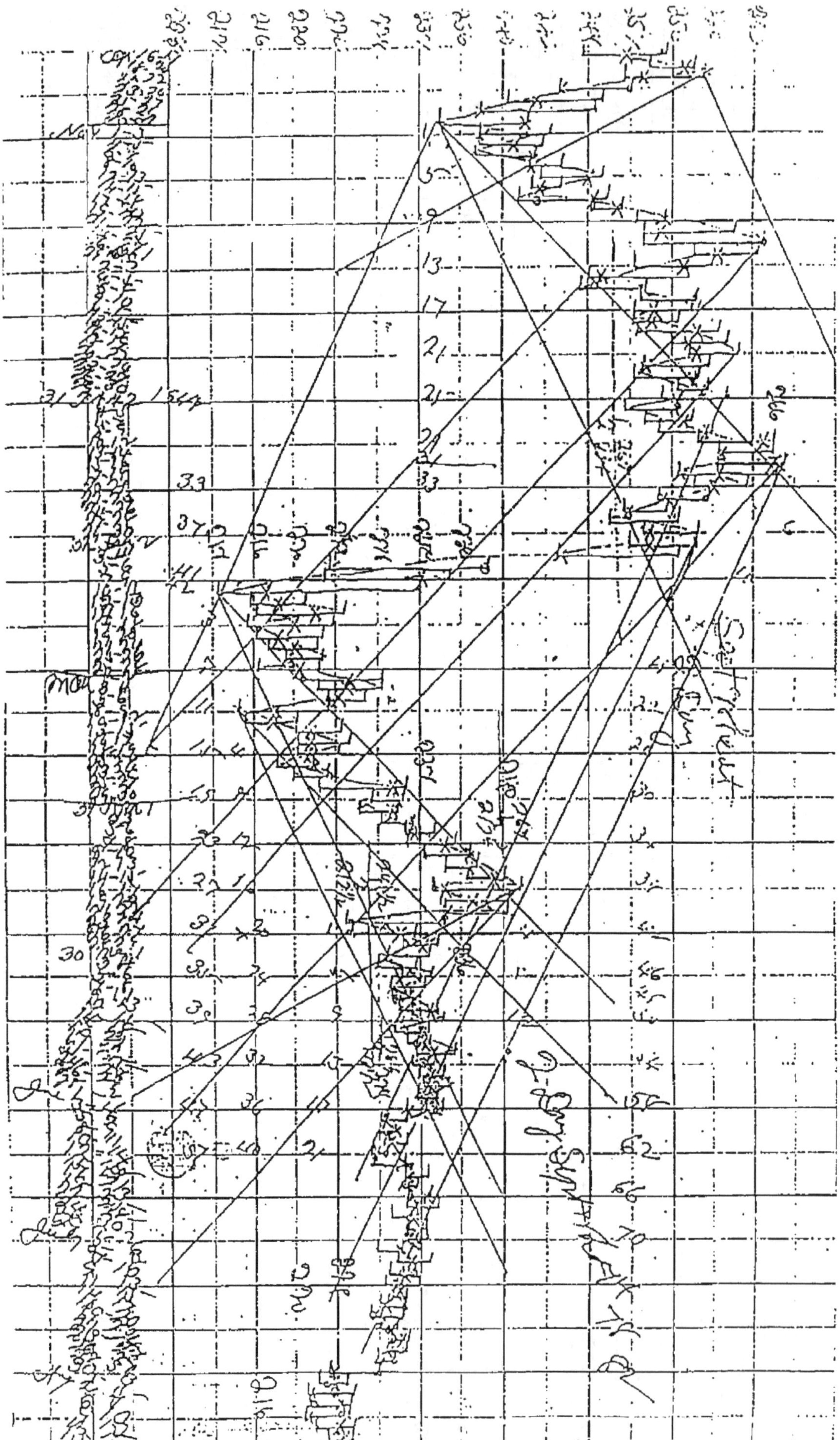

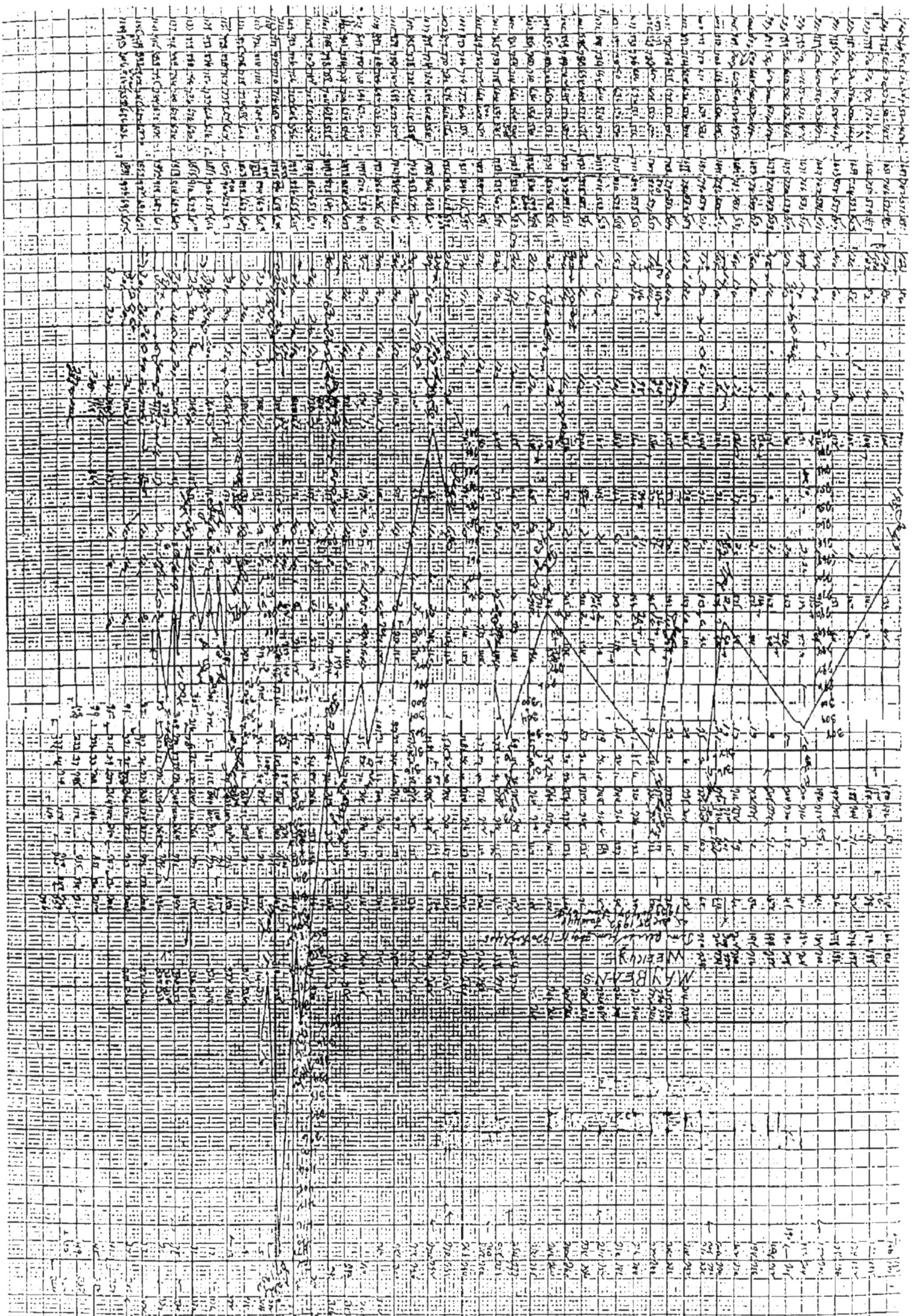

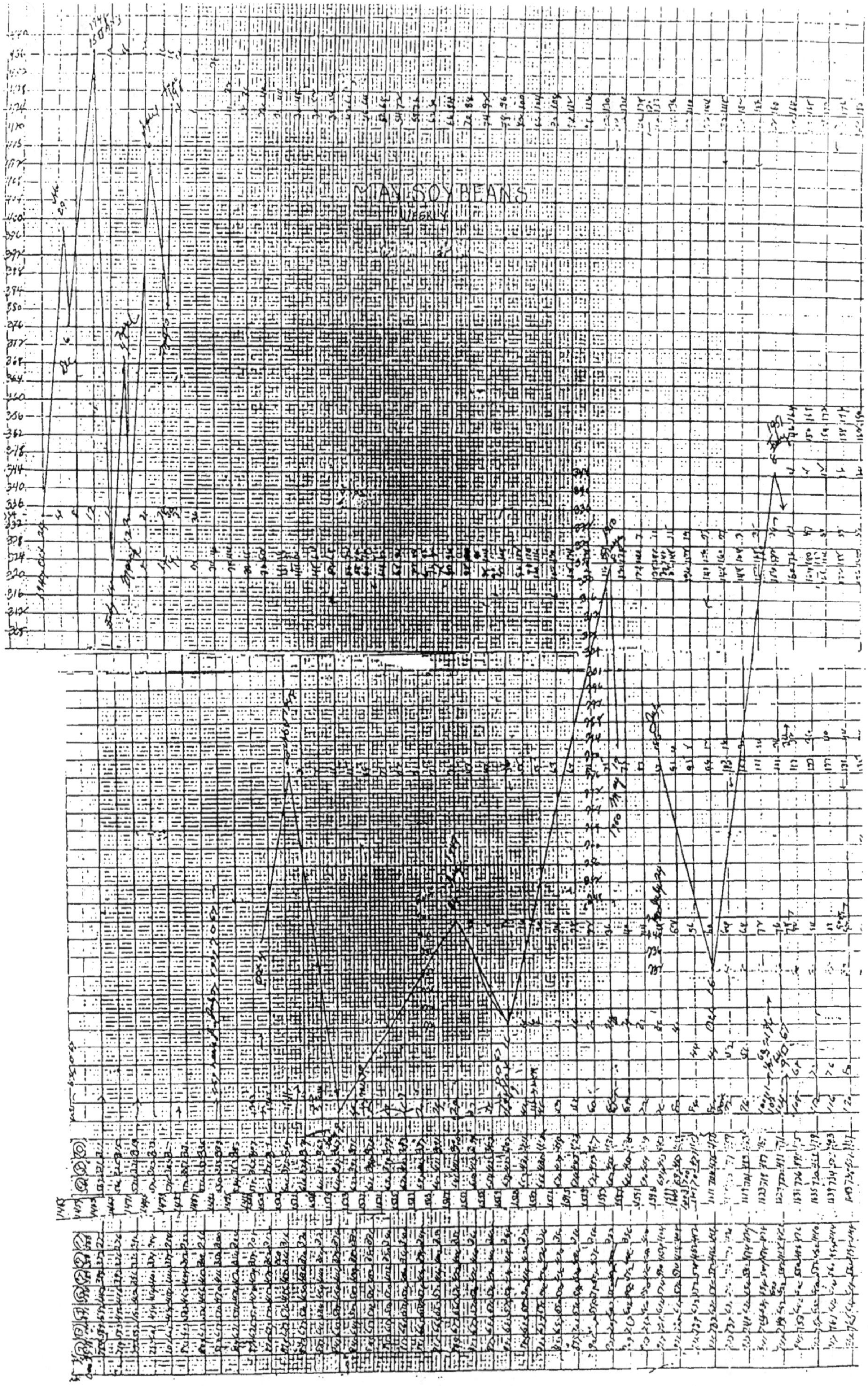
MAY SOYBEANS
WEEKLY

WEEKLY TIME PERIODS 7 DAYS FROM HIGHS OR LOWS. THE YEAR IS DIVIDED INTO 1/8s AND 1/3s.

CASH AND MAY SOY BEANS

		1	2	3	4	5	6	7	8	9	10	11	12	13	14	15	16	17	18	19	20	21	22	23	24	25	26	27	28	29	30	31	32	33	34	35	36
High and Low Prices		105	14	120	202½	60½	89	89	202	154½	203½	164	334	436 3/4	320½	426	239	274 3/4	201½	210	220½	224	323½	232½	344½	268½	309 3/4	281	314 3/4	279 3/4	309	259½	422	361	306 1/4	365 3/4	299
Dates		1920	1932	1936	1937	1938	1939	1940	1941	1941	1942	1942	1947	1948	1948	1948	1948	1948	1949	1949	1949	1949	1950	1950	1951	1951	1951	1952	1952	1953	1953	1953	1954	1954	1954	1954	1954
Mar 20		Feb 15	Dec 28	Oct 15	Apr 10	Oct 20	July 27	Aug 10	Sept 13	Oct 17	Jan 27	Oct 28	Oct 28	Jan 15	Feb 14	May 20	Oct 9	Nov 26	Feb 9	Mar 24	Nov 16	Dec 28	May 8	Oct 16	Feb 8	Jul 9	Dec 10	Apr 21	Aug 14	Feb 13	Apr 18	Aug 20	Apr 27	May 18	Jul 27	Sept 27	Nov 14
May 3	1/8	Mar 31	Feb 11	Nov 10	May 27	Dec 4	Sept 2	Sept 27	Oct 29	Dec 2	Mar 12	Dec 12	Dec 12	Mar 1	Mar 30	Jul 7	Nov 23	Jan 9	Mar 26	May 9	Dec 29	Feb 11	Apr 28	Nov 30	Mar 24	Aug 25	Jan 23	June 17	Oct 1	Mar 29	June 3	Oct 7	June 13	Jul 5	Sept 12	Nov 12	Dec 7
June 21	1/4	May 17	Mar 27	Jan 30	Jul 15	Jan 18	Oct 26	Nov 11	Dec 12	Jan 15	Apr 27	Jan 26	Jan 26	Apr 12	May 16	Aug 23	Jan 7	Feb 24	May 11	June 24	Feb 14	Mar 27	June 25	Jan 14	May 10	Oct 10	Mar 10	Jul 26	Nov 15	May 15	Jul 19	Nov 21	July 31	Aug 21	Oct 28	Dec 28	Feb 2
July 23	1/3	June 17	Apr 24	Feb 1	Aug 15	Feb 16	Nov 27	Dec 10	Jan 1	Feb 15	May 28	Feb 24	Feb 24	May 16	June 16	Sept 23	Feb 4	Mar 25	June 11	Jul 27	Mar 15	Apr 27	Aug 11	Feb 12	June 10	Nov 9	Apr 8	Aug 22	Dec 14	June 15	Aug 19	Dec 20	Aug 31	Sept 21	Nov 27	Jan 25	Mar [illegible]
Aug 8	3/8	Jul 3	May 15	Feb 10	Aug 29	Mar 3	Dec 11	Dec 25	Jan 26	Feb 28	June 12	Mar 11	Mar 11	May 30	Jul 2	Nov 8	Feb 20	Apr 9	June 27	Aug 9	Mar 20	May 13	Sept 11	Feb 27	June 26	Nov 24	Apr 22	Sept 6	Dec 29	Jul 1	Sept 17	Jan 4	Sept 13	Nov 6	Dec 11	Feb 9	Mar 18
Sept 22	1/2	Aug 19	June 29	Apr 2	Oct 14	Apr 17	Jan 25	Feb 8	Mar 11	Apr 14	Jul 31	Apr 25	Apr 25	Jul 19	Aug 18	Nov 22	Apr 9	May 24	Aug 13	Sept 26	May 24	June 29	Nov 10	Apr 13	Aug 12	Jan 10	June 7	Oct 25	Feb 12	Aug 17	Oct 09	Feb 16	Oct 31	Nov 30	Jan 25	Mar 26	May 9
Nov 8	5/8	Oct 4	Aug 13	May 18	Nov 28	June 12	Mar 9	Mar 23	Apr 25	May 29	Sept 14	June 10	June 10	Sept 2	Oct 3	Jan 6	May 22	Jul 9	Oct 28	Nov 12	June 29	Aug 15	Dec 25	May 28	Sept 24	Feb 19	Jul 23	Dec 9	Mar 27	Oct 2	Dec 4	Apr 5	Dec 15	Jan 4	Mar 14	May 10	June 17
Nov 22	2/3	Oct 19	Aug 31	June 3	Dec 12	June 18	Mar 24	Apr 8	May 12	June 15	Sept 30	June 26	June 26	Sept 15	Oct 18	Jan 20	June 7	Jul 21	Oct 13	Nov 26	Jul 11	Aug 31	Jan 8	June 14	Oct 10	Mar 6	Aug 14	Dec 23	Apr 12	Oct 17	Dec 19	Apr 18	Dec 30	Jan 18	Mar 24	May 26	June 29
Dec 21	3/4	Nov 16	Sept 30	Jul 4	Jan 11	Jan 19	Apr 24	May 9	June 12	Jul 10	Oct 30	Jul 27	Jul 27	Oct 10	Nov 17	Feb 10	Jul 8	Aug 25	Nov 12	Dec 25	Aug 16	Sept 30	Feb 7	Jul 15	Nov 11	Apr 6	Sept 5	Jan 22	May 13	Nov 14	Jan 17	May 16	Jan 28	Feb 17	Apr 24	June 26	Aug 12
Feb 4	7/8	Jan 2	Nov 14	Aug 20	Feb 24	Sept 4	June 10	June 24	Jul 28	Sept 1	Dec 14	Sept 12	Sept 12	Dec 2	Jan 1	Apr 4	Aug 24	Oct 9	Dec 26	Feb 8	Sept 29	Nov 14	Mar 23	Aug 31	Dec 26	May 23	Oct 23	Mar 17	June 29	Dec 31	Mar 2	Jul 4	Mar 13	Apr 2	June 10	Aug 11	Sept 17
Mar 20	1 yr 52	Feb 15	Dec 28	Oct 5	Apr 10	Oct 20	July 27	Aug 10	Sept 13	Oct 17	Jan 27	Oct 28	Oct 28	Jan 15	Feb 14	May 20	Oct 9	Nov 26	Feb 9	Mar 24	Nov 16	Dec 28	May 8	Oct 16	Feb 8	Jul 9	Dec 10	Apr 21	Aug 14	Feb 13	Apr 18	Aug 20	Apr 27	May 18	Jul 27	Sept 27	Nov 4

TIME AND PRICE PERIODS IN 7 DAYS, 1 to 40 Years.

DAYS	YEAR	1	2	3	4	5	6	7	8	9	10	11	12	13	14	15	16	17	18	19	20
46	1/8	6½	58½	110½	162½	214½	266½	318½	370½	422½	474½	526½	578½	630½	682½	734½	786½	838½	890½	942½	994½
91	1/4	13	65	117	169	221	273	325	377	429	481	533	585	637	689	741	793	845	897	949	1001
121	1/3	17	69	121	173	225	277	329	381	433	485	537	589	641	693	745	797	849	901	953	1005
136	3/8	19½	71½	123½	175½	227½	279½	331½	383½	435½	487½	539½	591½	643½	695½	747½	799½	851½	903½	955½	1007½
182	1/2	26	78	130	182	234	286	338	390	442	494	546	598	650	702	754	806	858	910	962	1014
227	5/8	32½	84½	136½	188½	240½	292½	344½	396½	448½	500½	552½	604½	656½	708½	760½	812½	864½	916½	968½	1020½
242	2/3	35	87	139	191	243	295	347	399	451	503	555	607	659	711	763	815	867	919	971	1023
273	3/4	39	91	143	195	247	299	351	403	455	507	559	611	663	715	767	819	871	923	975	1027
319	7/8	45½	97½	149½	201½	253½	305½	357½	409½	461½	513½	565½	617½	669½	721½	773½	825½	877½	929½	981½	1033½
365	1 yr	52	104	156	208	260	312	364	416	468	520	572	624	676	728	780	832	884	936	988	1040

DAYS	YEAR	21	22	23	24	25	26	27	28	29	30	31	32	33	34	35	36	37	38	39	40
46	1/8	1046½	1098½	1150½	1202½	1254½	1306½	1358½	1410½	1462½	1514½	1566½	1618½	1670½	1722½	1774½	1826½	1878½	1930½	1982½	2034½
91	1/4	1053	1105	1157	1209	1261	1313	1365	1417	1469	1521	1573	1625	1677	1729	1781	1833	1885	1937	1989	2041
121	1/3	1057	1109	1161	1213	1265	1317	1369	1421	1473	1525	1577	1629	1681	1733	1785	1837	1889	1941	1993	2045
136	3/8	1059½	1111½	1163½	1215½	1267½	1319½	1371½	1423½	1475½	1527½	1579½	1631½	1683½	1735½	1787½	1839½	1891½	1943½	1995½	2047½
182	1/2	1066	1118	1170	1222	1274	1326	1378	1430	1482	1534	1586	1638	1690	1742	1794	1846	1898	1950	2002	2054
227	5/8	1072½	1124½	1176½	1228½	1280½	1332½	1384½	1436½	1488½	1540½	1592½	1644½	1696½	1748½	1800½	1852½	1904½	1956½	2008½	2060½
242	2/3	1075	1127	1179	1231	1283	1335	1387	1439	1491	1543	1595	1647	1699	1751	1803	1855	1907	1959	2011	2063
273	3/4	1079	1131	1183	1235	1287	1339	1391	1443	1495	1547	1599	1651	1703	1755	1807	1859	1911	1963	2015	2067
319	7/8	1085½	1137½	1189½	1241½	1293½	1345½	1397½	1449½	1501½	1553½	1605½	1657½	1709½	1761½	1813½	1865½	1917½	1969½	2021½	2073½
365	1 yr	1092	1144	1196	1248	1300	1352	1404	1456	1508	1560	1612	1664	1716	1768	1820	1872	1924	1976	2028	2080

COSMOLOGICAL ECONOMICS

THE MASTERS OF TECHNICAL ANALYSIS SERIES

The Masters of Technical Analysis Series brings together a collection of the most important classical and modern works on technical analysis and financial market forecasting. These classic works from the Golden Age of Technical Analysis were carefully selected by the late Dr. Jerome Baumring of the Investment Centre Bookstore in the 1980's, as representing the most valuable and important works in technical analysis ever written. They were included as the foundational source texts for his program in advanced financial market analysis and forecasting, and serve as the ideal foundation for any analyst seeking a thorough education in market theory and technical trading.

The Golden Age of technical analysis was a period from the early 1900's through the 1960's where the foundational theories of modern financial analysis were initially developed. The ideas and technologies developed during this fruitful period have formed the basis for most modern technical market theory, which is considered to be mostly a repetition or reworking of these past ideas and techniques developed by the Old Masters of the Golden Age. In these historical works can be found the timeless trading wisdom which has laid the foundation for all modern investment theory and literature. These techniques are as useful in today's markets as they were in the past, providing rare and valuable insights, tools and strategies that give the modern trader an edge over traders and investors that are unaware of these time honored tools.

Each quality reprint of these classical texts has been reproduced as an exact facsimile of the original text, maintaining the original layout, typeset, charts, and style of the author and time period, helping to preserve and communicate a sense of the feeling of the original work that a reproduction in modern format does not capture. Many of these rare works and courses were originally printed in only very small private editions or as correspondence courses, so that the originals were easily lost or destroyed over time. Our reproductions of these important source works have been printed on acid free paper and bound in a quality hardcover format that will compliment any trading library and help to preserve this important resource for generations to come.

The series is also currently being digitized and archived for permanent digital preservation by the Institute of Cosmological Economics, creating a searchable reference library of market wisdom accessible globally and available in new digital formats to keep the knowledge fresh and accessible through new devices and technology as we advance further into the information revolution. To see our full catalog of hardcover reprints, new publications, and digital editions please visit our website at www.CosmoEconomics.com.

- **Samuel Benner, An Ohio Farmer** - Benner's Prophecies - *Of Future Ups and Downs in Prices* - (1879)
- **Geo. W. Cole, La Marquette** - Graphs & Their Application to Speculation - (1936)
- **Frank Tubbs** - Tubbs' Stock Market Correspondence Course - (1944)
- **R. N. Elliot** - Collected Works of R. N. Elliot - *The Wave Principle. Nature`s Law: The Secret of the Universe. "The Wave Principle": A Series of Articles Published in 1939.* - (1946)
- **Joseph A. Wyler** - Wyler Series on Stock Market Speculation - *Vol.1, The Application Of Scientific Principles To Stock Speculation. Vol.2, Trading And Trending* - (1960)
- **Edward Dewey** - How to Make a Cycles Analysis - *Correspondence Course in Advanced Cycle Analysis*- (1955)
- **Nikolai D. Kondratieff** - Long Waves In Economic Life - (1935)
- **Pickell & Daniel** - Pickell-Daniel Extension Course of Market Analysis - (1937)
- **Franklin Paul Jackson** - The I-S Method - *Individual Stock - Intermediate Swing* - (1972)
- **Richard Schabacker** - Technical Analysis & Stock Market Profits - (1930)
- **Richard Schabacker** - Stock Market Profits - (1934)
- **M. V. Woods** - Seven Studies In Stock Market Trading - (1943)
- **William Dunnigan** - Collected Works of William Dunnigan - *Gains in Grains. New Blueprints for Gains in Stocks & Grains; Barometers for Forecasting Stocks. One-Way Formula for Trading In Stocks & Commodities* - (1957)
- **Henry Ludwell Moore** - Collected Works of Henry Ludwell Moore - *Economic Cycles Their Law & Cause. Generating Economic Cycles. Forecasting The Yield of Cotton* - (1923)
- **Edwin S. Quinn** - Action - Reaction Signals - (1950)
- **Emil Schultheis** - Basic Trend Barometer - *A Long Term Stock Trend Study* - (1946)
- **Payson Todd** - The "Todd Theory" of Market Measurement & Price Projection - (1953)
- **Dr. Alexander Goulden** - Behind The Veil - (2010)
- **C. S. Johnson, C. P. A.** - A New Technique of Stock Market Forecasting - (1931)
- **William D. Gann** - The Collected Writings of W. D. Gann, Volume I - *Marketing Brochures, Interviews, Annual Forecasts & Trading Records* - (1909-1954)
- **William D. Gann** - The Collected Writings of W. D. Gann, Volume II - *The Master Time Factor: No. 3 Master Forecasting Method & Stock Market Forecasting Courses* - (1921-1954)
- **William D. Gann** - Collected Writings of W. D. Gann, Volume III - *Master Mathematical Formula & Calculators* - (1955)
- **William D. Gann** - Collected Writings of W. D. Gann, Volume IV - *The Complete Commodity Courses* - (1940)
- **William D. Gann** - Collected Writings of W. D. Gann, Volume V - *Introductory Stock Market Courses, Mechanical Methods, & Trend Indicators Courses* - (1935-1950)
- **William D. Gann** - Complete Collected Writings of W. D. Gann - In 6 Volumes - (1955)
- **Timothy Walker** - How To Trade Like W. D. Gann - *An Exploration of the Mechanical Trading Lesson on U. S. Steel* - (2014)
- **James P. Morton** - When to Sell to Assure Profits - (1926)
- **Daniele Prandelli** - The Polarity Factor System - *An Integrated Forecasting & Trading Strategy Inspired By W. D. Gann's Master Time Factor* - (2012)
- **Daniele Prandelli** - The Law Of Cause And Effect - *Creating A Planetary Price/Time Map Of Market Action Through Sympathetic Resonance* - (2010)
- **Perspectives, National Graphic Co.** - The Great Bull Market & Collapse - (1932)
- **Richard Martin** - An Introduction to Trend - Action - *A Scientific Method of Forecasting* - (1943)

- **George Bayer** - Money Investing In Stocks, Trading In Commodities, Or The Time Factors In The Stock Market - *The Art of Scientifically Detecting Direction & Distance of Swings* - (1937)
- **George Bayer** - The Egg of Columbus - (1942)
- **George Bayer** - Stock & Commodity Traders Hand-Book of Trend Determination - *Secrets of Forecasting Values, Especially Commodities, Including Stocks* - (1940)
- **George Bayer** - Gold Nuggets for Stock & Commodity Traders - (1941)
- **George Bayer** - Preview of Markets - *VOL. I, NOS. 1-10* - (1939)
- **George Bayer** - George Wollsten - Expert Stock & Grain Trader - (1946)
- **George Bayer** - The Collected Works of George Bayer - *9 Books In 2 Hardcover Volumes* - (1939)
- **Cliff Stewart** - Magic of Making Money in The Stock Market - (1951)
- **Dickson F. Watts** - Speculation as a Fine Art - *& Thoughts On Life* - (1865)
- **Henry Ansley** - I Like the Depression - (1932)
- **Henry Hall** - How Money is Made in Security Investment - *Or A Fortune At Fifty-Five* - (1908)
- **Dr. Jerome Baumring & Julius J. Nirenstein** - Gann Harmony: The Law of Vibration: The Complete Course Manuals & Lecture Notes - *The Complete Gann 1-9 Course Manuals. Compiled By Dr. Jerome Baumring With Notes On W. D. Gann's Hidden Material: The Complete Gann 1-9 Lecture Notes* - (1989)
- **Dr. Jerome Baumring** - Gann Harmony: The Law of Vibration. The Complete Course Manuals - *Course Manuals For Gann 1 Through Gann 9* - (1989)
- **Julius J. Nirenstein & Dr. Jerome Baumring** - Notes on W. D. Gann's Hidden Material: The Complete Lecture Notes - *Lecture Notes for Gann 1 through Gann 9* - (1989)
- **Alfred Friedman** - Lecture Notes from Baumring's Investment Centre Series - (1987)
- **B. Edlin** - Minor Swings of the Stock Market and their indications - (1924)
- **Henry Howard Harper** - The Psychology of Speculation - *The Human Element In Market Transactions* - (1926)
- **S. A. Nelson** - The ABC of Options & Arbitrage - (1904)
- **Daniel T. Ferrera** - The Gann Pyramid - *Square of Nine Essentials* - (2001)
- **Daniel T. Ferrera** - The Mysteries of Gann Analysis Unveiled! - *A Detailed Presentation of W. D. Gann's Technical Trading Principles* - (2001)
- **Daniel T. Ferrera** - Wheels Within Wheels – *The Art of Forecasting Financial Market Cycles* - (2002)
- **Daniel T. Ferrera** - W. D. Gann's Mass Pressure Forecasting Charts - (2004)
- **Daniel T. Ferrera** - The Keys to Successful Speculation - (2004)
- **Daniel T. Ferrera** - Spirals of Growth and Decay - *Exposing the Underlying Structure of Financial Markets* (2005)
- **Daniel T. Ferrera** – Gann for the Active Trader - *New Methods For Today's Markets* (2006)
- **Daniel T Ferrera** – Economic & Stock Market Forecasting – *W.D. Gann's Science of Cyclical Periodicity Sequencing* (2013)
- **Daniel T. Ferrera -** The Path of Least Resistance - *The Underlying Wisdom & Philosophy of W. D. Gann Elegantly Encoded in the Master Charts* - (2014)
- **Warren Hickernell** - What Makes Stock Market Prices - (1932)
- **William C. Moore (Market Expert)** - Wall Street - *Its Mysteries Revealed, Its Secrets Exposed.* - (1932)